Tales from the Road
Stories of Sex, Drums, and Rock & Roll from the Music Circuit of the '70s, '80s and Beyond…

by

Bill Bancroft

as told to

Colin Conway

Tales from the Road
Stories of Sex, Drums, and Rock & Roll from the Music
Circuit of the '70s, '80s and Beyond…

by Bill Bancroft and Colin Conway

Cover Design by Extended Imagery

All photographs courtesy of Bill Bancroft unless otherwise
noted.

ISBN-13: 978-1986650038
ISBN-10: 1986650030

I dedicate this book to my children –
Erin Marie, Cory John, and Casey William –
and to my wife, Sue.

And to my late wife, Becky Anne, (1952-
2011) who was an inspiration to me for the
thirty-three years we were together.

First and foremost, I am a drummer...
I didn't do it to become rich and famous,
I did it because it was the love of my life.

- Ringo Starr

... I think I liked every band I ever played in
because each band was different,
each band had a different concept, and
each band leader was different ...

- Buddy Rich

NOTE FROM THE CO-AUTHOR

Bill Bancroft is not who I expected him to be.

I first met him while we were members of the Spokane Building Owners and Managers Association (BOMA) – a non-profit organization focused on matters related to the commercial real estate industry.

At that time, Bill worked as Vice-President of Corporate Facilities with Sterling Savings Bank. He was always well-dressed in a suit and tie. His gray hair was cut short in an almost military manner. His eyes were often hidden behind his round glasses. He had a quiet and respectful demeanor. When I chatted with him, it was about property management or other BOMA related topics. Bill's reputation was that of a sweet, mellow guy.

The association executive at that time, Carla Warren, told me Bill used to be a drummer in various rock bands.

My first response was, "Bill?"

Carla swore it was the truth. I looked at her like she'd lost her mind. The most I could imagine was him possibly playing in some sort of soft jazz band.

When his wife passed away, he stepped down from BOMA. We all knew that he struggled with that devastating loss.

I filed "Bill Bancroft as drummer" away as one of those oddities in life.

Fast forward a couple years.

Carla and Bill had become good friends and then she and I began dating. One day, she mentioned Bill wanted to talk about writing a book.

Bill and I met over a couple beers. He shared some of his stories about being on the road. Sex, drugs, and rock & roll were all there, of course, but underneath those tales was a love story that would emerge and create a family.

He had recorded several tapes, filling them up with funny, interesting and wild tales.

"How many tapes?" I asked.

"Maybe fifteen," he said. "And that's not the entire story."

Finally seeing Bill Bancroft behind a drum kit was like witnessing the transformation of Bruce Banner into the Incredible Hulk. Off stage, Bill's personality is a mixture of humor and introspection. At times, he is quiet and reserved. On stage, working a drum kit with the lights gleaming down, he's a grinning wild man. His hands and feet move effortlessly, creating a beat his band will coalesce around into rock and roll glory. It's easy to see at these moments that this is where he's happiest.

I've read many rock star biographies.

Gene Simmons's *KISS and Make-Up*, Sammy Hagar's *Red* and Ozzy Osbourne's *I Am Ozzy* to name a few. I've lived my rock and roll fantasies through those accounts and many more.

I couldn't pass up an opportunity to participate in the writing of a book that would allow me to further live in the world of rock and rollers.

I transcribed every one of Bill's tapes and we met weekly to review the notes, clarify details and flesh out his story.

In the end, we crafted a tale that I believe will connect with musicians, lovers of musicians and music lovers. I also think it will surprise many readers.

When I read Motley Crue's *The Dirt*, it never once shocked me that Nikki Sixx and Tommy Lee could get away with their debauchery. They were on MTV and played stadiums. Strange things were supposed to happen at that level of fame.

Yet it surprised the hell out of me that Bill Bancroft and his various bands of youthful derelicts were marauding around in the late '70s and early '80s, consuming mass quantities of mind-altering substances while garnering the attention of local girls. They were getting away with the same stuff that bands like Aerosmith and AC/DC did.

Like most of my rock and roll heroes, Bill Bancroft was a beer guzzling, drug-abusing, skirt-chasing, dirty musician.

Until he met Becky Brewer.

And that's where the story and the man changed.

DISCLAIMER

As in many books that rely on one's memory, there is always the potential that dates, times, events, and names may get "misremembered." You could put many bandmates in a room and each of us would have a slightly different version of the same story.

If I have done this, I ask your indulgence and, in some cases, forgiveness.

Some names were changed to protect the guilty and the not-so-innocent (you know who you are).

-   Bill Bancroft, 2018

Tales from the Road
Stories of Sex, Drums,
and Rock & Roll
from the Music Circuit
of the '70s, '80s and Beyond...

CONTENTS

INTRODUCTION

PHILADELPHIA AIRPORT MARRIOTT – PHILADELPHIA, PENNSYLVANIA JUNE 23, 1997 11:00 PM

I've been thinking about telling my stories for some time. This weekend I rode home with Keith Lewis from Big Fork, Montana to Spokane, Washington. Our band, Café Blue, had a weekend gig and we were returning to our "normal" lives of family and five-day-a-week jobs. My job is Director of Corporate Facilities for Itron, Inc. where I oversee the real estate, security, construction, and maintenance for all Itron sites nationwide. This requires me to be away from home a lot.

While we rode, I told Keith some of the stories from my younger days in music. He always digs those anecdotes and, truth be told, I love telling them.

My family and friends have enjoyed my tales of being in rock and country bands, and some of the wild shit I lived through. The telling of those episodes always gets a laugh and a request for another.

From the mid '70s through the late '80s, I played full-time in the bar circuit wphich was something special at that time. I was lucky enough to play on some national tours, too.

Before MTV and the internet made music readily accessible and boringly safe, bands across America rolled into big cities and small towns to ply their trade. These musicians lived a fantasy many have only dreamed.

Behind a drum kit, I experienced the whole mind-altering trip. Sex and drugs were on steady supply everywhere we went. Adoring female fans treated us to all sorts of escapades. Acid trips, cocaine busts and psycho groupies are only a part of my story.

I narrowly escaped a shotgun blast from a jealous husband who later murdered his wife. A drunken behemoth pressed a gun to my forehead at a party gone bad. I fought in bar room brawls that didn't go my way and won a few that did. I survived a fire that completely burned down the bar that my band was performing in.

I played throughout the Pacific Northwest and mountain states. I made my way into Canada and toured through Nevada, Oklahoma, Texas, and Alabama.

I've opened for national acts such as Hoyt Axton, The Forrester Sisters and Robert Cray. I've backed up the legendary Bo Diddley and went on tour with Freddy Fender. I've partied with Heart and Alabama and drank beers with the guys from AC/DC. I was a studio musician when Garth Brooks cut an early demo tape. I even played a round of roadside golf in Texas with Willie Nelson.

Mine is a story of sex, drums, and rock & roll. Okay, there are some drugs in there, too.

Throughout my career as a musician I have experienced a variety of highs and lows. I've been respected and ridiculed. I've been abused and fawned over. Some have cheered for me and others have laughed at me. I've signed autographs for fans one night only to have those same fans not know who I was a couple days later.

This is my story of growing into a man while on the road and eventually finding that some things are more important than the pursuit of fame. It took me a while to discover what those things were, but once I did, it put my life on a different trajectory.

Many of these moments evoke a certain amount of shame, but there were also moments of great personal accomplishment.

My wife, Becky, suggested I record these stories before I forget them. It's amazing how time creeps in and robs little bits of memory. These are my recollections of events. If you ask one of my bandmates, they may recall it exactly as I have done, or they may remember it slightly different. Hell, they may not remember it at all. Regardless, there are two sides to every story and this is mine.

I'm not sure if these stories are going to lead anywhere, but here goes.

I'm sitting in my hotel room, dictating these stories into a handheld recorder. I've had a few beers to get up the courage to start this process.

I guess I'll start at the beginning...

THE BEGINNING

For a long time, I hated everybody.

Through all my school years, I felt like a little speck – never noticed, never special.

As a kid, I was small and skinny and if anyone *would* take notice of me it was because my mother was a teacher. That's not exactly the type of recognition a kid wants.

I grew tall in high school but remained thin which reinforced my insecurities.

By the time I was a senior in high school, I had been playing drums for several years. Still, I was unsure of myself when compared to a couple of other, younger drummers in the school band. I believed they were better than me and psyched myself out. As the only senior in the group, I believed I should have earned "first chair" or the best drummer of the group. I didn't, though, and it really hurt my confidence.

The last day of my senior year, Central Valley High School put on a big jazz band concert in the gymnasium in front of the entire student body. We had three drum kits lined up. The three of us played well and the kids dug it.

Afterwards, while we signed yearbooks in the halls, I couldn't believe how many of my fellow students came up to say things like, "I can't believe how great you are!"

Even Sue Davis, tall and beautiful in a short yellow jumper, noticed me.

Something clicked in me that day. I felt a new sense of pride.

Suddenly, I was noticed.

I was *somebody*.

I was born September 8th, 1956 and was the youngest of seven children – Chris and Chuck were my brothers and Bonnie, Cathy, Carol and Laurie were my sisters. Family was everything to mom. I'd like to believe that since I was the youngest she paid extra attention to me.

The first time I ever touched a drum it belonged to a neighbor. My mom, Velma, borrowed it, along with an Indian headdress and a bandana from the neighbor, thinking it would make a good picture. I was five years old. I cried the next day when the neighbor took the drum home.

I didn't think about a drum again until I saw Buddy Rich on *The Johnny Carson Show*. Buddy was a jazz drummer in his band, The Buddy Rich Band. I slipped out of bed and tip-toed down the hallway to secretly watch the show my parents had on television. Buddy was incredible. I couldn't take my eyes off him as he played. My dad snuck up and caught me watching the show. He immediately sent me to bed.

The next time Buddy Rich was on *The Johnny Carson Show* it was a Friday night and dad let me stay up to watch. I remember telling him, "I want to be Buddy Rich."

When I was seven years old, Ringo Starr and The Beatles played on *The Ed Sullivan Show*. That moment has become a generational cliché, but it inspired me in a way nothing before ever had. I bought toy rings from the grocery store and wore them to be like Ringo. I imitated my new idol by beating on pots and pans with sticks. When that irritated the family, I assembled a full drum set out of cardboard boxes, which I could beat on without making too much of a racket.

During elementary school, I joined the school band. To practice, mom and dad bought me a green sparkle Ludwig snare drum. I still remember the smell as I opened the case – wood, metal, grease from the lug springs, the rubber practice pad (which I still have and use to this day) and the shiny, new lacquered drum sticks. They also bought me a book that taught drumming basics and let me bang away.

My sister, Laurie, being a big fan of the band Cream, stopped by my room one day. She said, "You should play this," and, using her hands, tapped out the opening rhythm to Cream's song *Toad*. I quickly mimicked the rhythm she showed me. She clapped in approval and has taken credit for teaching me how to play the drums ever since.

One night, mom and dad were watching *Hogan's Heroes*. The theme song had a distinct drum riff that called the soldiers to order. I stopped and listened to it intently. When the intro was over, I walked to my room and played the riff over and over. Mom and dad came to my room shortly after that.

"How did you learn that?" dad asked.

I shrugged. "I just heard it."

My parents nodded in approval and left the room, so I could continue practicing.

In February 1968, my dad bought me my first full drum kit.

It was a Saturday morning and the region had recently experienced the biggest snow storm in Spokane's recorded history.

"Get your drum," dad abruptly said. He wasn't prone to long drawn out conversations with me. My dad, John, had been a Chief Petty Officer in the Navy during World War II and Korea. He'd served on the USS Jack, a submarine that patrolled the North Atlantic.

Just like that, he told me to put my snare drum in its now broken case and bring it along, so we could trade it in. Most of the roads were closed and several driveways were blocked in. My grandmother lived about forty yards away from us and her driveway was open. We walked over to her house and then drove to the Clark Evans Music Store.

It was a magical place, full of all sorts of musical instruments – drums, guitars, saxophones, and more. They were serious about music.

Dad pointed to several drum sets. "Which of these do you like?"

8

"What do you mean?"

"If you're going to be a drummer, you need a drum set."

I was euphoric. I studied all the kits and finally settled on a "Majestic" red sparkle drum set made in Japan. It had one cymbal, a snare drum, rack and floor toms, and a bass drum. A basic four-piece kit.

Dad and I carried the set from my grandmother's driveway, back through the snow, to our house. We held the various pieces over our heads as we stepped through the snow drifts.

We put the drum kit in the back bedroom and I banged away. Using my sister's radio, I would wait for songs from The Beatles, Paul Revere and the Raiders, The Animals, and The Monkees. I'd listen intently to those songs and learn to play them by ear.

I *still* have that drum kit and will occasionally gig with it today!

I continued to practice and when I entered Greenacres Junior High School, I joined the school orchestra. I also starred as the Little Drummer Boy in our church production because they found out I could actually play.

Thank God for music because I wasn't an athlete.

I tried out for baseball and was cut.

I went out for the basketball team and was cut.

In track, I ran the triple jump on the B-Squad.

Due to my size, I couldn't play on the football team, so I was made the manager for my sophomore and junior years. It wasn't until my senior year that I was able to try out for the football team and got my ass handed to me. The coach let me play on the 3rd string team. I guess he felt sorry for me, but I'd hung around the team long enough that he gave me a shot.

In 9th grade, the school had a Spring Musical and they let some of the kids' bands play. It was a chance for those students to show off their talent.

My friends and I decided to create a band for the show. A couple guys were on guitar while a couple other guys sang vocals. And I, Bill Bancroft, was on drums. We didn't have a bass player – what did we know?

We chose two songs from Creedence Clearwater Revival for the show: *Bad Moon Rising* and *Proud Mary*. We rehearsed those two songs for a month and we still sucked.

At the show, both guitar players rested a foot on a chair, so they could balance their guitars on their knees as they didn't have guitar straps. They plugged their guitars into the gym's P.A. system. The echo was so bad no one could hear anything clearly. Our vocalists sang together but didn't harmonize. We were all bunched together in the middle of the stage.

As for me, I didn't know about putting a rug under the drum kit. The bass drum skidded away whenever I kicked it. I would grab it and pull it back throughout the songs.

I don't even remember the crowd's response.

We were just there making noise.

It was an unmitigated fucking disaster.

COLD SMOKE
1974-1975

Central Valley High School Dance – I'm behind the drums
Photo taken by my friend, Jack Dial

Everything changed on my last day of high school after the jazz band concert. I finally felt noticed and a fire began to burn inside. Things didn't take off immediately, but it was enough to get me moving in a new direction.

In short order, I formed my first band, Cold Smoke. We had Jesse Bishop on lead guitar, Mike Coman on rhythm guitar and Dave Low on bass. Jesse and Dave handled the vocals.

For a time, it was just Dave, Mike and I sitting in my parent's living room and jamming. Dave and Mike were both playing single strings on their guitars and I was banging away. I really could play so I was considered the "professional" musician of the group.

Prior to Cold Smoke, Dave had gotten his bass as a graduation present but didn't know how to play it. He and Mike Coman had gotten together to practice. They were ecstatic when they were able to string three notes together at the same time, instead of a two-man cacophony.

Jesse helped teach them the basics to get them ready to play. Beyond individual notes and chords, he showed them how to fit them into a song. Jesse knew how to play both guitar and bass and was the bass player in our high school stage band.

Initially, we had a keyboard player, Rob Conway, who was Mike's next-door neighbor. He had a monophonic Moog synthesizer which means it could only play one note at a time. Later developments in synthesizers would allow them to play multiple notes at a time, such as a chord. The sounds that Moog made were very limited, but it was cutting-edge technology back then.

The band's name came from the time we dropped ice in some bong water and it produced cold smoke. Dave wanted to call the band Atomic Stagecoach – he was outvoted.

When we formed, we decided we would play original songs. This was a funny ambition, because Dave and Mike were still learning. The reality was that learning to play an original was just as hard as learning to play a cover.

After we hooked up with Jesse and Rob, we moved our practices to the barn at Mike's parents' house. Jesse and Rob clashed like two alpha males who both wanted to be leader. Jesse seemed older than the rest of us because he was married so he thought he should be in charge. Rob quit almost immediately, which left us a four-piece band.

Dave and Mike rented a house with a third roommate next to a funeral home. It ended up a party house in no time, so we naturally moved our practices to the basement there. By then, we had learned a few covers from Alice Cooper, David Bowie and Blue Oyster Cult, but what we wanted to play was originals. So, Jesse wrote some songs for us.

However, the originals weren't original.

Every song ripped off another popular song of the day. All our riffs sounded like a copy of something on the radio. It was respectable enough since we were teenagers and just learning to be musicians.

When we took a break from rehearsing in the basement, we'd run up upstairs to smoke a bowl from an oversized water pipe. We were so into the dope scene that we developed Cold Smoke's logo around a bong. Smoke drifted up from a pipe to form the words *Cold Smoke*. We painted the logo on my bass drum with black light paint so that when the lights went off it would look badass. Not very original, but it was definitely cool to a bunch of teenagers.

Black light posters hung on the walls and records played on the stereo whenever we weren't practicing.

We jammed in that party house while our friends and random strangers hung out. On Fridays, even more people would show up. Some of the visitors took advantage of hanging out and used the opportunity to sell weed. The local kids knew it was a place to buy illegal substances.

Eventually the cops noticed. Two of the guys who hung out in the house were undercover cops. We should have spotted them with their stupid haircuts. They had short hair while we all had long hair. They wore neatly pressed shirts and around their necks they wore white pookah shells. Nobody dressed that way in our world. Nobody. These guys even talked sports. Something nobody else in our world did. Nevertheless, we were too naïve to comprehend they were narcs.

Ironically, no one was ever busted out of that house.

For one of our first shows, Cold Smoke played an acid party. I was pissed off prior to the party so I was in a bad mood. I had about a half-case of beer with me at the drum kit. I stayed away from acid that night. Instead, I drank until I was puking.

My red sparkle drum set had problems by then, as well. The snare drum had a broken head. The bass drum was broken. I had even duct-taped a cymbal stand together. To get through the party, I borrowed some pieces from other drummers to assemble a complete kit.

We played some original songs we were working on over and over and then just jammed. It was enough to give us a spark to go after a real show.

After the acid party, we landed our first paying gig at the Valley Eagles club. A karate school held a private party for a bunch of little kids and a few grown-ups. Of course, I invited mom and dad to come watch us play.

For our sound system, Jesse laid a P.A. horn on the ground and ran wires to his microphone. Dave sang through a microphone plugged into the additional input on his bass amp.

So they could flash under the lights, Jesse, Dave and Mike sewed sequins and stars onto their clothes. To look like a rock star, Dave wore some homemade stage clothes that his sister had sewn together. I wore my cowboy hat, jeans and a t-shirt.

We opened the show with our original song *Welcome to the Party*. The chorus was something like

Welcome to the party,
Welcome to the show.

And, that was the gist of the entire song.

We were so nervous that we missed the car crash ending (the guitarists strumming and me banging the cymbals). We had to circle around to the beginning and start the song over. Unfortunately, we missed the ending once more. We circled back to the beginning again. We did this until we finally ran out of steam. That song lasted twenty-seven minutes! I'm not kidding. We didn't know how to end it.

We took a break after that one song. As I came off the stage, I walked up to my dad who said, "Well, Bill, that was a long one."

That was our first set.

Our second original song was *Cookin'*. As its name implied, it was fast and the lyrics were a bunch of blathering about partying. It was a 90 mile per hour clusterfuck.

The final original song we had was *A Place in the Future*. It had a nice guitar lick for its intro. It also had a cool back beat and was almost a funk song.

All told, we knew about ten songs which we played over and over through the night. We took long breaks to stretch out the time.

It was my first professional gig and we were paid for it.

However, we were shorted the agreed upon amount. After the show, we met the sensei of the karate school in front of a nearby junior high school to collect our pay. The sensei said how much he was now going to pay and Dave got upset. He said, "That's not what you promised." It was less than half of what was expected.

The sensei backed Dave down by telling him we weren't getting any more than he brought.

Dave didn't challenge him any further.

For that fact, neither the did the rest of us. We stood around looking dumbfounded as we accepted less than full payment.

What were we supposed to do? Tell our mommies?

He was a karate man, for crying out loud, and we were teenaged rock-and-rollers.

After our first gig, dad was upset about the condition of my set. He said, "How can you be serious about being a musician and have equipment like this?"

I didn't have an answer for him.

"Come on," he said.

16

We drove over to the Clark Evans Music Store. The last time we were there was several years prior when we walked through the snow to purchase my red sparkle drum set.

"Okay, pick one out."

I immediately went to the most expensive one.

"Nope," dad said.

I then saw a "Pearl" blue sparkle set. It was $200. It was an exorbitant price back then. I tried it out and said that was the one.

We took it home and I set it up. I scavenged pieces from the red sparkle kit. I grabbed the floor tom so I would have two of them. I didn't care if the set was now red and blue. I thought it was out of this world.

My sister, Cathy, suggested that Cold Smoke play the annual Flag Day teen dance in Fairfield about thirty miles southeast of Spokane. Some small farm communities pick odd holidays to make a big deal out of and Flag Day was what Fairfield had chosen.

Cathy lived in Fairfield and gave me the contact information of the guy handling the event. His day job was a salesperson at the local John Deere tractor dealership.

I phoned and introduced myself. He and I talked about the event and he asked how much the band needed to perform on Friday night to kick off the weekend festivities.

"We're going to need at least $200," I said, thinking we would get $100.

"Our budget won't allow $200," he said. "Would you do $175?"

I don't know if you can hear a smile across the telephone, but I was grinning ear to ear. We concluded our business and I set about becoming a professional musician.

The next thing I needed was a contract. I wrote one on a typewriter, making up the language up as I went.

> *I, Bill Bancroft, of Cold Smoke (band),*
> *agree to play at the Fairfield Teen Dance,*
> *June 14th, 1974, at the Fairfield Grange*
> *from 9 p.m. to midnight. We will play*
> *three sets with two breaks, fifteen minutes*
> *each. Payment of $175 is to be in cash*
> *on completion of the job.*

I put a couple signature blocks on the document.

My mom ran off a copy on the mimeograph at Greenacres Elementary School where she was a teacher. She gave me a folder to put both copies in. The smell of the ink made me feel important.

I drove to Fairfield and stood in the tractor show room, as the salesman read the contract. I had long hair, a button down long-sleeve shirt, flare jeans, and cowboy boots.

"We do checks," he said.

"Sir, we need cash."

He studied me for a moment. Finally, he nodded. "We can work that out."

The big man signed the contract and then I signed. We shook hands like equals and that was it.

When I drove out of Fairfield, I felt a new sense of confidence and accomplishment. I had taken care of business for our band.

A couple days before the show we rehearsed the set list at the party house.

When it was over, Jesse, his wife, and her sister headed to Jesse's house. They invited me to come along with them.

It wasn't long before the pot and beer came out. Then the black lights were turned on. Jesse and his wife disappeared into their bedroom, leaving me sitting in the living room with the sister. She was reclined on the couch, wearing white pants, her legs spread open. She had a lit cigarette in one hand and a drink in the other.

"They ran back into their cave," I said.

"You can crawl into my cave any time," she said with a smile.

I practically ran out of the house. I had no idea how to handle a girl coming onto me like that.

In Fairfield, on the night of the show, we dressed for the gig at my sister's house.

I wore brown corduroy pants and a hippy cowboy shirt I borrowed from my brother. Man, I loved that shirt. I also wore my beat-up cowboy hat and cowboy boots.

Jesse looked at me and said, "You're wearing that?" He was wearing silk and satin, and obviously didn't approve of my attire.

"What about him?" I said and pointed at Dave.

Dave said, "What the hell? I didn't say anything about your clothes." Dave wore a long-sleeve silver shirt with stars and moons on it. His bell-bottom jeans were satin and stars from the knees down. His sister had sewn that weird outfit together.

We argued about each other's clothes for a bit.

It wasn't obvious to us then, but the band was already fraying.

We played the gig that night and it went over well. Many of my family members were there including nieces and nephews to see their young, rock-star uncle perform.

We were a live rock and roll act at the Grange Hall in Fairfield. The kids loved it. Remember, this was the 1970s. There was no cable TV, no internet, no MTV. We were a rock band and, at that moment, we were something special.

For the dance, I insisted we learn a song, *Letter to the President* by Cat Mother (out of Northern California), a real country-rock song. The band hated it, but my sister loved it. I figured I owed it to Cathy for helping us get the gig.

The rest of the band split after the show, but I stayed in Fairfield and got my first taste of being a star. I continued to wear my gig clothes that night, in hopes of being noticed further.

The next day I kept going out on the front porch, hoping somebody would recognize me. Cathy lived on the corner of Main and 1st, so everybody walked past there. I wore my hippie cowboy hat around town so I could be spotted.

I was a celebrity that day. Several kids came up to say, "You were in the band last night!"

It was an awesome feeling to be regarded like that.

In September '74, we played our first big gig at Central Valley High School.

The guys and I had graduated from there in May so this felt like our triumphant return to the school. The show was immediately after a varsity football game.

We sounded tight by then and the crowd liked us. We borrowed a real P.A. system for that show. It was too bad that we hadn't thought out the show's lighting beforehand. The only light we had was the black light in front of the drum set and a small rotating lamp with a peace sign. Essentially, we played in the dark with our teeth glowing white.

Fortunately, the Cold Smoke logo on my bass drum looked awesome!

On breaks, the whole band would run to our cars in the parking lot. We'd smoke weed and drink beer to get messed up as quickly as possible.

By the time it was over, we were enjoying ourselves and getting more confident.

The school paid us $100 for the show.

After the school dance, we were full of ourselves as a band and as musicians. Because of this overblown self-worth, we decided to throw our own gig. We were going to hold a dance of our own to make some real money.

We rented the Trentwood Grange, made posters and bought two dozen liters of pop, cups, and ice.

At this time, all the guys had a girlfriend but me. The girls were tasked with watching the door, taking the money, and serving the pop.

On the night of the dance, the band and their accompanying family out-numbered the crowd. People showed up, looked inside and saw that not much was happening. They immediately turned around and left.

The band was devastated. Of course, we blamed each other for things like not putting up enough posters or not advertising enough.

The reality was we spent most of our days focused on other things besides the band. Dave had a full-time job and rent to pay. Jesse was married with a kid. Shit, I was heavily stoned. There was plenty of blame to go around.

It was around this time that I took to wearing platform shoes. I thought I looked dressed to kill, but I couldn't play worth a damn with them on. It was like trying to play a guitar while wearing a glove.

To better play the drums, I started playing barefoot.

Without warning, Mike took off to Hawaii. The band was suddenly adrift. One afternoon, the remaining three of us rehearsed on the deck at my parent's house. That practice went terrible. When we were done, I boxed all the gear up, which ended up including two microphones that Mike had left with me. I put the boxes in a closet.

A few weeks later, Mike came back to town to scrape some money together.

"Where are my microphones?" Mike asked.

When I went for the microphones they were gone. "I don't have them."

We argued for a bit and I accused Jesse of stealing them. Jesse found out and was pissed.

To settle things, Dave picked up Jesse and me in his Chevy Vega and took us to his place for a band meeting.

Dave acted as the moderator and sat at the kitchen table. Jesse and I sat on the couch. I had worn a hunting knife on my belt. I rarely carried it, but I was worried that something bad might happen.

We talked about the microphones for a while and it wasn't going anywhere. Finally, I said "I think Jesse took them."

"I didn't take them." Jesse said, clearly pissed.

"Maybe you lost them."

"If I lost them, I would pay Mike back for them."

I opened my mouth and said something stupid. "With what? A buck a month from your old lady's welfare check?"

Jesse grabbed me by the shirt, hit me in the face and then pinned my head in the corner of the couch. He continued to thump on me. Dave jumped out of his chair and got Jesse off me.

I grabbed for the knife on my belt, slapping at it several times, but couldn't get it out. Dave talked me down, telling me to relax.

In that moment, Cold Smoke was finished.

After the fight, Dave took us both home. Jesse sat in the back while I was in the front passenger seat. As he got out, Jesse shoved the front seat forward, banging me into the window. "Fuck you," he said.

Dave dropped me off at my house. Mom and dad could see I was upset when I came inside. I sat on our couch and cried.

Not because the band was over, but because I had been in a fight with a guy who was once my friend.

ORGANIZED CRIME
1975-1977

(L-R) Me, Brett Ashley, Linda Beach, Chet Martz, and Steve Hanna

After the break-up of Cold Smoke, I stacked my drum kit in the corner of my room. I wanted to get away from the band drama and the self-doubt about my worth as a drummer. My brother, Chuck, moved back from Seattle and we partied a lot together.

During this time, I was struggling to figure out what to do with myself and my life. I worked at the Pop Shoppe to pick up some cash, but knew I wanted something more. Dad told me that it was okay to want to be a drummer, "but you should have something to fall back on." It was a good piece of advice, but I didn't know what I wanted to do.

Dad had been a Navy man and I believe he wanted one of his sons to follow in his footsteps. Neither of my brothers, Chris or Chuck, joined. I toyed with the idea of joining the Navy to become a firefighter like my uncle. My family encouraged me to pursue it.

I drove my orange Volkswagen bus to visit the Navy recruiter's office to check out their program. A peace sign dangled from the rearview mirror and green shag carpeting was laid throughout the van.

With my long hair, I'm sure the Navy recruiters had seen my type before. I'm also sure they knew the battle that was going on inside my heart as they watched me through the windows.

After thirty minutes, having never gotten out of my van, I left the parking lot and went home.

I announced to my family that I was going to baking school.

While sitting outside the recruiter's office, I had remembered a field trip my second-grade class took to the Wonder Bread bakery. The smell was incredible. After I saw the giant vat of chocolate cake batter, I came home that day and told my parents I wanted to be a baker.

When I approached my grandmother about going to baking school she said, "You know, Billy, no matter how hard times get, people still need to eat bread."

The next day after sitting in the recruiter's parking lot, mom and I went to Spokane Community College (SCC) and I enrolled in the baking program.

Dad was happy that I selected a course of action that didn't involve me being a rock and roller.

I got the itch to start drumming again in early spring of 1975. I would lie in bed and look longingly at the drums in the corner of my room. One night, I sat on my bed with a spiral notebook and a black Magic Marker and made signs that read, "Experienced drummer looking for band or musicians to start a band. Serious inquiries only."

I made two dozen of them. I put one on each side my Volkswagen and hung them up at the baking school. Those signs also made their way into supermarkets, like anyone I would play with would ever see them there.

I got a call from a guy who invited me over to jam with him and his band. He said I didn't need to bring my drums.

Chuck went with me to the house which was in a sketchy part of town. There was a nice set of drums assembled which were more heavy duty than mine. Their bassist was cool, but the lead singer was a complete jerk and the lead guitarist was a major league asshole.

We played *Brown Sugar* by the Rolling Stones then rehearsed *Stairway to Heaven* by Led Zeppelin. All the while these guys smoked every bit of dope Chuck and I had brought.

When we finished playing, the guys put away their guitars and left the room. They left me sitting there at the drums. Chuck and I stared at each other as we were tried to figure out what the hell was happening.

I walked to the back of the house and found the band in a room, sitting on a mattress with some chicks, drinking and smoking.

"Uh, so, what do you think?" I asked

"Well, Bill, we'll call you."

The next call I received was from a guy on the north side of town. At his request, I showed up for a meeting. He said he was the lead for a country band and listed the songs he wanted to play.

Shit, I thought, *I have never heard these songs.*

It only took a bit before he decided I was too much of a punk kid to be in his band.

A few more days went by before I got a call from a band that played at the Veterans of Foreign Wars (VFW).

When I arrived, their pretty female singer handed me the sheet music to *Ain't No Sunshine* by Bill Withers. They wanted me to play the break in the middle of the song. I hadn't read music since high school band and I never could read it very well, anyway. I played with these guys for a couple hours before they said, "Thanks for coming by."

Basically, I had two auditions that I failed miserably. I was totally discouraged.

In late fall, I received a call from a band in Coeur d'Alene, Idaho known as Sailin' Shoes. I was a fan of Little Feat and I knew *Sailin' Shoes* was one of their songs so I immediately got excited.

I drove to Idaho and met the band. They were a little older than me and all wore long hair which made them authentic in my book. They told me they were into Little Feat and The Allman Brothers Band. They asked me to jam and it felt like I was coming home. They were doing lots of slide guitar stuff. I dug it. It went well and I got the gig.

We rehearsed one more time and afterwards went for a beer at The Rathskellers in Coeur d'Alene. Back then the drinking age in Idaho was nineteen which meant I could legally imbibe in the state.

The guys were talking about guitars and mentioned a Firebird. I was driving dad's Firebird at the time so to be part of the conversation, I said, "I have a Firebird, too."

They looked at me, oddly. One of them asked, "You do? I thought you were a drummer."

"Yeah, well, I can get my drums in there." I went on for a bit about the car and they laughed at me.

"Man, we're talking about guitars," the lead guitarist said.

One of them said, "Poor Billy." I felt so young and stupid.

A few days later they phoned to tell me their old drummer came back and they didn't need me.

I was crushed.

About a week later, a guy named Bob Allen called and said he saw my sign at Hoffman Music. He invited me to his house near the county courthouse to try out for a band.

Bob said he was the lead singer. He was an old guy in his early thirties.

His brother played acoustic rhythm guitar and supposedly lead guitar, but he couldn't jam to save his life. He also couldn't sing. He couldn't do anything.

On bass guitar was Chet Martz, a guy from the Air Force. He was another old guy, roughly thirty years old. I initially thought he was a doofus, but Chet turned out to be an okay guy. I became good friends with him.

Brett Ashley was on rhythm guitar and vocals. He was closer to my age. He was about twenty years old. He had long hair and a beard which made him cool.

We played several songs and the one that got me going was *Feel Like Makin' Love* by Bad Company. When it began, I copped the groove. It probably sounded like shit, but it felt good.

After playing for a bit, I was invited to join the band that Bob was forming.

Shortly after joining, I received a call from someone named Steve Hanna who said he played guitar and was looking for a band. After talking for a bit, I invited him over to Bob's house to try out for our new band. Steve was eighteen years old and fucking wailed. He liked us and we liked him. Bob's brother was resentful of Steve and quit which was fine with me.

In the fall of 1975, Organized Crime was born with Bob Allen on lead vocals, Steve Hanna on lead guitar, Brett Ashley on rhythm guitar, and Chet Martz on bass guitar.

Bob was a civilian working at Fairchild Air Force Base (FAFB) while Chet was an enlisted man. Both worked in the paint shop. Organized Crime was hired to play the paint shop's Christmas party. I don't remember how much we made, but it wasn't much.

For the show, the guys in the paint shop made us podiums. They built me a square one for the drum kit. The rest of the guys stood on round podiums. We rehearsed like crazy. It was incredibly exciting for us.

We learned a bunch of Eagles, America and other country-rock tunes. It was Steve's first gig. We even wore nice clothes. It went over well and we all felt triumphant.

In fact, Colonel Mar, Chet's commanding officer, liked us so much he let us practice on the base. He had a stage built in the cafeteria. It was a huge step up for us in terms of practice digs. Previously, we had been jamming in Bob's basement.

Before long, we were practicing five days a week. The colonel was such a supporter of ours he even hung a sign over the entrance to the cafeteria that said, *Colonel Mar's Bar*.

The base had a row of vending machines in the cafeteria with items like pop, candy, and ice cream. One of the neatest things I'd ever seen at that age was a beer vending machine – 50¢ a can.

Of course, Steve and I, being under age, had our pockets full of quarters whenever we practiced. We made it our mission to drink as much Olympia, Rainer, and Lucky as possible.

The band was talking about adding a female lead singer. Many of the songs we wanted to do were from Linda Ronstadt, Fleetwood Mac and Heart.

We put ads out, like my "Experienced Drummer" ones.

We auditioned one singer, Suzie. On the phone, she was nice and professional. When she came for the tryout, she brought along her own drummer.

"I want him to play during my audition," she said.

Being young and easily intimidated, I relented.

Suzie and her drummer were older, maybe mid-twenties. They got on stage and played *China Grove* by the Doobie Brothers. Steve and Chet covered it well enough to stay with them. The guy beat the shit out of my drums. When they were done, Suzie and her drummer took off.

We believed she was good, but she probably thought we were not to her level. She never called back.

Not long after that, Bob stopped showing up for rehearsals.

He and his wife were fighting often. She gave him a rough time because he was always practicing with the band after work. We kept fielding phone calls for female lead singers. One afternoon on break at school, I was sitting with all the other baking students, in our white clothes.

On the ads I had hung around the city, I had my home number, but for the ones I placed around the college, I said I was in the baking class, "come and find me there."

I looked across the cafeteria and saw a girl watching me, smiling. She was so beautiful, my heart jumped.

She worked her way across the cafeteria towards me. "Are you Bill Bancroft?

After stammering for a moment, I said, "Yeah."

"My name is Linda Beach. I hear you're looking for a singer."

"How did you know I was Bill Bancroft?"

"You look like a musician."

I puffed with pride.

We invited Linda to FAFB to jam with us. She sang a Bread tune along with a couple Linda Ronstadt songs. She sounded great, she looked pretty and she wanted to be in our band. That was good enough for us, so we hired her.

Bob had booked us at the Non-Commissioned Officers (NCO) club on the base. That was my first actual night club gig. This was Linda's first show ever, so she was only going to sing four or five songs since she hadn't learned that many. Even though he had missed most of the recent practices, Bob arrived wearing a fringe vest while we were setting up. We had a good show and the crowd responded well to Linda.

Afterwards, Bob told us he was quitting. His wife was nagging him about the band and he could see we no longer needed him. We didn't fight his leaving and we immediately centered the band around Linda.

I soon learned that line-up changes were a frequent challenge for bands and something I would deal with throughout my career.

The rehearsals continued at FAFB while Linda and I started to hit it off. We were both going to SCC and playing together.

In the meantime, I had begun dating seventeen-year-old Cindy. I would take her fancy things I baked at school. I'd go over to her house to play cards and listen to Joe Walsh albums. Her father was Chet and Bob's boss at the base's paint shop which is how I first met her. We went out for a couple weeks and I was smitten.

On the Bicentennial, July 4, 1976, the band was booked for an outdoor gig at the base. It was one of the biggest gigs we ever had as Organized Crime. Linda sang sixty percent of the songs while the rest of the band had started to sing some occasional songs. We had a great time.

At the show, Cindy cheered me on with real "he's my boyfriend" type stuff.

My sister, Laurie, and her husband were out of town. They let me use their truck to haul my drums to the gig. My plan was to take my new girl back to their house after the show. I figured we were at the point where we would have sex even though I was still a virgin.

When the gig ended, Cindy disappeared so I gave Linda a lift back to her car. She made a comment, "It's a shame you have to go." Being an ignorant kid, I didn't realize what she meant.

I drove back to the concert area to look for Cindy. I couldn't find her so I just started drinking. There was a fair amount of booze at the park. I don't remember how I got away with it, but I hung at the party for hours.

A couple of the guys left the party with two girls each. The lucky bastards. The life of budding rock stars!

I drove the truck back to my sister's house. I had to stop a couple times and get sick on the way. When I got there, I was too drunk to remember where she put the key so I broke into her house.

I fell asleep on the couch and slept off the booze.

In the middle of the following week, Cindy and I went for a drive and held hands. I asked what happened to her at the Centennial party.

"I have to tell you something," she said. "I'm married."

She said her husband knew about me and that he wanted to kill me.

I wish I would have said to myself, *Stop and think about this, Bancroft. She's seventeen and lives with her mom and dad.*

But I fell for it hook, line and sinker. I didn't call bullshit.

She dumped me.

As the resident band, Organized Crime was popular on FAFB. We were so well-known that when we approached the gate, we would wave at the guards and they would wave us through. Colonel Mar even gave us civilian ID stickers for our cars.

Every night, we practiced at the cafeteria, drank the vending machine beers and had a great time.

Outside of practice, Linda and I hung-out together. It was obvious that I had taken a liking to her.

The band signed up with Billy Tipton, a booking agent with the Dave Sobel Agency. Billy is a local legend in the Spokane area. Everyone thought he was a man, but after his death it turned out that Billy was a woman posing as a man for most of his adult life. Several articles and books have been written about him. It's a fascinating story.

Anyway, Billy took a shine to us. He thought we were a bunch of nice kids. He booked us into Baceceks Lounge at the top of Holiday Hills in Liberty Lake, WA. We were scheduled to play one week, Monday through Saturday. We were to be paid $600 for the booking. $100 per night for a five-piece band. That was phenomenal money for us.

The gig was even better than our Fairchild show because it was one we got through an agent.

No one knew us and we were ready to go kick ass.

It turned out we got the Baceceks gig because the house band wanted a week off. They came into the bar one night to drink and watch us play.

All the bandmates got to sing lead vocals on at least one song. My song was *Jumpin' Jack Flash* by the Rolling Stones.

The house band walked in as *Jumpin' Jack Flash* kicked off. That intimidated me and my mind froze. I suddenly couldn't remember the lyrics. I then got flustered and dropped the beat. The song fell apart about halfway through.

From the bar, the guys in the house band laughed. Patrons on the dance floor stopped to watch what was happening. My bandmates turned around and watched my meltdown.

It was horribly humiliating.

I felt like shrinking after that song, but we got through the gig and finished out the week. The club was empty most of the time and the bar owners, obviously, didn't want us back.

On Sunday, the band met at the lounge and the owners paid us in cash. I doled out the money to the band members, a hundred twenty bucks a piece, and they all took off, except Linda and me. We had dinner and danced at the Night Light, a club in State Line, ID.

Billy Tipton next booked us a wedding reception in Fernie, B.C. This was our first road gig.

We packed Chet's Chevy pick-up and my Rambler station wagon and headed to the Canadian border. Steve, Linda and I were in the station wagon. Chet and Brett were in the truck.

As we crossed the Idaho state line I honked my car horn and shouted, "I'm on the road." A tire blew on the station wagon then and wrapped around the axel. We pulled off to the side and jacked up the car. The only cutting tool we had with us was a small pocket knife I carried. We took turns cutting that tire. Steve did most of the sawing. Linda and Chet were down the highway, waving people around us. Once we got the tire changed, we were back on the road.

The border patrol delayed us at the Canadian crossing for a couple hours while they checked our papers. We took pictures and played Frisbee.

I had a simple, happy realization; *I'm a rocker and I'm on the road.*

We finally got to the wedding and played. The crowd liked the band, but they loved Linda. They kept saying, "Let the little girl sing!"

We rehearsed every day even though we didn't have many shows coming in. The band was getting tighter and we were having more fun on our practice stage. It was clear to the guys that a relationship was brewing between Linda and me. It bothered Brett Ashley since he also had a crush on Linda. As a result, he grew distant.

I invited the band to Priest Lake, Idaho for the weekend. My sister, Carol, worked for Fidelity Bank and they had three cabins she was able to rent. The plan was to go to the lake, play acoustic guitars around the campfire, fish and drink with Carol's friends.

Only Linda said yes. I wasn't disappointed when the guys bagged out.

On the Tuesday afternoon before the trip, I decided to head across the state line to get our fishing licenses. I phoned Linda to get her birthday and other particulars.

She answered the phone and told me she was just stepping out of the shower. She said she was dripping wet and wrapped only in a towel. That statement played havoc with my brain.

I explained what I wanted and she told me to wait. She'd head over to my house and we'd go get the licenses together.

About forty-five minutes later, Linda pulled up in her beige, convertible MG Midget sports car. She tossed me her car keys. "Why don't you drive?"

As we drove to Post Falls, Idaho, a town just across the state line, she waved to the truckers we passed and they honked back. We laughed and had a blast. We stopped at a hardware store and got the fishing licenses.

I mentioned this earlier, but in 1976, the drinking age in Idaho was nineteen. It was imperative we stop and get something to take home. Linda asked, "Do you like wine?"

I responded, "Yes," like there was any doubt of another answer.

Linda introduced me to Liebfraumilch, a semi-sweet white German wine. I thought she was so mature because of her taste in alcohol. She was not only beautiful, drove a sports car and sang in a rock band, but she liked fine wine. It wasn't until years later in life that I comprehended this was a shitty wine, but back then I thought it was the best. As a side note, literally translated, Liebfraumilch means *Beloved Lady's Milk*.

She went into the store and bought a couple bottles, a corkscrew and two plastic champagne glasses.

We drove to Coeur d'Alene City Park to look at the lake. It was early spring so there weren't many people roaming around. We sat on a bench and drank a bottle.

After that we drove out toward the town of Plummer until we found a long sloping hill with an old, dilapidated farm house on it. We parked the car and ran to the house. We finished the second bottle while we continued our talk.

As we walked down the long hill toward the car, Linda stopped us in the field to lie and watch the sun and the clouds in the sky.

We lay there for a bit, in that beautiful moment. Then I sat up and said, "We should probably get going." Now, all these years later, I fully grasp the moment I missed.

We went back to Coeur d'Alene and visited a few different taverns. At the last bar, there was a hotel next door. I said, jokingly, when I noticed it, "Hey, let's get a room." I was so naïve. Sex was on my mind but I didn't know how to make it happen or I would have been much subtler. I was astounded that she even wanted to hang out with me.

Inside, we shot pool and she touched me as we played. I didn't know what to do. We finished our game and headed home to Greenacres. We parked in front of my parent's house around 11:00 p.m. and went for a walk to continue talking. We cut through some nearby fields.

She finally got tired of waiting, grabbed me, pulled me to the ground and kissed me. The earth was rocky and we got up after a couple minutes. We headed home and into the backyard of my parent's house.

Linda stopped, wrapped her arms around my waist and kissed me again. A lilac hedge hid us from the house as we lay in the grass. She said, "Now, do you feel comfortable *here*?"

"Yeah."

And we made love.

For years, until I later met my wife, that was the best day of my life.

After that, the next few rehearsals were even more fun. We'd both arrive early. She'd bring a sack lunch for us and I'd grab beers from the vending machine. We'd go to the park on the base and eat together.

Linda and I spent most of the weekend alone in the cabin at Priest River. My family and friends were all expecting me to party hard, but we barely came out of our cabin. It was a new world and I was blissfully happy.

On the ride home from the lake, however, Linda sat next to the window and smoked. When I asked if she was going to move next to me in the car, she said, "Let me put out my cigarette and I will." She never did.

She quit bringing sack lunches after that weekend. I would come early for rehearsal, but Linda wasn't there.

A couple days later, Linda and Brett walked by together outside the cafeteria. They didn't say anything as they passed. I spun around and watched them, wondering *Were they together now?*

My head was full of confusion and anger. After experiencing one of the most profound moments of my young life, making love with Linda, it was like she didn't even see me. It seemed like I no longer existed to her. My heart was broken.

To make matters worse, Brett barely acknowledged me either.

It felt like I was right back in school with a couple of my own bandmates – a nobody, a speck on the wall. It played to my insecurities and I struggled with it for weeks.

Steve Hanna called one Monday morning in August to say Billy Tipton had a six-night gig for us at the Thunderbird Motor Inn in Ellensburg, Washington. They had a cancellation and we were a last-minute replacement. We were to start that very night.

I didn't hesitate. "I'm in," I said.

I went to my boss, Mr. Duckworth, to ask for time off, but he wouldn't agree to it.

I'd started my first baking job in the summer at the department store cafeteria of the Bon Marche. Located on the fifth floor, the Pear Tree was a small bakery inside a larger restaurant.

Mr. Duckworth was a suit and tie guy and quite full of himself. He wore thick glasses and was balding yet strutted around like a peacock. The guy thought he knew how to bake but clearly didn't. To a budding rock star, he was a turd.

I was making $5.50 an hour which was fantastic money for a nineteen-year-old, but I didn't hesitate to quit for the gig in Ellensburg.

Chet was able to get off from work and Linda wasn't working so she was in.

Brett was working at Volunteers of America for $2/hour and got pissed at the short notice. "I'm not quitting my job for this." We argued about it, but in the end, he wouldn't go. Steve said, "Bill quit a $6/hour job and you won't quit your fucking job?"

Brett wasn't swayed, however.

Steve, Chet and I went to the gig without Brett. We would figure out how to do the show without him. Linda didn't have to haul gear, so she said she would arrive later. When she did, she had Brett in her car.

My brain was on complete overload then.

What the hell was going on with them?

At the Thunderbird Motor Inn, we played in the lounge and Chet and Brett were the only members of the band over twenty-one. On breaks, Steve, Linda and I had to leave the lounge and either go outside or back to our rooms.

The thing with Brett and Linda weighed on me. I hoped Linda and I could spend some nights together at the Thunderbird, but that didn't happen. The four guys hung out and drank in our rooms.

On Friday night, my parents came to see us. This would be the first time they would see me play professionally in a bar. Before the gig, I brought them over to Linda's room to meet her. She was polite, but abrupt.

After the show, I followed Linda to her room and confronted her. "What's going on?"

She admitted that when we first got together she had a boyfriend. She had split with him to see me. Ever since the Priest Lake trip she felt guilty. She was also worried she might be pregnant.

I tried to talk more, but she didn't want to have anything to do with me.

"Good night, Bill," she said and closed the door.

After the gig, Brett and Linda drove back to Spokane together.

On Monday, Steve called and said Linda had quit the band. "You and Brett need to get some things straight."

Brett and I met at a burger joint. Brett said I had betrayed him by going after Linda. For some reason, Brett got teary eyed.

We talked some and then apologized to each other.

It was obvious that the band needed another female lead singer and, therefore, we made a pact - *neither of us would ever screw the lead singer again.*

We put an ad in the paper for a new singer and LuAnn Miller responded. She was cute, tall and blonde. She was also young and immature.

LuAnn rode with Steve and me to the base to audition. As we walked towards the cafeteria, she stated, "I'm so tired of people telling me how great I am."

She was trying to impress us, but I was a kid myself and it fell flat. All I thought about was how big her ego was and how much trouble she was going to be.

During her audition, she sang and boogied. She could definitely perform. While Linda was the girl next door, LuAnn acted provocatively. She just had that vibe while on stage.

It was a Wednesday when we auditioned her and we had a gig in two days in Smelterville, Idaho. LuAnn passed the try-out and we invited her into the band.

Brett and Chet rode in the pick-up to Smelterville while Steve, LuAnn and I were in Steve's Buick. LuAnn sat in the backseat with the lyrics for all the songs she was to sing. She practiced during the hour and a half drive. Our gig was in the Sandbox Lounge at The Sands Motel.

Smelterville was a hotbed of mining activity in the '70s and the club was packed on Friday. We killed it that night. We had a good variety of country-rock and current rock songs. We did *Hey, Baby* by Ted Nugent and the crowd flipped over it.

By now, the band was already dressing like gangsters. It was Billy Tipton's idea. LuAnn dressed like a flapper. She gyrated her hips as she sang and the crowd lost their minds. It was great and LuAnn cemented herself in the band.

The next weekend we had a show in Canada at TJ's Lounge in Creston, B.C. We stayed at The Kokanee Inn. That place was so disgusting it had rat droppings in the corner of the rooms.

The show was a disaster before it started. The club had billed us as a disco band from Chicago.

We were scared to sleep in the hotel because we didn't want bugs or rodents crawling on us so we stayed awake and partied through the night.

When we returned to Spokane, we continued to practice.

Bob Allen, our former lead singer, wanted his P.A. system back so we were stuck. We persuaded LuAnn to buy one. She was the lead singer, right? She convinced her parents to front the money, but they wanted to meet the band. They needed to know we were upstanding young men who would take care of their daughter. After the meeting, Mr. Miller reluctantly agreed to buy the P.A. system and we were back in business. It cost $300.

The Sandbox booked us for a return gig. There were a lot of women who came to our shows that were divorced from miners and very horny. The whole band had a great time.

I took a girl back to my hotel room on Saturday night and, at some point, she bit my neck. Hard! I didn't think much of it since I was drunk out of my mind.

I awoke Sunday morning with a hickey. Not a normal-sized, purple one. No, this son of a bitch was the size of a grapefruit and went from my neck to my cheek. To make it worse it was purple, yellow, and black. The girl must have been a vampire.

When we returned home to Spokane, I had plans to eat dinner with my parents. I wore a turtleneck in hopes of hiding the damn thing. It was spring so it wasn't cold. I know my dad saw the purplish mark, but never said anything.

I can still recall his wide-eyed look. Bless his heart.

The following Tuesday, we got a call from Billy. "They want you back at the Sandbox."

I thought, "Right on."

They put ads in the local paper that we were returning. The locals loved us and we killed it again.

We had such a great following at the Sandbox that when they didn't book us for one of the weekends, Steve, Brett and I drove back to watch the other band. We were celebrities there. People noticed us when we were in the bar, even though we weren't playing.

Billy booked our next gig at The Nickelodeon in St. Maries, Idaho.

Brett and LuAnn had gotten chummy and were drinking a great deal together. Brett would drink a six pack before rehearsal, sometimes a six pack during, and then we'd party afterwards.

The second night we were at the Nickelodeon, between our third and last set, the break stretched long because Brett and LuAnn were nowhere to be found. Chet eventually located them, completely smashed, together in a car.

We were late getting back on stage. The club owner was pissed. "You're here to do a job," he said.

It was the typical club-owner thing, but we couldn't blame him. The rest of the band was angry at Brett and LuAnn as well.

When she came back on stage, LuAnn was so drunk she could barely stand. We finished the gig and went back to Spokane.

We had it out with Brett and LuAnn and fired them on the same day.

By late '76, things were shaky.

We had outgrown the Sandbox. We figured we deserved more money and they weren't paying it. We had another gig upcoming at the Nickelodeon and immediately auditioned new guitar players.

United, the remaining band members decided, "To hell with female lead singers, we're done with them."

Around this time, our benefactor at Fairchild Air Force Base, Colonel Mar, was reassigned elsewhere and the new colonel quickly learned there was a rock band practicing on the base with no authorization to be there. He also discovered the permanent passes on our windshields even though we weren't playing the NCO club on a regular basis. We had worn out our welcome.

Without Colonel Mar, no one had our back anymore and we were told to stop practicing on the base. We moved our practices to Steve's house.

Our search ended when Randy Peterson entered our lives.

This guy was walking confidence. He had previously played in a band, One Shot Deal. They had some minor success when they once opened at the coliseum for Head East (*Never Been Any Reason* was their big hit song). One Shot Deal lived on that reputation for a while.

Randy blew us away. He played guitar as well as Steve. He could also sing lead. We immediately thought, "This is the guy!"

At that moment, Organized Crime became a four-piece band and dropped all country-rock songs. Randy couldn't stand that sound. We had already been moving toward more standard rock and roll so we didn't fight the change.

Randy certainly influenced us. He always looked sharp, wearing suits at times. He had a Marshall stack and a gold top Les Paul guitar. He was a rocker and taught us about stage presence.

Along with the change in line-up, Steve got his first perm and I got my first wavy perm. We also got some new clothes.

Poor Chet, being an older guy and an airman, still had his short hair. It was the '70s and he stuck out like a sore thumb in our band. He tried to dress sharp, but it never worked out right.

Steve bought a jumpsuit, but he could pull it off. He was that cool.

Then Chet bought one, too. His was made of denim and looked like mechanic's coveralls. Chet thought he looked sharp in it, but the denim jumpsuit was too tight. He also wore white high-top tennis shoes. With his close-cropped military haircut, he didn't look like he fit the rock scene. He played a Vox-replica of Paul McCartney's bass.

In this outfit, Chet would drop to one knee while playing in hopes of making it flashy. We would all cringe whenever he did it.

Chet was completely out of his element.

Billy continued to book us shows including high school dances and private parties. We played gigs from Canada to Walla Walla, Washington to Lewiston, Idaho and all the little towns in between. We even played in Montana.

Things got scary in Potlatch, Idaho. Most of the places we played had lights for the show. I had some lights that I attached to the cymbal stands to aim at my drum heads. All they had above the stage in one Potlatch club was a single 60-watt light bulb.

We played and the crowd hated us.

They were cowboys and we were a rock band.

It wasn't the right place for us.

Afterward, as we loaded the gear, a big four-wheel drive truck pulled up with a bunch of cowboys in it. They yelled things like, "You guys suck," "Hippie girls with your long hair," and other stupid shit like that.

Of course, being the polite young man I was becoming, I told them to "fuck off" along with some other not so nice things they could do to their horses.

The lead cowboy threw a beer bottle from the truck which hit me in the forehead.

When I regained my senses, Steve told me they were going to go get some friends and come back to kick our asses. We finished loading the gear in a hurry and got the hell out of Potlatch.

With a big knot on my forehead, we hauled ass all the way back to Spokane.

In November of '76, Billy booked us a gig at the 121 Club in Boise, Idaho to open for Heart, whose debut album, Dreamboat Annie had recently come out and was making a big splash. Heart still had responsibilities to play many smaller venues they had previously booked. Also opening for them was Child, a popular Seattle band that we totally respected.

We piled into Chet's truck and drove the eight hours to Boise. To save money, we had recently adopted the practice of cramming the four of us into the front of Chet's pick-up. It was cheaper than driving two vehicles everywhere.

We drove all night to get there.

When we walked into the club, we were blown away. Heart brought their big sound system. There were huge speakers on both sides of the stage. Mike Derosier, the drummer for Heart, had a monster drum kit on stage.

We hauled my drums in and set them in front of Mike's huge set. Heart's sound check guys put a microphone in front of the kick drum and a mic over the top of the kit.

We went on stage at 6 p.m. Now here is a tried and true fact; *Nobody is ready to rock and roll at that time of night.*

We were essentially the sound check band. We played a variety of songs including some from Head East and Ted Nugent. All of us tried and failed to dress like rock stars, especially me.

Beyond the sound check guys, the crowd consisted mostly of the bartender, the waitress, and a few other people.

When we were done playing, the club gave us a reserved table to watch the other bands. After us, Child came out. The place was packed by the time they started. We were so impressed with them that we would later cover a couple of their songs in our act.

When Heart came on, they rocked the venue. Their show was awesome.

I thought Mike Derosier was a rock god. When he played, he wore a pair of drummer gloves. I later bought some to be like him.

That night we stayed in a cheap hotel. The after-party was in the room of Lance Baumgartel, Child's bass player. He wore red satin pants, a white shirt and Jovan *Sex Appeal* cologne. Our band thought he was so cool that when we got home, we all went out and bought a variety of Jovan scents. I would later start wearing knee high moccasins because of Lance.

Ann and Nancy Wilson from Heart were also at the party. I tried to move next to Nancy, but she continually flicked me away like an annoying fly. I followed her around the room all evening. She was nice enough, but dismissive and I can't really blame her. I was an awestruck kid trying to get next to a newly minted star.

We hired a sound guy, Robert, who was the cousin of Brett Ashley, our former member. Robert worked at a music store and that somehow qualified him in our minds to be a soundman.

Organized Crime was headed next to Troy, Montana for a two-night stay at the Little Opry Hall.

Around this time, I had purchased a red and white Ford Econoline van.

The band crammed into the Ford, along with our new soundman. Two guys in the front and the other three sitting in the back on whatever equipment they could.

We were on a two-lane highway. I sped up to 70 mph to pass a car and the driveline came off the front U-joint. It bounced along the ground. We were lucky it didn't dig into the road and kill us.

I immediately pulled over. We didn't have any tools to fix the thing.

A sheriff stopped by to see what happened and make sure we were okay. He gave Robert and me a lift into nearby Bonners Ferry, Idaho to buy a new U-joint.

Robert was a good mechanic and figured out how to fix the van without the necessary tools. He pounded the driveline back in place with a rock and a 2' x 4'. It was astounding how he got us back on the road.

We still made the gig albeit a little late.

The Little Opry Hall treated us like rock stars. It was a large log cabin building on Highway 2 in the middle of nowhere. It was a popular place for bands and fans.

People literally hung from the rafters. Girls climbed on the railings and pulled up their shirts. Some of them shook their breasts in my face while I played. I was twenty years old and could hardly stand it. It was so much fun!

Organized Crime was booked to play a couple nights at The Mint Lounge in Wallace, Idaho. On the second night, the band tore down our equipment after the bar closed. Our mixing board was an old Peavey system which stood on four very heavy aluminum legs.

Randy had flipped me shit through the night because I'd started dating a girl named Sherry. I previously went out with Sherry once in high school – she was my prom date. She agreed to go out with me again, but she didn't like the fact I was in a rock band. Because she was a cowgirl I got heavily into country music. That's why Randy razzed me.

I finally had enough and grabbed one of the Peavey legs. I raised it above my head and threatened him with it.

Randy yelled, "What are you doing, you stupid motherfucker?"

The rest of the band froze, watching us.

I pointed the Peavey leg at Randy. "You give me any more shit and I'm going to break this over your head."

On the drive back to Spokane, the band joked about my argument with Randy. The running gag became "Don't give me any shit or I'll get you with a Peavey leg."

We pulled off the highway and took side streets for a round of mailbox baseball. We each took turns leaning out of the passenger window of our van with the remaining guys holding onto the batter's jeans for support. The batter used a Peavey leg as his baseball bat.

We knocked over a shit-load of mailboxes that night.

On Christmas Eve and Christmas Day, we were booked to play The War Bonnet Saloon in Nespelem, Washington. The town is located on the Colville Indian Reservation.

This was the first Christmas I would not spend with my family.

At the saloon, the band set up on the floor next to the bathrooms.

On the first night, the bar was full of drunk, sad people. We played and those in attendance liked us fine. Through the night there were several fights and several patrons who puked in the bar.

One large man, roughly 300 pounds, leaned on one of our speakers. He was drunk and swayed to his own rhythm while we played. Eventually, he passed out and fell behind the speaker. The only thing between him and the floor was my drum kit.

He fell on the floor tom and broke off a leg. He also knocked over a cymbal and pushed me from my stool.

The song ended abruptly.

The bar staff quickly got the man out of there. The club owner came over with $100 to replace the broken equipment.

I duct taped the leg of the floor tom together to make it through the gig.

At the end of the night, we left our equipment at the saloon since we were due to play the next evening and drove home to Spokane.

I got about an hour and a half of sleep before waking to open presents with mom and dad. Afterwards, instead of having dinner with family, I had Christmas dinner with Sherry.

Then I drove back to Nespelem with the band to play the Christmas night gig.

We were also booked for a New Year's Eve gig.

Sherry was going out to the Slab Inn in Post Falls and I wanted to go, but I had to work as a rock and roller – at a church youth dance, no less.

The band was scheduled to go to the youth center around 7 p.m. to get ready. It wasn't too far from Sherry's house so I figured I had plenty of time and hung out at her house all afternoon.

About 7 p.m., the band wasn't at the youth center so I drove to Steve's house. When I arrived, I saw the guys sitting in his living room.

When I walked in, they told me they were wondering where I was at. A booking agent named Mary Lou had scheduled the show for us. She double booked us with another band and then cancelled us.

"You've got to be kidding," I said.

I was pissed, but the other guys had already dealt with their anger. They were resigned to the fact that we were out some dough.

"Let's go party" was the new plan.

"No. I'm going out with Sherry," I said. "Why would I hang out with you ugly fuckers, when I could hang out with her?"

Steve laughed and made the sound of a whip. The other guys chanted "pussy-whipped." Steve continued his whip sounds and laughed harder, eventually falling to the floor.

That pissed me off. When Steve finally stood, I pushed him back to the ground. He was laughing too hard to get mad.

I stomped out of the house, like a punk, and went to the Slab Inn to be with Sherry.

A shake-up was brewing in the band.

Randy thought Chet was holding us back. He was about ten years older than the rest of us and wasn't keeping pace with the changes in the band. We wanted to play Aerosmith and Zeppelin and Chet wanted to play country-rock.

One day I came into town to meet with Steve. We were going to listen to music and select new songs for the band to learn. We listened for a couple hours and then Steve said, "By the way, Chet quit."

"What?"

"Yeah. He quit the band. We've got to do something fast."

I immediately got in touch with Dave Low, the bassist for Cold Smoke. He had previously been in a band known as Krystal Kidd but was now free of musical commitments. He jumped in right away. No audition necessary.

At the beginning of '77, Organized Crime sounded tight. We bought some new gear and had made the decision to get a new soundman. Dan Murphy, a friend of mine, hit the road with us to work the mixing board.

We went to Nelson, B.C. for a gig at The Golden Drift. I had a rough night. The band was improving, but I felt like I wasn't. I was dropping beats I shouldn't. I still felt easily intimidated and thought the bartender and waitress hated me.

I missed a beat and I saw the bartender say, "See what I told you? He's terrible."

The waitress said, "Yeah, he sucks."

It devastated me.

After the show, a bunch of girls came back to our hotel room. There was a husky girl who liked me. She wasn't my usual type but didn't say no to a groupie throwing herself at me.

The waitress from the bar also came to the party. I was drunk and laid into her. "How dare you say shit like that?"

She didn't know what to say. I continued with my tirade.

"Opinions are like assholes, everyone's got one," I yelled. I used every cliché I could think of and tore into her until she cried.

One of the guys came to her rescue and got her away from me. She rewarded him the way groupies do.

The band decided to make a change in agents. We were no longer a country-rock band and Billy Tipton wasn't connected to the big rock and roll clubs. It was becoming clear that we were leaving him behind.

Billy treated us well. He was never condescending even though we were young and a little goofy. We never went wrong working with him, and I have nothing but respect for the guy.

We auditioned at The Judge's Chambers, a bar near the Spokane County Courthouse to get the eye of an agent, Jeannie Carter of Freade´ Sounds.

Even though I had my perm, I didn't dress like a rocker for the show. I was still doing my cowboy thing. I took off my cowboy shirt and hung it on my microphone stand and played in my t-shirt. The rest of the band was nicely dressed.

Jeannie was a bit unimpressed but saw enough to take us on and start scheduling some gigs. She also said we needed to change the name of the band.

In March, the band was booked for a two-night return gig at The Mint Lounge in Wallace, Idaho. We stayed at The Down Towner Hotel.

Dave and I bunked together and Randy, Steve and Dan were in the other room. Due to our time in Smelterville, we were very popular in the Silver Valley, a region of Idaho known for its mining and brothel heritage.

We had a solid show on Friday night. After the gig, Dave and I partied hard, but I didn't chase any women since I was dating Sherry. I would go through this on-again, off-again argument with myself while on the road. Sometimes I'd be faithful to my girlfriend and others, well, you get the point. I was young and women were plentiful. There was a part of me that wanted to be a good guy and there was a part of me that wanted to do what every rock and roller does.

Dave and I went back to our room and continued drinking. We still wore our slip-on platform shoes. When Dave kicked his shoes off, one flew to the ceiling and hit it, causing some paint chips to flake off and fall to the carpet.

That gave us an idea for a contest.

We sat on the edge of our own beds, kicked our shoes skyward and tried to see who could get one to stick into the sheetrock ceiling first.

I tried, and my shoe bounced off. Dave tried with the same amount of success. We drank some more and attempted the challenge again. Platform shoes continued to bang off the ceiling as we laughed and yelled, having a great time.

Finally, Dave swung his leg hard and his shoe launched like a rocket. It buried itself, toes deep, in the ceiling.

We cheered our success and ingenuity until there was a knock on the door.

I opened it to see the hotel manager standing there.

"What the hell is going on?"

He looked over my shoulder at the beer cans and bottles scattered around the room, the chunks of ceiling that had fallen to the floor and on the beds. His eyes went to the ceiling and saw the marks from various failed attempts and the lone platform shoe stuck deep in the drywall.

"You're out of here," he said. "Now!"

Dave and I packed our stuff and loaded the truck. Dave snuck into Randy and Steve's room to sleep. I slept in the truck.

In the morning, the manager kicked out Randy, Steve and Dan. They were guilty by association.

Jeannie Carter really let us have it when we got back to town. The hotel manager had called her and told her what we had done.

When we played the Nickelodeon in St. Maries again, I brought Sherry and her little sister, who was nineteen.

Randy got drunk and made a spectacle by hitting on the little sister. That pissed off Sherry. The next day, I took the girls back home. Sherry hardly spoke to me because of my bandmate's behavior.

I went over to her house later that week so she could trim my hair. In the middle of the haircut, she said, frustrated, "How am I supposed to cut this? This isn't what I want."

And that was it. She broke off our relationship.

Our next big gig was in Pocatello, Idaho at the Hotel Yellowstone, part of a three-week summer tour. We played a couple shows in Bozeman and Missoula, Montana before finally arriving in Southern Idaho.

On the last few miles into Pocatello, our Ford Econoline Van began leaking oil profusely from the rear main seal. It was spewing quarts of oil!

We limped the van into town, but we weren't going any further until it was repaired. Dave spent most of our free time in Pocatello under the van. As the band's duly appointed mechanic (meaning he was the only one who understood how to fix cars), he spent hours under the van in a wind-blown dirt parking lot with limited tools repairing the rear main seal. He complained about us running around town while he had to fix our ride.

For the gig, the club insisted we change our name to "Small Change" for the week. They said our name of Organized Crime "might bring in trouble." We suspected that there may have been some shady dealings going on with ownership. At night, we'd watch fancy cars and limos pull in front of the club. Nicely dressed guys came and went. Speculation on what they were doing is simply that.

It was a scary place. Bikers and generally strange people hung out there.

Each one of us had our own room, but we had to share communal bathrooms.

On our first day there, I was sitting on a toilet and a bearded lady walked in. She was dumpy with big boobs and a full beard. For a moment, she stared at me and I stared back, aghast, as I sat on the toilet. She eventually turned and left. She seriously looked like someone in a *bad* circus act.

I walked back into Steve's room. He said I was white as a ghost. I was totally freaked out.

But what a sex-fest Pocatello turned out to be! Most of the action revolved around a pack of groupies that worked at the club. For that week, each one of us had our own squeeze. Mine was a waitress at the club who had the cutest butt. She gave me the first blowjob of my life.

During one of the days there, I went over to her house. She gave me a handful of Niacin pills and said, "These are a lot of fun, try it." Of course, I did. What a rush. I broke out all over in red bumps and my mind raced, but it went away after about ten minutes.

On Sunday afternoon, we were invited to a biker party in the woods. Dave was still under the van trying to get us ready to flee Pocatello.

Most of the bikers were eating mushrooms, but the rest of us didn't consume them because we had to head to Twin Falls later that night.

The bikers and their girls jumped into a creek. They decided they also wanted the band to get wet. They grabbed Steve, the baby-faced guy in the group, and threw him in the stream. Randy was off in the woods with a girl.

When they focused on me, I ran for my life. I jumped a bush and landed in a bonfire pit, cracking a rib. I also was gashed from a branch that dug deep into my skin. I still have that scar. The guys left me alone after that.

I did get some attention from a couple girls who tended my wounds. Poor me.

The whole band was totally smashed by the time the party ended around 10 p.m. and we still had to head to Twin Falls, about 120 miles away.

When we made it to Twin Falls, we had to find a hotel room in the middle of the night. No one wanted to rent to us. We reeked of alcohol and I looked like I had been in a fight.

We finally made it into one hotel room and set about cleaning ourselves up. A few minutes later, there was a knock on the door. It was the manager.

"I want you out."

"We weren't making any noise," I said.

He handed us back our money. "Get out."

That provoked a shouting match between us and him. He finally threatened to call the police.

We moved on and found a hotel that rented us a room with three double beds. For the week, I wrapped my ribs as tight as I could. Playing the gigs was tough.

On our first day, some of us sought out medical attention at a free clinic. We knew the girls that we had met previously in Pocatello had been with anybody and everybody so we wanted to get checked out. I figured a cotton swab down the tip of my dick was the price of rock and roll.

That's a hell of a price to pay, by the way.

After the tour, we came back to Spokane and had a week off.

My sister, Laurie, and her husband were going out to Twin Lakes, Idaho. A long-time family friend, Donna, was going along so I joined them.

We rode in the front of Laurie's big orange truck. Donna rode on my lap. I didn't think anything about it since Donna was close with my other sister, Carol, too. Besides, she was four years older than me so I figured there was never a shot.

After boating, we went back to shore. I said I had to go for a walk and use the bathroom. Donna said she'd join me. When I came out of the restroom, she was waiting.

"We need to talk," she said.

"Okay."

She put her hands on my shoulders.

What the hell is going on? I thought.

"I want to talk about us," Donna said.

My jaw dropped. Donna had a nice figure that was now dripping wet in a low-cut swimming suit. She definitely stirred me up. Donna moved in close, pressed against my body and kissed me.

This was a girl that I fantasized about for years when our families hung out together. I was stunned for the rest of the day.

After the lake, we went back to mom and dad's house. Carol invited Donna to stay for dinner. Mom and dad sat at the heads of the table, Carol and Donna were on one side and I was on the other. While we ate dinner, Donna ran her foot along my legs. I could hardly eat. I had to excuse myself and take a walk. When I came back, both Carol and Donna had left.

Carol lived on the opposite side of town by then. I had to talk to my sister about the whole Donna incident. I grabbed my car keys and announced to mom and dad, "I'm going to visit Carol."

"I want to visit her, too," mom said.

Being the good son, I couldn't say no. We went over and mom talked with Carol for a half an hour before we left.

When we got home, I said I needed to go back to Carol's. "I forgot to talk with her about something."

Dad said, "Is it about Donna?"

Mom smiled, knowingly.

Back at Carol's house, my sister said Donna had a crush on me since I was in high school. She was worried about it since Donna was older than me and I was still immature.

Organized Crime was preparing for a four-week tour. Pendleton, OR, Twin Falls and Pocatello, ID and then to Bozeman, MT. It wasn't good money, but a return trip to places we'd played showed we were advancing.

The night before we left, Donna was house-sitting and she invited me over. I was a nervous wreck as we sat in the kitchen, talking. When we made-out in the living room I felt overwhelmed. This was my fantasy girl. Then she said, "Let's go to bed."

She was older than me and she knew what she was doing. This wasn't like the groupies. It was amazing. I figured this was what passion was supposed to be like.

We set the alarm for 5 a.m. since the band was hitting the road at 8.

She walked me to the door in her robe shortly after we awoke. She let it fall open to show her body.

In less than a second, I had the robe off her as we tumbled back into the house.

I barely had enough time to get home, shower, and race to Steve Hanna's place so we could head out. I hadn't gotten any sleep, but that didn't matter.

I had a grin on my face the rest of the day.

Our first stop on the tour was in Pendleton, Oregon at The Rathskellers (a very popular name for clubs during that time). It was a basement club with low ceilings. By then, the band was using smoke bombs and flash pots for added stage presence.

We had two different types of effects with our flash pots. The first was caused by packing the pots with flash powder. We did this on our Led Zeppelin covers. The result was loud, concussive booms with bright flashes of lights.

The second type of effect was caused by flame powder packed into the pots. The result was a shot of flame when ignited. We positioned four of these at the front of the stage so we'd have a wall of flames on certain songs. During *Jumpin' Jack Flash*, Dan would set these flames off, and Steve, Dave, and Randy would jump through them. It was awesome.

We'd been booked at The Rathskellers for two weeks and started on a Monday. On Thursday night, Dan packed the flash pots with a little too much flame powder. He set them off during *Jumpin' Jack Flash*. Unfortunately, the guys didn't have a chance to jump through the flames because the ceiling was ablaze.

The club owner ran over with a fire extinguisher and put out the flames. The pressurized carbon dioxide, the white stuff from the fire extinguisher, rained on our gear and got all over my drums. It pissed me off and I yelled at the club owner to aim the extinguisher in another direction.

It was a fucking debacle.

The club owner was seriously pissed. Veins stuck out of his neck as he screamed at us. "If you ever set those off again, you're fired! I outta fire you right now!"

We took a break and let things calm down. We didn't use the flaming flash pots the rest of the week.

On Saturday morning, at the end of the first week, our agent, Jeannie Carter, called us at the club.

"I've got a great gig for you at the David Thompson Motor Inn in Kamloops, B.C. They'll pay you $2,000 and rooms for two weeks."

For a four-piece band with a soundman, in the late summer of 1977, that was outstanding money.

A band previously booked for the Kamloops gig had fallen out. We were an emergency replacement. Jeannie booked another band to take over the rest of our tour through Twin Falls, Pocatello and Bozeman. We were disappointed that we weren't going to visit those clubs because there were some nice girls in those cities who we had lots of sex and drugs with on our previous tour.

However, we figured we couldn't pass up the career move of playing at the David Thompson Motor Inn.

The owner of The Rathskellers was more than happy to not let us play the second week.

On Sunday morning, we headed to Kamloops. At the David Thompson Motor Inn, they were accustomed to bands like Ship of Fools, Apple Jack, and Blind Willie. Those were quality regional bands that were much more experienced than us.

We took the stage on the first night and the crowd hated us. Our equipment wasn't to the standards of the other bands and they played more oldies. The place wasn't packed that night, but we had an okay time.

We bought a bag of dope and spent our free time drinking Canadian beer and smoking shitty weed.

I turned twenty-one while we were in Kamloops. The guys asked what I wanted for my birthday and I said, "A bottle of Jack Daniels and to get laid."

They bought me a bottle of JD and I was lucky enough to meet a girl who helped make that birthday wish come true. We wrote each other for a while after that trip.

On a side note, I would give groupies my address and they would write me. But it was, in fact, Jeannie's business address. When we would get home, she'd hand me a stack of mail from various girls. I didn't want them to know where I lived. This also saved me work when I came back into town the next time.

When they got too serious, I ended various pen pal relationships by saying I was engaged.

While in Kamloops, we made friends with some local girls and had plenty of extra-curricular activity. Even though I thought I was madly in love with Donna, I was cheating on her constantly while on the road. Today, I can't defend these actions. All I can say now is that I didn't know what it really meant to be in love then.

On our one day off, we went out and bought a song book of oldies so we could learn some tunes that the locals might like. It was full of 1950s hits from bands like Buddy Holly and Bill Haley and the Comets.

The band would practice earlier in the day so we could be a little more professional. This was a time when the band matured because we set out to do our job right. We developed the mentality to do the best job in the face of adversity.

It didn't matter. The locals still didn't like us.

On a midweek night at the Motor Inn, we were sitting in our hotel room partying after our gig. There was a girl there who wasn't very attractive, but she was clearly horny. She had her sights set on Dan. He was sitting on the floor and she was on the couch. She started combing his hair and he shrieked before running out of the room.

The girl was totally shocked.

I told her not to worry about Dan – he was just incredibly shy.

She got over it quickly because we hooked up without much effort.

After the Kamloops experience, we returned to Spokane and set to rehearsing like animals. We were going to sound our best and be the most professional band we could be. Around this time, we met with Jeannie at the Judge's Chambers. She challenged us again to change the band's name from Organized Crime and alter our look.

She wanted the band to have a professional rock and roll image. I still had a country appearance and stuck out like a sore thumb.

We had a return gig at The Golden Drift in Nelson, B.C. The Golden Drift was a basement club whose ceiling and walls looked like rocks but was actually made of soft insulation. The owner of the club was an old guy who dressed in a tuxedo every night. He spoke in a crazy, German accent and acted like he was introducing Dean Martin at some swanky club.

He would also say, "Welcome to the Golden Drrrrift," rolling his r's with his accent. Then he would announce, "Ladies and Gentlemen, Organized Crime, playing all the hits that you love!"

During the show, a fan gave Dave a Hunchback of Notre Dame mask and he put it on. Dave grabbed his billowy coat and wore it backwards. He looked like a crazy, guitar-playing Frankenstein. The crowd went wild and some of them "gatored" on the floor, like they did in the movie *Animal House*.

The club owner ran out and immediately stopped the music. He pointed at us and yelled, "You do that again and you're fired."

We finished the gig and the club owner said, "You'll never be back here."

There were plenty of times when we deserved some form of punishment, but I wouldn't say this was one of them.

The band was also performing at frat parties and high school dances. One gig was booked by a musician's fraternity at the University of Moscow.

We were especially concerned with this performance and if they were going to like us or not. These kids were going to college to learn how to play music and we were playing for them.

We had a great time, though, and they went crazy for us. When the show was over, the party moved upstairs. We didn't even pack the gear. We left it where it was.

I met this girl nicknamed The Duke and we had sex in an upstairs broom closet. We had to kick mop buckets out of the way to make room for ourselves. We wrote each other for a while afterwards.

I broke up with Donna when we returned home.

Every time we were together the sex was incredible. It wasn't like it had been with any other girl. However, the emotional stuff was too intense. I kept thinking she wanted to get married.

We went out for a date and she gave me a late birthday present: a blue t-shirt that read *Columbian is the best* and an ounce of pot. Then we went to a tavern for a beer.

Afterwards, we drove back to her where her was car parked at the University City Mall. We made out in her car for a bit and then I broke it off.

"I can't do this," I said. "This is too quick."

She cried and I left.

Don't get me wrong, I felt shitty. I wasn't an uncaring bastard, but I wanted to be in a band and she wanted a family. I wasn't ready for that.

RAVEN
1977-1978

(L-R) Me, Steve Hanna, Dave Low and Randy Peterson
Photo by Richard Heinzen Photography

In the fall of '77, Organized Crime had a band meeting at Steve Hanna's house. We got thoroughly stoned for this discussion. Jeannie had pushed for us to change our name and we finally came to terms with that suggestion.

After much debate (and weed), we agreed to change our name to Raven.

The band also needed to upgrade our ability to move equipment so we bought a former <u>Spokesman-Review</u> newspaper delivery truck. It was a big orange box with tires.

Gray primer paint hastily covered the former owner's logo. We put a bench seat behind the driver and passenger's seats so the entire band could travel in a single rig.

As Raven, our first gig was at the Nickelodeon in St. Maries, Idaho and we killed it. We had our soundman on the mixing boards and we were using all sorts of pyrotechnics.

Then we went to Lewistown, Montana and played a show.

That night, still trying to find my "rock look" that Jeannie Carter insisted I adopt, I wore a black French-cut t-shirt I borrowed from a female friend that said *Teaser* in sparkly letters on it. I also wore red pants, black platform shoes and my afro. I was probably 115 pounds then.

Some guys called us faggots and threatened to kick our ass after the show.

We barely got out of there alive.

On the way through Spokane to our next gig, we stopped at Hoffman Music to get a repair done on our P.A. board. While that was going on, I visited my dad in the hospital.

He'd been diagnosed with emphysema and it was getting worse. He was having a good day and gave me some major shit for my newly permed hair.

When I decided to chase a career in music, my dad was disappointed. I spent two years in baking school and got a degree. After graduation, I got an offer from Safeway for a good paying job.

He was a man from the 1940s. What I was doing was not stable. We argued over it in the early days, but he slowly came around.

Dad had a logistical mind. He would help me plan our road trips by pulling out maps and plotting our courses across the various states. He was kind of our de facto road manager.

After our visit, as I walked through the door of his hospital room, he smacked me on the back of the head with a newspaper. I turned to see a playful smirk on his face.

Raven had a Christmas Eve gig back at the Nickelodeon. We went there and performed well. We came home and got a few hours of sleep. Our family opened presents that morning at the foot of dad's bed.

We also had Christmas dinner together as a family in dad's bedroom.

On December 30th, my dad's birthday, Raven performed a show at the Coeur d'Alene Hotel. It was a teen dance and 500 kids were estimated to be there in the big ballroom.

Mom and dad were supposed to come. We learned dad had only a year to live as his emphysema had taken a serious toll on him. His coming to the show meant a lot.

The show was wonderful as the band was on fire. Our flash pots and fog machines were a big hit with the kids.

After the show, the band dropped me off at home and I found a note on the door that read, *Dad's really bad. We've gone to Deaconess Hospital.*

The phone rang as I entered the house. I answered it and Carol told me dad wasn't doing well.

"I don't know if there is anything more they can do," she said. "He might not make it through the night."

"What are you guys doing?" I asked

"We're just waiting. Are you going to come down?"

"Yeah," I said and hung up.

I went into my bedroom. I didn't pray too much back then but I said a prayer for my dad. I remember thinking *my dad is dying tonight.* Then I fell asleep.

My whole life, I've felt guilt over not going to the hospital that night.

The phone rang in the morning. Carol said, "Dad made it. He's doing fine."

She never asked why I hadn't come.

When dad came home we all gathered around him. He said, "I know all you kids were there and I appreciate it."

I was so ashamed that I wasn't there, but I didn't tell him.

I felt like such a selfish son of a bitch.

That night, New Year's Eve, we played at the Youth Center in Lewiston, Idaho. South of Spokane, between Colfax and Pullman, in the middle of farm country, we blew a tire on our big truck and we didn't have a spare. A tow truck hauled us to the gig.

The crowd was irritated by our tardiness, but once we got rolling, the kids got into it.

We were housed that night at The Tapadera Motel.

On New Year's Day, '78, there were no mechanics or repair shops open to get a replacement tire. Randy's girlfriend and Steve's girlfriend had both joined us and brought additional girls with them. We held up in The Tapadera all day and partied.

Since we didn't have a rig, we called cab drivers to buy us beer and they actually did! We did this all New Year's Day and the next day. The tire repair was delayed since we couldn't find the correct tire size and the tire would cost $300, more than we had with us. Steve's parents were sending money, but it was going to take a couple days.

At that point, we didn't care. We were partying.

I was in bed with one girl when the rest of the group walked in. That caused some problems since I was with her friend the night before. It was practically an orgy for those couple of days.

There was one tall, leggy blonde who loved showing off her body. We stuck her in a rollaway bed, the type that folds up for easy transportation. She was wearing only her panties. Her top half, with naked breasts, hung out one side of the bed while her legs stuck out the other side. We rolled her down the hallway, put her on an elevator, pushed the lobby button and ran.

The girl thought it was funny and laughed with us.

The hotel, however, had enough of that shit and kicked us out.

We all went next door to the Denny's as the truck was repaired. When it was done, Raven headed back to Spokane.

Our next gig was at The Penticton Inn up in Penticton, B.C. – essentially a hotel club.

After our show, we partied like animals. I met this one little Earth girl who wore coveralls, a thin top underneath and no bra. She wasn't beautiful but was super nice. I went home with her.

We chatted about plants, about life, and about dad. We smoked some pot and she played some songs she was writing. Many of the girls we met on the road wanted to play their music for us.

She had a mattress on her floor. We slept together but didn't have sex. In the morning, she drove me back to the hotel.

When I passed the front desk, there was a phone message from the girl I had met previously in Nelson. She said she was going to come and see me.

I immediately called her back and got her answering machine. "Don't come," was essentially what I said.

By the time I'd gotten her message, she was already in Penticton.

She was in the crowd that night while we were playing. I thought, "Oh, my god," when I spotted her.

After the show, the girl came up to the room for the "requisite" after-party. She sat next to me, kissing my wrist and cooing words of affection. It creeped me out, but I let it go. Things went over the edge when she started sucking my little finger.

I pulled her into the hallway.

"I'm sorry," I said, "I can't be with you. My fiancé and I got back together."

It was a complete lie, but I wanted her to leave me alone.

She looked devastated and cried. One of the guys came out into the hallway and consoled her. He continued to comfort her in his room, all night and very loudly, I might add.

On Monday morning, January 23rd, Raven auditioned at Goofy's, a Spokane club Jeannie had been trying to get us booked into. This was where the "real" bands played.

We did a set and the club owners liked us. We were hired.

I went home that afternoon to find dad in his bed. He was trying to read the paper, but not having much success.

"Dad?"

He could barely open his eyes.

"We got the gig at Goofy's. I think we're on our way."

He held out his hand and I took hold.

"That's good," he said. "That's good. I knew you could do it."

I walked out of the room and let him be.

Later that evening, he passed away.

I never told my dad I loved him. It's something for which I'm ashamed.

My father was from "The Greatest Generation" to be sure. He worked so hard for many years at a job he really didn't like, but he was damn good at it because he "did what he had to do." That was his favorite saying and the one I remember most fondly.

I didn't see much of my dad growing up. He was a swing shift dispatcher at Garrett Freightlines. On Friday nights, he'd come home early, around 9 p.m. On those evenings, he had a tradition of bringing a bag full of candy bars from the vending machines at work.

Two for each kid! We called it "Friday Night Surprise."

It's funny to think about now, but we thought every family had "Friday Night Surprise."

Dad would call mom before heading home. She would then prepare his dinner and put on a pot of coffee. She would let me scoop the grounds into the percolator. The smell of coffee still reminds me of that.

Before he would get home, we'd watch our little 12" black and white TV. Shows like *77 Sunset Strip*, *12 O'Clock High*, *The Flintstones*, *The Addams Family*, and *Twilight Zone*.

I'd stand by the front window, watching and waiting to see the headlights of dad's car as he pulled into the driveway.

While dad sat at the table eating, I'd stand next to him, my head barely higher than the table top, just to watch him eat.

As I grew, dad and I had our issues but we always had football in common. We'd always watch the NFL on Sundays.

When he became ill, I was most certainly wrapped up in my own world as a budding rock star.

Looking back, I was seemingly unable, or unwilling, to grasp just what he was going through and what he was facing. I missed a real chance to connect and relate to him as an adult. What I do know with absolute certainty is that I loved him with all my heart as he loved me and, in the end, he was very proud of my convictions and pursuits as a musician.

Raven was booked to play a teen dance at the Outlaw Inn in Kalispell, Montana on Friday, January 27th, the day of dad's funeral.

I went to Jeannie Carter and discussed the matter. She advised me to stay on the horse, suck it up and do the gig.

"It will keep your mind off things," she said.

I don't believe she was callous. She was trying to give me the best advice she could.

The band would head out to Kalispell without me and I would fly in later to join them. The band paid for my plane ticket.

After dad's funeral, I went to the airport with my cousins and Chuck. This was my first time ever on a passenger jet. I had already dressed for the gig in Kalispell. I wore my dad's double-breasted navy coat and sunglasses to hide my eyes.

We killed time in the airport's lounge until the plane arrived. My cousins pretended they were my manager and publicist and they acted like I was a rock star.

"When you land, the van will pick you up and get you to the gig," one of them said loudly.

"They'll have you on stage in no time," the other joined in.

People stared at us, trying to figure out who I was.

When I landed in Kalispell, I took a cab to the Outlaw Inn. Due to a snow storm, my plane didn't arrive until almost midnight.

The Outlaw Inn Hotel was hosting a ski club with almost 200 kids packed inside. Randy was playing the drums and really slopping his way through it. The band sucked, and the promoter was pissed. I jumped on the drum kit and we played five songs. The band had arranged my drum kit backwards so playing was a disaster.

That was Friday night.

On the other hand, Saturday was great. I re-set the drums and we rocked.

After the show, the promoter refused to pay us for Friday night's performance.

The band came to my defense and explained to the promoter that my dad had recently passed away.

We got Jeannie on the phone but that didn't change his mind. We got the local musicians union from Missoula on the phone and still struck out.

I was distraught at affecting the band and then the promoter went too far.

"I don't give a fuck if his dad died," he said. "I'm not paying you guys."

I crossed the room, ready to kick his ass. The band intercepted me and pushed me out of his office into a dimly lit ballroom. They went back to talk with the promoter and left me sitting alone.

I was pissed and in a weird headspace. I sat there talking out loud to dad.

The band came to a negotiated agreement.

We would do a two-hour show on Sunday afternoon for the kids. Instead of heading out first thing Sunday morning for our Monday show in Revelstoke, B.C., we didn't leave Kalispell until 6 p.m. Sunday night.

I drove all night while the band slept since I was wired from the emotional rollercoaster.

On one stretch of highway, there was a steep downhill grade. It was January so the roads were still slick. I was going about fifty miles per hour and the band was asleep. The tires hit a patch of ice and the truck turned completely sideways. We slid that way for what must have been fifty or sixty feet until I got the nose of the truck pointed back in the right direction.

No one woke up.

I pulled over and shook.

Dan lifted his head. "Are we already there?"

"No," I said and got out of the truck. I needed to calm myself before I continued the drive.

I didn't tell the band about that for a year.

We arrived in Revelstoke at 4 p.m. and were scheduled to play at 9 p.m. Unloading and arranging the gear along with sound testing took three hours. It was a huge club and we were booked for a six-night gig.

They lodged us in a series of small cabins away from the club. Dave and I shared one of the cabins. I quickly showered before the show. I had enough time to grab a bag of corn nuts and a pickled egg from behind the bar for dinner before Monday night's show.

Two older women, both about forty, came to the club on Wednesday and hit on Randy and me. We never got anywhere with them, but they had us on the line for sure.

On Friday night, there were roughly 300 people in attendance as we finished the show. Randy and I ran to the restroom as the crowd chanted for an encore.

At the urinals, a random fan moved in between Randy and me.

"I love you, guys."

We nodded our thanks.

"I have some great acid," he said. Then he offered me a pill. It seemed like everyone at the party was wacked out on acid, so I figured what the hell.

I popped a purple microdot of acid in my mouth with the other. Randy did the same thing.

The crowd continued their chant of "Encore, encore."

We went back on stage. About halfway between the second song of our three-song encore, Randy and I looked at each other with wide eyes. We were both starting to trip.

That night's party was in my room. We were tripping hard by the time we got back there.

For a few nights, I'd been working on a girl we nicknamed Jitterbug and she came to the party. Jitterbug had black curly hair and was always tripping on something, hence her nickname.

During the party, someone dropped a cigarette in a trash can and ignited a fire. For what seemed an eternity, no one did anything about it. I finally grabbed the trash can and ran outside into the snow. I was hysterical and yelled, "Fuck you! You start a fire and you don't put it out."

The party went to the other guys' room after my tantrum. When I mellowed, I went to their room and heard them laughing. After banging on the door for several minutes, they let me in.

Jitterbug and I were all really tripping. I said, "I need some sleep" and lay on someone's bed.

She stared at me for a while. "Wow, you look like a dead guy in a coffin."

I freaked out over her comment. A week before I'd seen my dad in a casket. Tears ran down my face.

To save me from my trip, Jitterbug took me for a walk at 4 a.m. It was obvious that she had a better handle on her drugs.

In January '78, there had been a blizzard through this part of the world. We walked amongst snow banks that were five and six feet tall.

Suddenly, I tunneled into one of those banks of snow. While I dug, the snow turned from purple to green and back to purple. I must have dug through six feet of snow, but it felt like thirty feet before I popped through the other side. I was soaking wet.

When we got back to my room, Jitterbug toweled me off. I crawled in bed and curled in to a fetal position.

A few minutes later, Jitterbug took off with one of the other guys. I laid there and didn't feel jealous.

On Saturday night, the forty-ish year-old woman that I'd flirted with earlier in the week came back. This time she didn't back out.

We went to the cabin and after we were done, she talked to me like I was her son.

She said things like, "You're such a nice boy."

It was weird and ended things in a hurry.

Jeannie booked us next at The Night Hawk on the old, winding Lewiston Grade highway above Lewiston, Idaho.

At the bottom of the Lewiston Grade sat the Evergreen Hotel and a three-bedroom house where they put the bands. The house was very nice and kept clean.

On our second evening of the stay, as I covered my drums for the night with a blanket, I noticed a girl with long black hair watching me. She was an Emmy Lou Harris type. Randy had been hitting on her but she eventually brushed him off. She introduced herself as Lexie. We chatted for about ten minutes before she left.

Later, a group of "friends" followed us back to the band house to continue partying. There was a mixture of girls and guys. It wasn't a wild scene, just a nice get together.

I didn't meet anyone that interested me and was playing *Pong* on the TV by myself.

Someone behind me mentioned how Lexie was a real bitch and on the outside of the group. They'd started talking about her because she'd shown up at the party. I went over to talk with her some more. It was about 4 a.m.

To get her away from the group, I asked, "Do you want to get something to eat?"

We went to Denny's for breakfast and had a nice conversation. Afterwards, she accepted my invitation back to the band house where we all had our own bedrooms.

All of the guys had girls with them. Dan was alone.

From the room next door, one of the girls moaned extremely loud, "Oh, God!" over and over.

"Oh, God!" I yelled.

"Oh, God!" another guy yelled back.

Quickly everyone in the entire house was yelling, "Oh, God!" and laughing.

Lexie laughed and tried to cover my mouth as we all yelled at the moaning girl.

The next morning, the girl who was moaning loudly wasn't embarrassed about it at all. It all seemed normal in the rock and roll life.

The next several days and nights were spent with Lexie. When I had to do my laundry, she went with me. During our conversation, I said, "Ever since dad died –"

Lexie interrupted, "Oh, how long ago was that?"

"Two weeks."

Lexie's demeanor suddenly changed. She hugged me and bawled.

The minute Lexie wrapped her arms around me, I started crying.

Until then, I had not cried for my dad. I didn't cry at his funeral. I didn't cry on the drive to the gig in Kalispell, the week in Revelstoke (except during my freak out while on the purple microdot which didn't count), nor the whole week in Night Hawk.

At that moment, I knew I liked Lexie a lot.

I gave her my phone number and address (my *real* address) before the band left for our next show.

I'd grown a goatee by then. If you look at my pictures, you can see how much I had changed in those couple of years when we started off as Cold Smoke to the first days of Raven.

Our band was happening in the Lewiston, Clarkston, Moscow, and Pullman areas. Even in Spokane we were doing well.

We next played The Dispensary in Moscow, Idaho.

Our agent, Jeannie, came and saw us there. We had new gear by this time. The band was tighter than ever and the show was solid. Jeannie was impressed with how the crowd responded to us along with our new attitudes and appearance. When she last saw us, we *played* our songs.

We were now *performing* our songs.

Jeannie's advice had resonated with us.

Our next stop was a Monday through Sunday gig at The Hotel Allen in Rossland, B.C., on the 1st of April.

Steve, Randy and Dan traveled in the truck with most of the equipment. Dave and I drove in my Pontiac Ventura, which I parked in front of the club.

The hotel had a basement club – The Loose Cabooze, where we played, a main floor tavern and a hotel/apartment on the second floor where the band stayed. Remodeling was underway on the tavern when we arrived.

The basement had a series of twists and turns before it opened to the actual club. The initial hallway turned left where it dumped into a small bar with an acoustic guitar player. Then the hallway continued with a series of twists before it got to the main club.

There is no way, in today's world of building and fire codes, the club could exist, but this was 1978 and it was essentially the Wild West for rock clubs.

In our hotel room, there was a central common room that led to four bedrooms and a kitchen.

I had brought along some of dad's clothes. He had a baby blue leisure suit jacket that I would wear occasionally during a show along with my t-shirt and jeans.

Or I would wear his double breasted, mid-calf, navy overcoat with my jeans. It made me look like a rock star.

When I was hanging out, I'd wear the brown slippers that he wore. These were some of the ways I held onto his memory.

When we met the owner of the club, we shook hands. His was limp and he didn't make eye contact. He was flakey and I didn't trust him.

Almost immediately, he argued the price of our contract that he had negotiated through Jeannie. He complained non-stop about paying an American band.

Jeannie inserted a rider in our contracts that we got a case of beer from the venue. All of the major rock bands had contract riders. Jeannie was treating us like budding rock stars which the owner of the club complained about upon our arrival.

The bartenders and waitresses groused about the proprietor and wondered if *they* would get paid.

It was a bad omen.

Randy was working on a pretty girl with short black hair.

She came across incredibly slutty and, of course, we all loved her.

After the gig on Tuesday night, she came to our room where she was the lone girl hanging out with a few of us. We listened to music, drank beer, and smoked joints.

At one point, she jumped up and danced to the music which led to her stripping. Dan quickly left the room.

She must have stripped for a living. She was wonderful!

She got completely naked and wasn't ashamed to stand in front of us all.

Randy took his half-full bottle of Budweiser and put it in the middle of the floor. She squatted and picked it up, with no hands, of course.

She continued to dance, holding the bottle in the holiest of places. The more she shook her hips, the more it foamed and dripped down her legs.

For her finale, she rolled onto her back, lifted her hips in the air and let the bottle drain inside her.

Randy and I went nuts for her. We clapped and cheered. She climbed on top of Randy and they made out. I felt like a third wheel, but she was naked and I was drinking so I figured I'd hang out for a bit longer. Then she went down on him.

I didn't stick around after that.

On Wednesday, a couple of box fans sat on the side of the stage, gusting in our direction to keep us comfortable. As a bonus, we thought we looked extra cool with our hair blowing in the wind as we played.

We were in the middle of *Balinese* by ZZ Top when smoke poured in through the fans.

Randy yelled, "Fire," and quickly unplugged his guitar from an amp. He grabbed some extra gear and ran off the stage.

Fire alarms had sounded, but our playing had completely drowned them out. People started fleeing from the building.

The rest of us dragged some of our gear outside. Once in the open air, we could see the main floor of the building was on fire.

Dave and Steve hurried to get the truck and bring it into the alley to load our equipment. Randy, Dan and I ran back inside to get more gear.

The smoke was thick.

I went for my drums first. Time moved in slow motion as we ran in and out of the club. It was less than five minutes before I went back in for my third trip.

Randy was still inside and I was worried about him. I went back in without thinking. The smoke was so thick on the dance floor I couldn't see a foot in front of me.

"Randy, you've got to get out," I yelled. As I tried to say another word, I dropped to my knees.

"Get out," Randy hollered.

There was no more oxygen in the room. I couldn't catch my breath.

My last conscious thought was, "I guess I'm going to see dad again."

I awoke to a fireman standing over me with an oxygen mask pressed to my face.

Near me, Randy yammered a mile a minute as he yelled directions to everyone. It was a steady stream of orders to whomever was nearby.

Randy said that I had crawled on my hands and knees out of the club. I have no memory of doing such a thing. It was a miracle that I made it out of that maze. They didn't take me to the hospital.

The band huddled together and watched the building burn.

I noticed smoke coming from the second floor where our room was located. *Our stuff is going to smell like smoke now*, I thought.

Then flames blew out the windows.

I realized then that all our clothes were in the fire.

The hippy shirt I always borrowed from Chuck, along with a long-sleeved t-shirt I'd taken without asking, was gone.

The stuff from dad was forever lost.

I also remembered that I had a half-eaten submarine sandwich left in the room.

"It's over toasted now," I muttered as tears welled in my eyes.

The owner of the hotel stood next to me, straight-faced.

Someone yelled that the building's front wall was going to collapse.

My car was parked in front and my keys were in my jacket which was on stage in the basement. A fireman told me to stay back. Someone would have to break a window to get into the car so they could move it out of the way.

At that moment, another fire engine pulled on scene to join the fight. As the engine rounded the corner, it swiped the left rear quarter panel of my car.

Due to the danger, they told me the car was staying in place.

At about 4 a.m., the fire was brought under control.

The interior of the building had collapsed into the basement. The walls didn't buckle and collapse and they didn't tow my car away. It was covered in soot and debris and had an ugly crunch in its side.

Some of the girls we befriended the previous days took us to their house on a nearby hill. We could watch the fire department battle the remaining flames from there.

Being skinny rock stars, we could wear some of their clothing while they laundered ours. I wore one girl's jeans, t-shirt and jacket.

They brought out some hash. Regardless of how good the drug was, it still was anti-climactic. We were all in shock.

The group went to sleep, but I stayed awake and watched the fire department continue to pour water on the smoldering building as the sun came up.

I could smell the smoke that was still stuck in my nose.

Two different arches of water were sprayed into the building. Sunlight hit the water streams and produced a very pretty rainbow.

I sat there quietly crying.

I thought the band was done.

I waited until about 6 a.m. to call mom.

Chuck was there. He'd come home when dad got sick and stayed there after he died.

I explained what had happened and told them I was okay.

I had only gotten my drums out, but not my cymbals. I figured my cases and microphones had burned.

For wrapping my kick drum, I had a quilt that my grandmother made me when I was a little boy. I lost that in the fire, too.

Later that morning, the firemen continued to drag things out.

The first floor had collapsed at an angle over the basement so not everything was crushed or burned. They pulled out our P.A. and speakers which had both water and smoke damage. We also had a Yamaha 2200 amp that we were able to save. My cymbals and their stands had survived intact.

We put the salvaged items in the back of the truck and headed home.

We didn't get a dime for the shows we had played.

On the Thursday evening after the fire, Dave and I didn't go home right away. We stopped off at Jeannie Carter's home. Steve, Randy and Dan were in the truck and they didn't make the detour with us.

Jeannie got out her "very special" pot and we smoked it with her. We laughed and cried as Dave and I retold the story of what happened.

Jeannie followed the news of the fire for a while. She told us the authorities determined the cause of the blaze was arson. The club owner supposedly torched the place and later left the country. I don't know if he was ever caught.

The next couple days we unloaded our gear at Steve Hanna's house and set about repairing the damaged gear in his driveway.

We tore apart the speakers and bought replacement parts from Hoffman Music. We repainted the boxes. Randy cleaned out the Yamaha amp and saved it. We cleaned my drums and bought new cases.

I ran my account at Hoffman Music to $2,500 with new mics, new equipment, etc.

The fire was big news back home. We were a well-known local rock band that had been burned out.

Mom let me use her credit card to go to Bluebeard's and Hamer's to get a new wardrobe. I lost most of my clothes in the fire. She let me spend $500.

Bluebeard's was downtown, across from what is now Riverfront Park, and was where the local rock stars shopped. You could buy satin clothes, scarves, and platform shoes.

Mom was reimbursed for some of the loss through her homeowner's insurance. She really came to my rescue.

On Wednesday, exactly one week after The Loose Cabooze fire, we were back on stage at The Dispensary in Moscow, Idaho. Whatever equipment we didn't have, we begged and borrowed from our friends.

Tuesday and Wednesday nights were ladies' nights and marketed as Tilted Tuesday and Wilted Wednesday. The place was always packed with women. The bouncers would only let chicks in for the first two hours. This way the ladies were liquored up before any guys got inside.

As the band, we had a two-hour head start and got to pick the girls we wanted before any other guys were let in. It was awesome!

There was sex in the dressing rooms, between sets and after the shows.

Whenever Lexie wasn't around, I wasn't lonely, that's for sure.

On Thursday morning, the band got a call from the owner of The Dispensary. "The liquor control board is shutting me down," he said.

The "official" story was he hadn't correctly transferred his liquor license. We never found out the real reason, but his story was always fishy.

We played two nights of a four-night contract that was supposed to pay $1,000. The owner paid us $400, which was all he had. He then grabbed a keg from the bar and we went to his house to party.

Afterward, I drove to Lewiston to see Lexie. I crawled into bed and we held each other.

Back in Spokane, Lexie phoned while I was at mom's house.

"What are you doing?" I asked.

"I'm sitting here itching," she said, her voice full of displeasure.

"I don't know what you're talking about."

"Sure you don't."

I knew exactly what she was talking about, since I was itching, too. I had given her scabies, a contagious, super itchy skin condition caused by burrowing mites. A rash develops due to the skin's reaction to the mite. I'd been with a girl in Canada who'd given me scabies and I'd given it to Lexie.

She didn't easily get over this – who could blame her?

I made things worse when she wanted to come to Spokane and spend a night with me before we left for an upcoming tour. I said, "Before you come, let me check with mom and make sure it's ok since it's her house."

My answer was weak and disappointed her. In reality, I had a squeeze on the side. I should have told her to come or been straight with her and said no. Instead, I strung her along and further hurt her feelings.

No girl should have been treated like that.

The Spokesman-Review wrote an article about the band.

It mentioned my father's death, the fire in Canada and the liquor board's closing of The Dispensary. The gist of the article was that the band had a rough start to the year and was playing Goofy's on the weekend which was a big deal.

We were booked for a week and then would immediately hit the road for four weeks. We were touring through Rawlins, Casper, and Cheyenne, WY as well as Salt Lake City, UT.

On the final night of our week at Goofy's, I took my suitcase and transferred it to the band's truck. It felt so good to hit the road again.

We had a big crowd and the show was wonderful. After the gig, we had breakfast with some friends, one of whom gave us some speed pills known as Black Beauties.

I took the driving responsibility for the first leg of the journey. I ate a Black Beauty and drove the entire way to Salt Lake City.

For thirteen hours, we listened to music and talked about being rock stars.

The gig in Rawlins was horrible.

The club owner was a freak. On the first day, he came out with a decibel meter during our sound check and said, "Nothing over ninety."

I purposefully dropped a drumstick on my snare and the needle spiked to 102.

We played Monday night and he hated us. The place was empty anyway.

Tuesday and Wednesday nights were a little better, but not much.

On Thursday, we were on the phone, begging Jeannie to get us out of there.

"Stick it out," she said, "This is a good learning experience. You're a young band. Learn how to tough it out. Besides, what am I going to do with you, now?"

Near the end of June, we moved on to Our Place Too in Cheyenne. On the way to the gig, we stopped and bought a bunch of fireworks.

We arrived on Sunday. Our room was an apartment above the club. The only access was by a staircase outside. Upon entering, there was a long hallway. I took the first bedroom and dropped my gear. The rest of the guys funneled down the hallway. I was the only one with a single bedroom. The other guys had to share rooms.

Our Place Too was a big club with a large stage and we were excited to be there. There were pictures of bands we knew on the walls. Cheyenne, Big Horn, Fiver, Randall Rosberg, Child – all Seattle bands.

The bar was closed Sunday night so the bar owner invited us out to his house, a rancher on the outskirts of Cheyenne. He was big guy built like an out-of-shape linebacker – 6'3 and 280 pounds, most of it in his gut.

The owner broke out some high-end pot and, after we all took a deep hit, he put on an opera record. No shit. It was odd. It didn't matter, though, since the dope was so good – we were all soon digging the opera sounds.

As we continued to smoke and drink, the conversation turned to how strong Dave Low was. Dave was 5'9 and 160 pounds but he was a strong son of a bitch compared to the rest of us. The bar owner took this as an affront and challenged Dave to arm wrestle him.

Dave didn't bite on his challenge so the bar owner bet "double or nothing" that he could beat him. We were getting paid $2,000 and rooms for the week. If Dave won, we would get $4,000. If he lost, we'd get nothing.

Randy went into overdrive and told Dave, "Do it! You know you can take him. Kick his ass!"

The bar owner laughed at Randy's egging Dave on and really loved the scene.

Dan and I weren't buying into it. "Don't fuck with our pay" was the general message.

Dave didn't do it for fear of losing the band's money, which I totally appreciated.

We all smoked another bowl, put on a new opera album and soon forgot about the bet.

On Monday, we leisurely set up as we didn't have much to do.

Our fog machine had developed some problems. While Dave and Randy worked on it, Dan went to get some dry ice.

Steve and I walked into the outer lounge to have a beer. There was an attractive girl sitting at the bar. I wanted to hit on her and made my move. I failed miserably and left to go tinker on my drums.

When I returned, Steve was sitting with her and they were hitting it off.

We played the first part of the week and it was mostly uneventful.

After spending our money on fireworks, we all spent the whole week mostly broke.

I bought a loaf of bread, a hunk of cheese and jar of mayo. That's what I ate for breakfast, lunch and dinner for the first week. I would slice the cheese with a coat hanger and spread the mayonnaise with my finger. In those days, I figured that was life on the road.

On Friday, it was Randy's birthday so we had a big party after the show.

I met a woman named Connie with long, black hair that reminded me of Lexie, who I still thought of as my "girlfriend."

We spent the night together until 4 a.m. when Connie had to hurry home before her husband returned from his hunting trip.

Dave and Dan joined me in driving Connie home. When the truck ran out of gas, we walked her the rest of the way.

I was still in my gig clothes including my knee-high moccasins. We stopped a block away from Connie's house and said our good-byes.

On our way back to the truck, we noticed a nearby creek. A tree stood near the water and a rope swing hung from it. It was now 5:30 a.m. and we were all still drunk and high. There was only one thing to do. We ran to the rope and took turns swinging out over the water and back to land.

On my third time with the rope, I had a moment of inspiration while over the water and let go. The creek was deeper and swifter than I had anticipated. I was fortunate that the current took me back to the bank, albeit the other side of the river.

I was soaking wet and still drunk. Dave and Dan walked to a gas station, got a gas can, filled the truck, and drove around the creek to get me.

We headed to the club and slept half the day away.

On Saturday afternoon, Randy, Dave, Dan and I fought boredom by shooting off some bottle rockets from our room. We put them in an empty beer bottle and fired them out of our window.

Soon, we tired of that. Someone got the bright idea to make a bigger explosion, so we taped two together. Two led to three but that entertainment didn't last long either and we were soon bored again. One of us got a notion to tape firecrackers to the bottle rockets. We laced the fuses together and shot one out of the window. Success led to bigger experimentation.

In short order, we built the mother-of-all bottle rocket/firecracker hybrids. I knelt by the window to aim this monstrosity with its big-ass fuse. It sparked and burned my hands and I dropped the bottle. It fell the couple of stories and crashed against the sidewalk and broke apart.

The bottle rocket hybrid, released from its guidance system (aka the beer bottle), took off from ground level and launched into the street and hit a passing car – a passing *police* car.

They say timing is everything in rock and roll.

The cop car immediately hit its brakes and came to a screeching stop. Its emergency lights turned on and its sirens blared. He knew exactly where it came from.

"Holy shit!" the four of us yelled.

We scattered. Dan and I ran to the roof. Dan hid behind an HVAC (Heating/Ventilation/Air Conditioning) unit. I crawled under the flashing of another HVAC unit and thanked God the fan never came on inside. It might have chopped me to pieces.

Randy and Dave hid somewhere in the apartment.

Steve was with his new woman somewhere so he didn't have any worries.

We suspected the cops came into the apartment and searched but didn't find us.

There were firecrackers and beer everywhere. It smelled like pot and sulfur from the fireworks. They might have only poked their heads in the room, but we were convinced they thoroughly searched for us.

Dan and I stayed hidden for at least an hour. We were afraid to move. Dan finally came out of hiding and went back to the room. He found Randy and Dave inside the apartment, laughing and talking about the incident. They came back and got me.

We never got caught, but we never shot any more bottle rockets – well, in Cheyenne anyway.

Later that afternoon, it rained hard. To escape our hot and stuffy apartment, I went outside to enjoy the rain. I stood on the sidewalk with my face raised to the falling water.

A four-wheel drive truck drove by. Connie, the woman from the night before, was behind the wheel and there was a guy in the passenger seat beside her, looking down. She must have gone and gotten her husband.

The truck slowed as it passed and Connie stared at me intently.

I didn't think about it before I did it, but I waved.

At that instant, her husband lifted his head in time to see me smiling at her. He responded by slapping Connie hard across the face.

The truck sped away.

At the end of the week, Dan had a family reunion so he couldn't go with us to our next gig in Casper. He would meet us in Salt Lake City. We took Dan to the airport and pushed on.

Steve and his new woman were hitting it off nicely. Steve rode with her in her dented Barracuda.

The rest of us were in the truck.

The Victorian in Casper was a cool club. As the name implied, its style was indicative of the Victorian era, but it was odd for a rock and roll club to look this way. It had a corner stage and an outer room with backgammon and chess tables. The tables were made of dark mahogany wood with ornate scroll work. There was another room that acted as a smaller club.

The Victorian's band house sat in a residential neighborhood. We stayed in the basement and an employee of the club stayed on the main level.

This was the week of July 4th.

On Monday night, I noticed the bartender closely watching me.

When she had a chance, she'd get on the dance floor and move provocatively. On our first break, I complimented her about how she moved. She responded well to that and we hit it off. She introduced herself as Katrina and said she was the daughter of The Victorian's owner. She pulled me into the club's office and brought out some cocaine to share.

Even though she was in her early twenties and only a couple years older than me, she already had a few strands of gray hair. I imagined it was due to the all the coke she did.

We spent the night together at her house. She had a great body and moved in bed like she danced.

I woke in the morning and walked out to her living room. Katrina was in her bathrobe, smoking a cigarette and drinking wine. That surprised me. I was a hard partier, but her drinking that early threw even me off.

She made me breakfast and took me back to the band house.

Tuesday was a beautiful day so we decided to visit a nearby canyon and stream.

On the previous night, Dave met Racheal, a strange but cute girl. He fell head over heels for her.

Randy met a girl that first night and was still spending time with her. Steve had his new girlfriend from Cheyenne with him.

Randy, Steve and Dave's girls brought additional girls with them to the canyon. Dave, Randy and I went mountain climbing. We climbed the seventy-five feet to the top. I was wearing my knee-high moccasins.

We got to the top and waved to the girls. The view was impressive.

Then we did what came naturally to us. We smoked a joint until we all ended up so stoned that we scared ourselves from climbing back down. Had we tried in that condition, we might have killed ourselves. Instead, we hoofed it along a trail which was probably two miles long. It was a great way to spend the rest of the day.

It was a moment that I still remember as one of my favorites. It was beautiful. I was hanging out with my friends and talking about how we were going to be rock stars. More importantly, we were trying to find our way through life as men.

After the gig that night, we brought the party home.

We still had plenty of fireworks left over from the Cheyenne incident. At 1:30 a.m., with Randy and me on one side of the road, and Dave and Steve on the other side, we fired off bottle rockets at each other. This was especially stupid, not only because of the physical danger, but we'd hit a police car during our last bottle rocket experience. I'm still amazed no one called the police.

When we ran low on bottle rockets, we went into the backyard where the party continued to get crazier as we lit off firecrackers.

One jerk in the group was 6'5 and 250 pounds. He was a noisy son of a bitch who got off on being the biggest guy in the room. He figured he would top us all and pulled out the biggest, shiniest .45 automatic pistol I'd ever seen in my life.

Actually, before that moment I'd never seen a .45 pistol.

When that gun fired it sounded like a fucking cannon. Everyone ducked for cover. Being drunk on Jack Daniels, I was now ten feet tall and bullet proof, or so I thought.

I tried to tackle him and only succeeded in bouncing off. I stood there, dazed. When I opened my eyes, he pointed the gun at my head. He pushed the muzzle against my forehead and kept pushing until I stood straighter.

His exact words are still clearly etched in my mind.

"You fucking little cock sucking faggot. You touch me, I'll kill you." Spittle flew on my face as he spoke.

That was the scariest moment of my life and I thought I was going to piss myself.

Calmer heads quickly prevailed and they pulled him back.

The party was over then.

There were pats on the back from other party-goers for taking a stand against the shooter.

I parlayed that moment of heroism into some sex with an adoring groupie. Regrettably, I can't remember her name.

The only thing I can remember is that gun pressed against my brow. For a day, I had a little circle on my forehead from the heat of the muzzle and how firmly that asshole pushed the gun against my head.

I hope I screwed his girlfriend on one of our trips through Casper.

I spent Friday night with Katrina, the bartender. She was a raving alcoholic and that creeped me out. She wanted to spend all day Saturday with me. I told her no because I wanted to hang out alone in my room. That didn't sit well with her.

I walked back to the band house that morning.

When I got there, I had horrible stomach cramps. I laid in one of the bunk beds.

Diet, booze, excitement and fear finally caught up with me. I hurt so badly that I whimpered. The band thought I had an ulcer or was having appendicitis. By the night, the pain eased.

I dressed for the gig and played. On my first break, I made eye contact with Katrina as she stood behind the bar, holding an empty bottle of whiskey. She hefted it a couple times in her hand before she slammed it to the ground while staring at me.

We finished the gig and I avoided Katrina until we left town.

Six months later, Katrina was killed in a car accident. We heard this news from another band that had played The Victorian. I've tried to verify this tale over the years and for this book but have struck out every time. Nevertheless, this was the tale we were told.

Supposedly, her car was rigged for the accident. The story went that the incident was related to her drug dealing. Allegedly, she had been a coke dealer which was why she always had so much cocaine with her. The police had determined her brakes had been tampered with prior to her head-on collision with a semi-truck.

On Sunday, we prepared to take off to Salt Lake City, the destination of our next gig.

Randy was staying another day with the girl he'd spent time with all week. He would catch a flight and meet us in Utah.

Steve's new girlfriend headed home to Cheyenne.

Before we left, one of the bartenders drained several mescal bottles and got the worms out. The rumor was if you ate the worms, it was like eating mushrooms or acid. Steve and Dave ate their worms immediately. I didn't. My experience with the purple microdot effectively cured me of any psychedelics, even the rumored ones. The worms had no effect on Steve or Dave.

We took off mid-morning. While I drove, I kept thinking about how I was creeped out by Katrina, the gun to my head, and the stomach problems. Due to those things, I reflected on my life while behind the wheel.

As we passed through Rawlins, Steve and Dave wanted to stop and flip the owner of the club some shit. He was an angry man and we couldn't do anything to please him whenever we were booked there. He wasn't around and I was glad he was gone. We didn't need the headache. We had a beer and then went through a drive-through liquor store and got a half rack of beer. There were only three of us on the road trip so it was a light order.

Steve and Dave were mellow by then. We were drinking slow and driving slower at fifty-five miles per hour.

We pulled off the freeway in Evanston, Utah. Ahead was a big green sign that read San Francisco to the left while Salt Lake City was to the right. I felt so far away from home.

While I drove, I listened to Neil Young's Harvest on 8-Track. *Old Man* started while Dave and Steve talked amongst themselves. As Neil Young sang, I thought about my dad.

I didn't want to be like my father and work a job my whole life that I hated. I saw what it did to him and I resolved it was not going to happen to me. I wasn't being disrespectful to my dad in those thoughts. I just wanted my life to be different in some areas.

The sun rose behind us and we pulled off alongside the road.

For a moment, I felt peaceful and happy. I thought, "I'm doing what I want to do." I drove the entire trip to Salt Lake City without amphetamines.

I was young, happy to be alive, and on the road. Life was good.

We were next booked to play The Silver Cloud and to stay at The Capitol Motel in Salt Lake City.

We got three rooms. Randy and Dan would share a room when they arrived. Steve had his own. Dave and I shared the final room. I slept most of the day on Monday.

We were wrung out and tired that first day. The bar was closed and we didn't know anyone so we hung out in the room and had a night without partying. It was probably good and healthy for us to have that little break.

The Silver Cloud was an odd club in that it was long and narrow. The bar was on the left and the stage was on the right, but they were offset from each other.

During our show on Tuesday night, a nice-looking woman in her early forties hit on me. On my last break, as we made out, she grabbed my crotch. I thought this was going to be a slam dunk.

Before I was set to go back on stage, she said, "Well, bye. I've got to go."

"Wait, where are you going?"

"I wanted to see if I could seduce a younger man," she said with a smile. Then she turned and walked away.

On Wednesday night, I wore light-colored jeans tucked into my knee-high moccasins, a sky-blue woman's French cut t-shirt, and wide suspenders with rainbow colors. I looked like a hippie version of Mork from Ork.

I thought I was wild and cool. Some guy in the bar gave me shit for it. In hindsight, I looked silly, but back then I thought it was hip.

On the dance floor, which was left of the stage, I noticed a tall, good-looking redhead. During a break, we introduced ourselves.

I took her back to The Capitol Motel where there was an indoor pool. While the redhead and I made out, a manager busted in and kicked us out of the water.

We then went to Red's house and she and I spent the night together. In the morning, she cooked us breakfast and treated me like I was something special.

The next night, Red invited me back to her house. I brought Steve along since she had a bunch of friends over. In the late '70s, a live rock band was special so that made us something different in their lives. Red barbequed steaks and we drank some wine. Steve and I went back to The Silver Cloud afterwards for the gig.

Red came to the club later. She wanted me to come home with her again, but I wasn't into her anymore.

"I don't want to," I said and then I blurted out an unusually lame excuse. "I usually only spend one night with one person."

"So, you've had your one night and now you're done with me?" she shouted and then slammed her glass on the table. Beer splashed upwards and landed on my hair, face and shirt. She made a scene, but I shrugged it off. I was tired.

After the gig, I killed some time tuning my drums, cleaning the kit and polishing the cymbals. This was my normal activity when I wanted to be left alone.

When I was done, I went back to the hotel room to find a party going on.

There were five girls there from Ogden, Utah with the band. The girls were introduced before I got there so I never learned their names.

There was a blonde who stood out but she wouldn't have anything to do with us. She was cold and aloof, but she was still the prettiest thing I'd ever seen. After a while they all left.

No one scored with the girls from Ogden.

Two nicely dressed women who looked like models came to our Friday show. I went after the gorgeous blonde. Randy, the other.

Later in the night, we went back to Randy's girl's house.

The blonde, Melanie, and I were on the floor in sleeping bags. She was a beautiful woman, but I couldn't get it up. Holy shit, was I embarrassed. That had never happened to me before and I was losing my mind. I did my best to explain it away – being on tour, too much alcohol, being tired. The more

I talked the more I mind-fucked myself. Melanie was patient and finally got me there even though it took some effort.

In the morning, Melanie drove us back to the hotel in her orange VW. She and I promised to see each other on Saturday night.

Melanie came back as promised and we spent the night together, hitting it off. We liked each other. That was the last night of the tour but we had an extra day before we had to move on so the band decided to stay in Salt Lake City. Randy and I were having fun with the two girls and Steve had met a chick.

We rented the rooms one more night. Randy and I, along with our girls, went to a jazz club on the top floor of the Salt Lake City Hilton. It was easily the nicest hotel in town.

The girls were beautifully dressed. I wore nice clothes that were not part of my performance attire. The crowd was an older, professional mix. Melanie was more mature than other girls I'd been with.

I watched the drummer in the jazz band. He was an older, black gentleman. He played smoothly while I tended to break sticks all the time. He made it look effortless.

We went onto the balcony which overlooked Salt Lake City. Melanie asked if I would forget her and I told her I wouldn't. We went back to her friend's house for the night. We exchanged addresses and promised to stay in contact. I gave her Jeannie Carter's address.

In July '78, we returned to Spokane after more than four weeks on the road.

The guys dropped me off at home. I wore light blue jeans tucked into my knee-high moccasins. I had a denim vest on with no shirt underneath. Five necklaces were strung around my neck. My afro had fallen into long, wavy hair as it had grown out.

I came around the corner of the backyard and my family was on the deck having a summer get-together. They were drinking beers and laughing.

I felt like a successful rocker returning from the road.

After a couple beers, I went in the house, lay on my bed and cried. To this day, I'm not sure why.

Of course, I was tired and I missed my family.

I'd been so busy since dad had died.

I might have still been tripped-out about the gun to my head.

Thoughts about how I treated Donna several months before entered my head and I felt bad.

Then I also felt bad how much I liked Lexie but couldn't help myself out there on the road.

Everything overwhelmed me.

Raven's next gig was at The Cotton Club in Hayden Lake, Idaho.

As part of our sets, we performed Queen's *We Will Rock You* followed by Ted Nugent's *Storm Troopin'*.

In between the two songs, I played a drum solo that worked up the crowd. During the solo, Dan would run to the drum kit and squeeze lighter fluid on the crash cymbals. He'd then light them on fire. The cymbals would flare whenever I hit them. When I came out of the solo, Dan would run back to the sound board and hit the flash pots as the band roared back in with *Storm Troopin'*.

If too much lighter fluid was on the cymbals it would flick off.

That's what happened at The Cotton Club. Some of the lighter fluid flicked off, landed on my head and lit my hair on fire.

That ended our set fast.

The hair on the right side of my head was burned.

The next day, I had a new hair style. My curls had to be cut to match the shorter length of my singed hair. It was now shoulder length and looked stupid. Like Sampson lost his strength, I'd lost my cool.

After the fire in Rossland, the band moved to harder rock music like Led Zeppelin. I'm not sure if that experience changed the way we perceived life, but it affected our music.

In August, Raven broke into the Seattle market via Baldy's Apartment in the neighboring city of Milton-Fife. It was a tiny, but prestigious club.

Every Wednesday night, Baldy's held a wet t-shirt contest. It was at one of these contests when I first saw Rhonda. She was a black-haired, Italian girl with a fantastic body. She ensured she won the competition by dropping her pants and showing the crowd everything.

After a gig, the band went to a party. Rhonda was there and she had her sights set on Randy. Unfortunately for her, he was after someone else. Fortunately for me, I was her second choice. Steve and Dave had brought their latest girlfriends with them on this trip.

I took Rhonda back to my hotel. In my room, I immediately went in and clicked off the lights.

"God, fast action," Rhonda said.

We spent the night together and I took her home in the morning.

We finished the rest of the week at Baldy's. Rhonda came in every night, but we didn't sleep together again even though I tried. On the last night of our stay, Rhonda sat at the end of the bar with me, drinking.

"Bill, I'm in love with you," she said. "I want to go home with you."

"Okay," I said.

All I was thinking of was sex.

Five days after meeting her, Rhonda was driving with me back to Spokane.

Once we got home, I introduced this sexy little number to my mom and said Rhonda was going to live with us now.

Please understand that I never asked my mom permission. I just told her that Rhonda was going to be living with us. What a disrespectful dumbass I was then.

Mom took it in stride by cooking a nice dinner for us. When she put a bowl of cooked cauliflower on the table, Rhonda pointed at it. "What's that?"

Mom gave me a look that I'll never forget. Without uttering a word, mom communicated quite clearly, "Bill, what have you done?"

When it was time for bed, Rhonda stayed upstairs, and I slept in my room. House rules.

The next day, I took Rhonda with me to Jeannie's office, but she wasn't allowed in. Jeannie had strict guidelines against groupies being in her office.

She made Rhonda wait in the car while we conducted business.

Our next gig was a return to The Dispensary in Moscow, Idaho. After the show, we headed to our hotel rooms where the party continued.

Rhonda said, "I'll be right back. I've got to go take my make-up off."

When she didn't return, I went to our room and she was asleep. I tried to roust her but couldn't. I thought she was faking it. It felt like things between us had gotten weird.

Back at the party, some attendees said she had given head to the club owner while I was on stage.

The next morning, I took her to the Moscow airport, paid for her ticket and flew her home.

Rhonda and I weren't destined to be soulmates after all.

Raven moved on to Missoula for our next gig. No one had a girlfriend with them on the trip so the band was ready to throw down.

I ate a Black Beauty for the three-hour trip.

We played The Dumpiest Hotel Around. Yes, that was its real name and aptly so – it was a real dive. While we played, a fight broke out between two women. One gal repeatedly slammed another woman's head on the stage rail. It was completely vicious but we didn't stop playing.

I didn't chase a single girl that week. A good friend gave me eight ounces of dope before I left town. Dan and I spent most of our time in our room, smoking our brains out to see how stoned we could get. We called this type of activity a "smoke out." It was a ritual we repeated many times in other cities.

On the hotel's second floor was a balcony. Neon lights could barely be seen through the floor drain. One night, Dan was so high he started shrieking because he thought he was going to slip through that balcony drain.

The rooms we had were divided by a living room and an actual kitchen. There was a little pass-through window between those two rooms. While high, Dan challenged me to climb through the pass-through window. I was a skinny guy and decided to take his dare.

I pushed my head and one shoulder through the small window and got stuck.

My butt hung out in the other room.

I was so high I didn't know what to do.

Dan was so stoned and laughing so hard he couldn't help.

He left me hanging there while he went to get the other guys to rescue me.

I ate some speed and drank beers while we drove to our next gig at The Red Barn in Great Falls, Montana. By the time we arrived, I was so fucked up that I immediately puked when I got to my hotel room. Not a great way to start a week-long gig.

The club lodged us in a hotel with a three-bedroom basement apartment under the laundry room. They were smart to do that. We could be loud and no one would complain.

The Red Barn was a big club and there were good crowds every night.

On Tuesday night, a bunch of people came to our room after our gig. I didn't have a woman and I wasn't drunk so I was more aware of things than normal. I noticed a few people in our room looked extremely young. I didn't remember seeing them at the bar.

I discovered one Native American girl was only fourteen and she'd been drinking our whiskey.

The amount of trouble we could get into worried me.

"You've all got to go," I said to the young girl and her friends. "The party's over."

The band supported me in kicking the kids out. There were limits to partying that even we – a horny group of rock-and-rollers – wouldn't cross.

The girl got mouthy while I escorted the group to the door. I walked them up the stairs and out of the hotel's glass door. As I walked back to the basement apartment, a cinder block crashed through the glass door, shattering it. I was showered in clear shards. The block bounced down the stairs and landed at my feet.

I ran up the stairs and looked outside. There was the girl and her friends.

I chased her across the street and into a funeral home yard. When I caught her, I shook her by the arms and yelled, "What the hell were you thinking?"

The other guys caught up to me as she spit in my face. I threw her to the ground.

"My brothers and I are coming back and we're going to kill you, white man."

Randy dragged me back to the room.

Our next series of shows was scheduled back at Baldy's near Seattle. When our gig started, I was thankful that my former, unfaithful fling, Rhonda, was nowhere to be found. Getting upset with Rhonda for being unfaithful was the proverbial pot calling the kettle black. However, I was young and self-absorbed. *How dare she do that to me?* I thought.

On Wednesday night, it was the wet t-shirt contest again. Like our visit before, I was the lucky recipient of the competition winner's affections. She came back to the room with me.

Dan and I shared a room on this trip. He did me a favor and slept in the truck to give us some privacy.

We stripped completely naked and she put the coolest, gold necklace around me which I kept for years. Then she stretched out on the bed, in a Playboy pose, and I lay next to her. And we talked. That's all we did – talk. We never had sex. I don't know why. She was a nice girl with a beautiful body. I can't explain why it happened that way. We had a great conversation and a great time. There was something oddly refreshing about that moment which I really enjoyed and still remember fondly.

Of, course, it didn't last long. She came back on Friday night and all we did then was screw.

On Thursday, Rhonda reappeared, but I didn't want anything to do with her. After the gig, I went to a big party and saw Rhonda. I spoke to her for a minute but that was all. I couldn't get over the fact that she'd blown the owner of The Dispensary while I was on stage.

I later fell asleep on the couch while still in my gig clothes – black slacks, black platform shoes, velvet vest, and no shirt on underneath, satin black jacket. When I awoke, everyone was gone, like the apocalypse.

I had no clue what part of the city I was in.

I walked around, looking for my hotel as it poured rain.

Imagine a 6'0, 120 lb. guy on the street in gig clothes, platform shoes, fifteen necklaces around my neck and completely rain-drenched. What a fucking sight!

Before we went back to The Dispensary for our next show, we returned to Spokane for a couple of days.

Dave Low and I went to an underground club. When we were done, we headed to Moscow before the rest of the band. We already had the truck packed, so we took off. We were impatient to get back on the road.

When we arrived in Moscow, we unloaded the equipment ourselves. We carried the gear up a flight and a half of stairs to The Dispensary, but that didn't bother us. We were excited to be back.

Raven had a shit load of gear – lights, speakers, fog machines, drum riser, all sorts of stuff.

When we were done, we hung out with the bar's owner. He and I had made nice since he'd gotten the blowjob from Rhonda. Even though I could hold it against her, I cut him a break. He was paying us and that was common behavior for a groupie. It's what happened in our world.

Randy was currently juggling two women – one in Spokane, one in Moscow. He shared a house with the girl in Spokane. She was a strange one, into mysticism and Egyptology.

Both girls showed up at the end of the first set on Tuesday night. One was on the left side of the room and the other was on the right side of the room. Randy didn't know what to do.

When the set was done, Randy fell onto his back and lay there, staring at the ceiling. When the lights lowered, I got off the drum riser and stepped over to him.

"Come on, Randy. Get off the floor"

"Give me fucking break," he said. "Leave me the fuck alone."

The crowd cheered for us to continue as I walked off stage.

Randy lay there for the entire break.

For some unexplained reason, neither girl came to the stage to talk to him.

Randy's "Moscow girlfriend" stayed away the rest of the night. Ironically, he would marry her some years later.

After the show, I tried to make it with a girl who claimed to be a virgin. The club was locked and the music was turned up loud. I tried unsuccessfully to get it on with her in the band's dressing room.

Still being a somewhat decent guy, I didn't pressure her. Instead, I drove her home. As I returned to the club, I was bummed over not having met a girl. It was The Dispensary, for crying out loud! We were legends in Moscow and always making new "friends."

As I got back to the club, the after-party was ending. I met some of the girls leaving the club that the other guys had let walk out. They were the leftovers, you could say.

I wasn't proud, at that point. The girls knew who I was and I charmed the best looking one of the bunch into bed for the night.

Like I said, it was The Dispensary and I had a reputation to maintain.

When Friday's show ended, I drove to Lewiston to see Lexie and we made up.

She came back to Moscow on Saturday and spent the night with me. Then she came to Spokane when our booking was done.

Raven had a couple days at home before the band had to be in Missoula.

Lexie and I went to a party at my sister's house on a Sunday afternoon. Carol had invited my former girlfriend, Donna, who glared at me throughout the night.

When we broke up, I'd given her the excuse that I didn't want to get tied down, but I looked to be in a committed relationship with Lexie. Donna got drunk and slapped people in a joking manner. Then she slapped me hard and with meaning behind it. I grabbed Lexie and we left.

The band headed to Missoula to play The Trading Post. The gig was uneventful. I didn't chase any women. Believe it or not, I was trying to be good. Nothing crazy went on.

After this show we were scheduled to go to Casper, Wyoming for a return to The Victorian. I was worried about our shows due to the volatile experience I had with the cocaine-dealing bartender, Katrina (we hadn't heard the news of her death yet). Randy and Dave were both excited about visiting Casper because of the girls they had there. Steve's latest girlfriend was going to drive up from Cheyenne to meet him. Dan Murphy hadn't been there so he had no idea what to expect.

The second to the last night in Missoula, we received a call from Chris Roberts at Meadowlark Ventures. He was a talent agent that worked with Jeannie Carter and co-booked some of our Montana gigs.

"You guys have been bumped at The Victorian."

He explained they had scheduled a band in there that Meadowlark Ventures managed at the same time, so we got the short end of the stick.

"We've got something else for you in Helena," Chris said. "It's for six nights. It will be a good gig."

We called Jeannie. "If it's the same money, then do it," she said.

We were all disappointed, but it wasn't as far to go and we were going to make more money because of reduced travel. We piled in the truck on Sunday morning and headed to Helena, Montana. When we got to the club, it had a tiny corner stage. We were a big show by this time and this wasn't going to work.

When we approached the club owner, he looked at us like we were from another planet. "What are you talking about?"

We explained that we were booked to play his venue for the week.

"Boys, I run weekend shows and we only feature country bands."

"If you call Meadowlark Ventures," Steve said, "we're sure they can straighten this out."

The club owner shook his head. "I have never heard of Meadowlark Ventures. You're on your own, boys."

By then it was too late to turn around and head back to Spokane. We had to get a room for the night.

The next morning, Monday, we drove to Missoula and stopped by the offices of Meadowlark Ventures to have it out with Chris Roberts.

"We're not paying you the commissions for those other gigs you booked," I said. "You cost us a lot of money."

As we walked out, he shouted, "You're cutting off your nose to spite your face".

After a quick meeting in the truck, we crammed around Steve in a phone booth as he called Chris.

When Chris answered, Steve said, "Here's what we'll do. We'll pay you a third of what's owed. We feel that's more than fair after the trouble you caused."

Chris replied, "No. I'll sue if I don't get the whole amount."

Steve said, "Okay, then sue us." He hung up the phone without another word.

We headed back to Spokane with an abruptly ended tour.

Over the next months, Raven had return gigs at The Dispensary and Goofy's and then we were on the road again to Missoula, Billings and various spots in Montana. When were done with the Montana road trip, we returned for another stay at Goofy's.

The first night there, I had a message at the club from the manager of a local band known as Kracker.

There were four big bands in Spokane back then – Hot Stuff, Starbux, Flash and Raven. Kracker was an up-and-coming rock band and they wanted to make me a proposal.

This was the first time I was ever offered a job as a drummer – no audition necessary. I didn't know what to say.

"Why don't you come to High Bridge Park this weekend and watch us play?"

I agreed to give them a listen.

On Saturday afternoon, I went to High Bridge Park to listen to several bands play an afternoon concert. Kracker was one of them and they did a solid job.

The lead guitarist did a fair amount of slide work and I was impressed with his playing ability. The other guitarist was also memorable, but the bass player was just plain weird. The drummer was weak which was why they wanted me to join.

After the show, I was talking with the lead guitarist when Randy walked over. He had also been there watching the show. He had no idea I was there to talk about potentially jumping bands.

I hung with Randy the rest of the day and drank beers.

I flirted with the idea, but in the end, never joined Kracker.

After an uneventful stop at The Dumpiest Hotel Around, Raven pushed on to Billings for a stay at Gramma's.

The venue was so large they broke it apart into two clubs. After you entered, if you turned to the left, you were in a rock club that sat about 400 people. If you turned to the right after entry, you would be in a country bar that sat 150 people.

We were slightly intimidated because Gramma's pulled in bands from Seattle that we idolized. We didn't pack the wallop that some of those bands did. We wanted to do a good job at Gramma's and be asked back. They were paying us $2,000 plus rooms for a five-night gig.

Saturday night, AC/DC was in town playing a concert with Aerosmith so our crowd wasn't very large at the start of the show. Most of the people who would want to hear our music were at that concert.

When the Aerosmith and AC/DC show ended, Gramma's packed out and things got rocking. As we finished the first song of our fourth set, Dan Murphy ran to the stage and said, "You're never going to believe who just walked through the door!"

"Who?" we asked

"AC fucking DC!"

We all tripped out, but we kept it together and finished the show which included an encore.

Following the show, we were relaxing in the dressing room when Angus Young and Bon Scott walked in. They said they liked our band. The guys flipped out that these rock stars were even talking to us. I didn't have much to say so I kept my distance. The other guys fawned over them, nonetheless.

Angus and Bon stayed for a while and helped us drink a shit load of beer. They were drunk and kind of arrogant, but if I'm honest, I would have acted the same if I was ever that famous.

Earlier in the day, Steve had gone to the Aerosmith soundcheck with some others. When his group approached security, he told them he was with the band from Gramma's. Security waved his group through. AC/DC, right behind them, couldn't get in because security didn't know who they were. They were still relatively unknown to the world at-large.

From Billings, we had four days off before we were scheduled to be in Cut Bank, Montana for a Thursday through Saturday gig. We didn't want to drive back to Spokane and turn back around a few days later. The band decided to take a short vacation to Yellowstone.

We found a little country bar outside the west entrance. As we approached the bar, we heard *thump-thump-thump* like someone was warming up a bass guitar.

We walked inside and saw Eric Lindstrom of Stone Johnny Mountain Band on stage, sound checking his bass.

Stone Johnny had a gig that wasn't set to start until the weekend so members Rick Roadman and Dave Dieter drove back to Spokane to go home while Eric and Dave Griffith hung out.

Since I knew them through our mutual agent, Jeannie Carter, Eric and Dave joined us for camping. We were all broke, though. We basically had enough money to buy a few bundles of firewood, some burgers and beer.

The Stone Johnny guys drove a Ford Econoline van and we drove the orange newspaper truck. We pulled into a camp site and began cooking burgers.

The guys hauled out their acoustic guitars and started playing. I didn't want to be left out so I jumped in the back of the Raven truck to get my snare drum and high hat. I made a horrible racket as I banged around, opening and shutting cases.

I got my things arranged and joined them.

It never registered to us that we were in the middle of the woods at midnight. Finally, other campers complained about the noise we were making. A park ranger came by and told us to knock it off. We didn't argue with him, but he still told us to check out of the park the next day.

We had three days to kill before we needed to be in Cut Bank so the group decided to camp alongside the road until then. We were almost totally broke by now. We didn't eat much and instead focused on scraping enough money together for beer.

But it was still fun.

After a couple days, we said goodbye to the Stone Johnny guys. As we parted, Eric said, "We still can't believe you're playing Cut Bank."

"Why?" I asked.

"I heard it was a country bar."

"Jeannie booked us," I said. "She knows what she's doing."

We had $5 left after we put gas in the truck. We pulled into McDonalds and the entire band ate on that measly amount until we arrived in Cut Bank.

Steve's girlfriend joined us there and brought along Dave's girl, Rachael.

The stage had wagon wheels as a bannister around it. No doubt about it, the place was a country bar.

Being who we were, we hauled in our entire P.A. system, our lights, and our fog machine. We were going to put on our Raven show. Fuck it.

On Thursday night, we played and were considered too loud. The crowd hated us. Worse, the bar owner hated us.

On Friday, we tried to turn it down and we couldn't make anyone happy. People were booing.

First thing Saturday morning, we went to a store and bought a cassette tape of country music hits. That night, I grabbed Randy's guitar and Randy sat behind my drums. Dave put on Steve's guitar and Steve wore Dave's bass.

Dan played the cassette tape through the sound system and the band proceeded to lip sync to the country songs pumping out.

We made it through three songs before people realized we were faking it.

The club owner freaked out. She screamed, "You think we're all a bunch of dummies here? You do what you're supposed to do. Just keep it down."

On every break, we went outside to smoke a few joints and drink Peppermint Schnapps I'd stolen from the end of the bar when the bartender wasn't looking. The club's owner wasn't giving us free beer and was charging us for soft drinks, so we figured the liquor heist was a way of getting even.

On our last set, we collectively said, "Screw this, let's play like Raven."

That set kicked off loud, aggressive and fun.

It didn't last long. The club's owner quickly threw a circuit breaker to cut the sound and told us to get out.

She fired us with one hour left on our booking. Damn if she didn't dock our pay by one hour as well.

After the show, Randy, Dan and I were tanked. Steve and Dave kept things in control because they had girls in tow. We checked out of our hotel room that night because we couldn't afford to stay there any longer.

From Cut Bank, which is on the other side of Glacier National Park, Steve and Dave, along with their girls, headed immediately to Spokane – more than a seven-hour drive.

Dan, Randy and I were going to sleep in the truck and leave in the morning. That sounded like a solid plan, but, of course, we partied more. We drank more schnapps and beer and smoked more weed.

There wasn't room in the truck so Dan slept under the truck in the dirt. Randy slept inside the cab and I slept on top of the metal truck roof in a sleeping bag.

At roughly 10 a.m., I woke with the summer sun beating down on me. I thought my brain was sizzling. I was hungover beyond belief.

I had great difficulty getting off the top of the truck and fell the last several feet to the ground. I puked all the way to Bonners Ferry, Idaho before I began to feel a little normal.

By the fall of '78, Raven had a bunch of local gigs rolling in.

In Spokane, Goofy's changed its named to Gatsby's and became a haven for hard rock bands. New rock clubs like One Bridge North, Ichabod's and Doc Holiday's opened. Jeannie booked us into the Judge's Chambers, Rathskellers in Coeur d'Alene and the El Patio in State Line, ID.

We spent the late fall and early winter of 1979 around Spokane. That might sound great, but it allowed us to get complacent as we settled into daily routines.

Steve's girlfriend moved in with him.

Randy was on again/off again with his girlfriend.

Rachael shacked up with Dave. He'd been living with his dad and called him to ask for permission for her to move in. He was shocked when he said yes. They were living together for a few weeks when he announced he was quitting the band to settle down and have a more normal life. We couldn't believe it. We were devastated. I went over to their house to find out what the hell he was thinking.

He said, "A lot of musicians fall by the wayside, Bill. I guess I'm one of them."

Raven had to scramble for another bass player for a few high school gigs and frat parties we had booked in the area.

The first one was Wallace High School and we sucked. The guy we landed to replace Dave was an arrogant prick and didn't even know our material. The kids were excited for the "famous" Raven to come to their school and blow their socks off.

All we blew were our flash pots that knocked some insulation from the gym's ceiling. We were awful.

Amid those small gigs, Jeannie said, "Gramma's wants you back. The money's going up. That's good for you. You've got to get this bass player situation figured out."

That should have excited me, but it didn't. I was feeling unsatisfied with the band.

I went looking for a country-rock band because I always had an affinity for that sound. I met Jimmy McElwain through a mutual friend and jammed with him. He was in the original line-up of Stone Johnny Mountain Band and was now in Sidewinder. The guys from Sidewinder wanted to bring me on. I announced my departure from Raven, but said I'd give them a month to figure out what to do so they could still cover their shows.

Dave was gone and I leaving. Raven was in disarray.

Things had gone so well for the band while we were on the road but derailed as boredom set in at home. We gigged all the time, but there was no new challenge.

We were all restless and young.

The more I jammed with Sidewinder, the more I knew I didn't want to do that, either.

A wife of one of the guitar players was best friends with Donna. I'd arrive at rehearsal and Donna would be there. We'd flirt a little, but I knew it was a bad idea. I still pined for Lexie from Lewiston and didn't want the distraction of Donna.

Jeannie was in the process of booking the tours for next year. She came to Raven and announced she had several contracts coming in that needed signing. "What are you guys going to do?"

Things sorted themselves out when Rachael left Dave.

She wasn't interested in him after he quit being in a rock band. Funny how that works. Rachael moved in with Dave's sister for a short time, before ripping her off and moving to Texas.

Dave and I met to talk. We both wanted back in Raven and we figured a united front was better when we approached Steve and Randy.

We told the other guys that we'd like to come back. They were cool with the idea. "Let's get this thing going again."

We hired Rick Wise to run our lights while Dan Murphy continued to handle our sound board. We paid those guys a full cut and they became our roadies. They hauled our gear and arranged our equipment.

Winter was in full effect and we weren't traveling outside the area anymore. We were true Spokane rock stars now and played only the best clubs. We got comfortable and full of ourselves.

We completely quit rehearsing. Dave would run in a couple minutes before the start of a show, his hair still wet from a shower, and plug in his guitar to play.

I was dating three girls at the same time. Calling it 'dating' is a stretch. We'd go to a movie and then have sex. They were groupies who I occasionally spent some time with outside of bed.

Since the band wasn't rehearsing, I had time to fill, so I took a job.

My neighbor was Dan's uncle and he owned Joe's Paint and Body Shop. They were looking for a shop boy. I took the job to earn some extra money. I would clean, make dump runs and take cars to the car wash. I still had my long hair so I had to tuck it under a baseball cap.

We were playing the Judge's Chambers and I met this girl who came on stage and sang with us. She was persistent about getting up there, but that was okay since she was cute and had a nice ass. That went along way. She wasn't that good of a singer, but we hit it off and spent time together.

We had a lot of sex. It wasn't great, but it was frequent and that's what counted back then. On my off nights, we would hang out at her place. She shared a house with two roommates. We would have sex in any room including the living room with the shades not drawn. Whatever she wanted to do, I went with it.

I later discovered that she was only eighteen and was underage for the clubs we were playing in.

I spent my nights with the eighteen-year-old and then went to work at the paint and body shop. They treated me like shit there, but I didn't care.

I was bored with my life.

In the middle of this, Jeannie said there was a possibility Raven might get booked for a month in Hawaii. Many clubs were bringing stateside bands over there. We got together and partied at Squire's. It was what we needed to get us of out of our rut.

That high lasted for a day before we learned the Hawaii gig wasn't going to happen.

When it fell through, we went back to our doldrums.

A couple days into the new year, Jeannie held a party at her house.

Since all the bands she represented had to work on New Year's Eve, Jeannie planned this party to get her clients together. I was the only one from Raven to attend.

Stone Johnny Mountain Band was there as was the band Black Jack. Restless from Moses Lake, Washington also attended.

We partied and had a great time. There was a jam session with double drums.

I enjoyed playing with the Stone Johnny guys. I told Eric Lindstrom, "If you ever need a drummer, give me a call."

Raven had gotten mundane.

Hell, life itself had gotten mundane.

Offers to join other local bands came my way, but none of them seemed better than Raven.

Then Jimmy McElwain called. He'd moved to Utah and joined a successful country band, Clear Sky. They needed a new drummer and wanted to hire me. They took Jimmy's word that I was a solid drummer. He put guitarist Jeff Benson on the phone and Jeff listed a bunch of the songs they did. They were also writing original songs. Jeff said they were opening soon for The Marshall Tucker Band and they also had financial backing. It sounded good, but I said I would think about it.

I didn't jump at the offer since I was in one of the most popular bands in Spokane. I was up to four different girlfriends by then.

Life might have been mundane but it sure as hell wasn't horrible.

I played the early part of January until I had a meeting with Jeannie. I laid out what I was experiencing and what I was faced with.

"Maybe you need a change of pace," Jeannie said. "Maybe you need to get out of town for a while."

Even though I had a handful of girlfriends, I was having women trouble. It's not like I couldn't get them. I just didn't like the ones I kept getting.

I felt like a wanted a relationship, but Lexie finally dumped me. I couldn't blame her when she quit returning my calls.

A new girl I met wanted me to quit the band. There was potential with her but we were only beginning and she wanted a white picket fence. "You're being childish by being in this band," she once told me. It never took off with her.

Raven played Doc Holiday's on Saturday, January 13th, 1979.

Afterwards, I told the band I was quitting.

Steve Hanna was pissed. "There isn't a third time to come back."

Dave Low said, "Wow, good luck to you brother."

Randy Peterson said, "Fuck, you're quitting? When?"

"Tonight was my last night," I said.

Then they all got pissed and deservedly so.

I didn't handle my exit well.

On Sunday morning, I took my drums to the airport in my Volkswagen bus and dropped them off at the freight section. I was excited and scared at the same time. I felt bad leaving mom, but my brother, Chuck, would be there for her. I was always on the road anyway.

On Monday morning, January 15th, 1979, I boarded one of the bright yellow planes from Hughes Airwest and flew to Salt Lake City.

CLEAR SKY
1979

(Back L-R) Me, E.J. Bell, and Jeff Benson
(Front L-R) Jimmy McElwain, Chuck Montes, and Frank Hewitt

Jimmy McElwain and Jeff Benson picked me up at the Salt Lake City Airport in Clear Sky's black Dodge van.

Jeff had long hair under his cowboy hat and Jimmy's long hair was under a fedora.

Before heading north to Ogden, my new home, we stopped at a strip club for a few beers. What once seemed like taboo behavior was now perfectly normal.

When we arrived in Ogden, they took me directly to The Public Affair restaurant which was the unofficial hangout for Clear Sky and referred to by the locals as "the P.A."

My first visit to The Public Affair was at 11 p.m. on a Monday night so it was dead inside. The décor of the P.A. was

126

accented with tacky fake medieval swords and shields hanging on the walls. Dark wood and trim were everywhere.

We had a few beers before leaving for Jeff's uncle's house where we spent the night.

Clear Sky had an upcoming gig booked in Moscow, Idaho so there was only a week and a half to practice and get me ready. I met the rest of the band and saw their line-up. Frank Hewitt sang lead vocals and Jimmy McElwain played lead guitar. E.J. Bell also played lead guitar while handling some keyboard duties. Jeff Benson covered rhythm guitar and Chuck Montes played bass. Along with Frank, some vocal duties fell to Jeff, Chuck and me.

It was the guys in Clear Sky who started calling me "Billy." It was a country thing. Up to this point, I'd been known as Bill, but for years after I would be known as Billy Bancroft.

The band rehearsed during the day at Sweetwater Station, a club around the corner from The Public Affair. Sweetwater Station was such a dump that when the lights were turned on cockroaches would scamper away.

At night, Frank and Jeff would perform an acoustic duo at The Public Affair. On Tuesday, we rehearsed and then headed over to The P.A. to watch Jeff and Frank do their show. The club was hopping.

Folks would come by and the band would introduce me as their new drummer. My head continued to swell with all the new introductions.

Then a waitress walked by that caught my complete attention. She had the cutest ass I'd ever seen in my life. She had small breasts that were covered with a t-shirt that displayed a Mounds Bite-Size candy bar logo. Her long blonde hair was almost white.

She was introduced as Becky Brewer.

Wow, I thought, *what a babe.*

Everyone was friendly that night, except Becky who was cold and aloof. She didn't talk to me. I don't think she even noticed me.

I expressed my appreciation for how she looked to the guys.

Jimmy nodded, "Yeah, she is a cute one."

Jeff said, "I had her. She'll scratch your back good, but don't waste your time with her. She's a cold bitch."

I didn't challenge Jeff's statement, but it was obvious he was full of shit.

Frank and Jeff later performed on the small stage. After a bit, the crowd egged the whole band up there. By the end of the week, we were all up on stage, sitting on stools and singing. I even sang lead on *24 Hours at a Time* by The Marshall Tucker Band.

It turned into quite a party. It was an acoustic gig, kind of a "Clear Sky Unplugged."

On the 21st of January, Jimmy and I went to The Public Affair to drink some beers. The Super Bowl was on a small black & white television in the upper corner above the bar. The Pittsburgh Steelers were playing the Dallas Cowboys in Miami.

At the end of the bar sat an old derelict. He was seriously drunk but wasn't disruptive.

Some jocks were in the bar to watch the game. They were the stereotypical arrogant, obnoxious type who bully the most defenseless person around. When the drunk walked to the restroom, the jocks teased him.

One of them asked him, "What's your name?"

He stammered, "Bu...," several times.

"Bu?" they repeated and giggled.

He finally said, "Buck."

Jimmy told the assholes to leave the guy alone. For interrupting their jock-like fun, they angrily glared at us through the rest of the game.

I take great comfort in knowing that at some point one or all my bandmates screwed the girlfriends of those jocks.

On January 23rd, the band was invited to The Swamp Root, a private club. The guys all got drunk and tempers flared.

I didn't know this, but when I first arrived in Ogden, Clear Sky was on the verge of a break-up. There was a great deal of in-fighting between Chuck, Frank and Jeff. There was always tension in the band except between Jimmy and me.

That day sticks out in my mind because it was exactly a year after my dad died. I had been sad the entire day. As the guys continued arguing, I left the table since I had planned to call mom.

We talked about dad and life for over thirty minutes.

I told her I was doing great even though I wasn't.

The band had a gig in Moscow less than a week away and the guys were lackadaisical about it. My head was filled with thoughts of doubt. I was seriously questioning what I had chosen to do. *I left a popular band and lots of girls for this?*

We rehearsed the next few days and then headed out to the Moscow gig.

Clear Sky had two rigs, a red Chevy van and a black Dodge van. We headed north to Moscow on I-15. Outside Deer Lodge, Montana on I-90, it was extremely cold and the Dodge broke down. We all piled into the Chevy and drove into Deer Lodge. We had the Dodge towed to town to get fixed. We didn't leave Deer Lodge until late afternoon.

We rolled through Spokane in the morning.

The guys were going to head straight to Moscow, but they dropped me off at Greenacres Elementary School to visit my mom. I would meet them in Moscow after I got my Volkswagen bus.

This initially pissed them off since I wasn't going to be with them to unload the gear. Chuck Montes threatened to charge me fifty bucks since I was skipping out on this work. Chuck always threatened this but it never happened.

I saw mom, but since she was in the middle of class she couldn't leave. She let me take her car home. My brother was gone at work and I was all alone.

The house was cool inside and it smelled clean. It felt like home. I stood in my parent's bedroom and thought about dad for a bit.

I then took a shower and cleaned up.

My VW bus sat in the driveway and still had my drum riser in it. I packed a few more clothes in the van.

I spent a couple hours by myself enjoying the quiet. It felt so good to be alone and quiet.

There was no silence amid the chaos known as Clear Sky.

In Moscow, Idaho, we played the Capricorn Lounge which was inside the Eagles Club.

I still had been talking with a girl I'd met before leaving Spokane and had a decent although distant relationship going with her. I drove back to Spokane to spend the night with her after the first gig. That's roughly a two-hour trip one-way. In the morning, I would head back to Moscow. I did that every night until Saturday when she came and stayed with me.

The Capricorn wanted a country band and we were a country-rock band. The crowd hated us. At the end of Saturday night, when we figured we had a whole other week to go, the owner fired us.

It was my first road gig with Clear Sky and we got fired.

The night we were fired, my girl came to spend the evening together. She made me wear a condom. It was the first time I ever wore one.

"I don't want to get pregnant if you're not going to be around," she said.

In the morning, we drove my VW back to Spokane. She then drove me back to Moscow in her car so I could join the band for the return trip home.

She stood on the sidewalk as we packed the band's gear. She wore a light brown, leather jacket and knee-high, leather boots.

We kissed before she left. I watched her walk toward her car. She turned around and waved. She looked fantastic. That was the last time I would ever see her.

There were many moments like that on the road.

Back in Ogden, the partying kept on. One girl showed me a quarter gram of cocaine and asked if I wanted a taste. Even though I was skilled at partying, I was still a novice when it came to harder drugs. I went into the back room and proceeded to snort almost all her powder. I came out and handed her the nearly empty vial. She got mad, but I pleaded new guy innocence. She forgave me and I let her seduce me. The sacrifices a budding rock star must make to keep willing fans happy.

We went to the North Ogden house she shared with a girl named Melissa. In the morning, we lay in bed together. I rolled over to her and said, "Jimmy told me to watch out for you. He said that you'd come for me next. What did he mean by that?"

The girl smiled. "I was with Jimmy last week."

"Oh."

"He was number thirty-nine. E.J. was thirty-eight."

"What?"

"You're number forty."

She was so proud of her accomplishment.

I later learned she'd been with every guy in the band.

Needing a place to stay, Jeff, Jimmy and I moved in with Jeff's friend, a big, heavy-set girl who fed us and acted like our mom.

Her cooking was the first decent meal I had since I left Spokane. We had great dinners every night. Turkey noodle soup. Meat loaf. Real food was something the three of us desperately needed.

The only thing tainting her "Mrs. Cleaver" routine was her cocaine dealing. She had a shit load of the white stuff in her house.

The three of us slept on the living room floor. We'd wake in the morning with customers stepping over us to make a coke deal in the backroom.

I walked in one day and the girl had what looked to be a pound or more of cocaine sitting on her dresser. She was cutting it with a laxative.

I'm not complaining since we snorted a lot of coke with her.

In March of '79, Meadowlark Ventures, the booking agency that occasionally co-brokered gigs with Jeannie Carter, got us a gig in Missoula followed by a show in Casper. They were the same booking agency that screwed over my former band.

In Missoula, Clear Sky played The Top Hat, and after the gig they put us in the same hotel I'd stayed in with Raven. We were in an apartment room over the office of this hotel.

Chris Roberts, the booking agent with Meadowlark Ventures, brought his girlfriend to the show. She was too young and too cute for him, but absolutely perfect for me.

Chris had sued Raven after the fallout over the scheduling fuck-up and our subsequent refusal to pay him a commission.

The lawsuit with Raven was still pending so I was none too happy to see him at our gig.

I tried to ignore the guy, but Chris pressed the issue and said, "Let's let bygones be bygones." He was suing me and my former band and he wanted me to somehow be okay with it. The guy was a moron.

Chris and his girlfriend later showed up at the after-hours party and I flirted with his girl almost immediately.

We were smoking dope, snorting cocaine, and drinking whiskey.

It didn't take long for the band to get Chris involved in a drug-induced argument and the dumbass made the best/worst compliment ever.

Chris thought he was complimenting Frank Hewitt when he said, "You're the Mick Jagger of country-rock."

Now, Frank hated Mick Jagger with a passion and took this as an insult.

They got into a heated discussion.

While that was going on, Chris's girlfriend and I slipped into a bedroom down the hallway.

We were in there thirty minutes and when we came out, the guys were still having a coke-addled argument.

Chris never noticed his girlfriend was gone.

For those keeping score, the lawsuit against Raven was later dismissed since we all went our separate ways and time allowed it to fade away.

We finished the gig at The Top Hat and moved on to Charlie's in Casper.

When we arrived we immediately assembled our gear. We were a six-piece band so we had quite a set-up. A grizzled, old guy sidled up to us and leaned on the railing that ran around the stage.

"Look at all those goddamn microphones. Merle Haggard doesn't use that many goddamn microphones. What do you girls need that many for?"

We all had long hair and I had the longest. We stared back at the old man. Immediately, we knew this was going to be an interesting week.

Monday was our first gig. The bartender, Cary, was a cute blonde. Frank took her home that night. The next night I took her home.

On Wednesday night, Jeff and Chuck got into a fist fight in the hotel room. They simply didn't like each other. Jeff was an acoustic guitar player and Chuck was a rock and roller. They were oil and water. Those two were always flipping each other shit. It was nothing in particular.

It happens frequently when you mix a couple guys with attitudes fueled by cocaine and booze. There's bound to be a fight. I ignored them and spent another night with the bartender, Cary.

On Thursday night, Cary and I had planned to spend the night together again, but we stopped first at an after-hours club to do some dancing. Cary and I danced until the club closed at 4 a.m.

As we walked towards her truck, we absently chatted about how much fun we'd had. I opened the passenger door to her big four-wheel drive truck to let her in. She was going to let me drive.

Behind us, someone screamed, "He's got a gun!"

I spun around. One hundred and fifty feet away, a guy was aiming a shotgun at us.

Cary yelled, "No!" and jumped into the truck.

The gun went off. Boom!

I dropped to the ground as the passenger window shattered. Glass was everywhere. I rolled under the truck, came out the other side, hopped up and sprinted over a bank.

I raced like a motherfucker away from that truck. My heart was pounding so fast, I could hardly breath. All the cocaine I'd ever done couldn't compete with the adrenaline surging through me. The fringe hanging from my jacket whipped wildly as I ran. I had no idea where I was running to or if her husband was behind me.

I'll admit I didn't even think about Cary as I took off.

I eventually made it back to the hotel.

Cary didn't come into work on Friday and I was worried that something might have happened to her. I was scared to death that night as we played. I kept worrying that he was going to come in and blow me away. I worried all day on Saturday, too.

It was shitty.

A couple weeks later, after we had returned to Ogden, we learned that Cary's husband had come into the bar one night with his shotgun and killed her.

Our next stop was the Bronze Boot in Cody, Wyoming.

Clear Sky had played there before and the other guys were excited since they planned to visit some girls they'd partied with previously.

We arrived on Sunday night, but weren't scheduled to start until Tuesday. We were staying in a trailer for the week.

I had a severe case of depression due to the gun scare in Casper, the band fight a couple nights before and the cold outside (it was March). I wasn't happy. The things that had been promised when I joined Clear Sky weren't materializing.

On Monday morning, I went to a local grocery store and bought some supplies because I thought I could save some money. I came back with a fridge full of food. I was acting a little different from the rest of the band because they wanted to party and I had already done that with Raven. I was searching for something different.

Later in the afternoon, we went to the famous Silver Dollar Bar where everyone drank peppermint schnapps except me. I chose not to drink that night. The band then moved on to acid. The guys made fun of me because I brooded most of the night. A group of girls joined us, some of them having been squeezes from earlier tours through Cody. One of the girls introduced herself as Lisa.

When we returned to the band trailer things went bad.

Jeff was blitzed and acted like a jerk. He reached into the fridge and grabbed a head of lettuce that I had bought for sandwiches. He broke it on E.J. Bell's head and then bit into it.

"What are you doing?" I yelled.

"Bite me," Jeff said.

I punched him in the throat, knocking him out. He was so drunk he simply fell backwards into a chair and passed out.

E.J. freaked. He yelled, "I can't stand this fighting!"

He broke a mirror, grabbed a chunk of glass and came after us. E.J. cornered me in the far bedroom, screaming and yelling. When I could get around him, I ran out of the trailer.

Someone called the police. When they arrived, they tackled E.J. and subdued him. He continued to fight until they put him in a straight-jacket.

Later, an ambulance transported E.J. to the hospital. Jimmy, Chuck and I followed them. Frank had taken off with a girl when the police came. We left Jeff passed out in his chair.

At the hospital, E.J. had squirmed out of the straight-jacket and was lying in bed, smoking a cigarette. He was totally calm.

When the police officer saw the look on my face, he chuckled.

"What are you laughing at?" I asked.

"Boy," he said, "we see this stuff all the time. You just have to laugh at it."

Chuck was tweaking from his acid and it was evident he was fried. The cop pointed at him and said, "Do you want that boy to go to jail?"

I shook my head.

"You better take him out of here."

We went back to the band's trailer house and cleaned up the broken glass. E.J. spent the night in the hospital.

In the morning, surprisingly, no one was mad.

It was one of those strange, yet typical, band experiences.

We played Tuesday night's gig. It was at The Bronze Boot that Jeff told me Lisa, one of the girls from the first night, had previously been his squeeze.

Jimmy was hitting it off with a girl while Frank got with another one. Frank was separated from his wife during this time.

At our band trailer later, I sat between Lisa and another girl. The three of us were talking and I kept thinking I had a chance with one of them. I had to make a choice, so I could direct my efforts.

I turned my attention to Lisa and made a date. She wouldn't be a groupie, she said, but she would pick me up for breakfast. I liked her and agreed to wait.

The next morning, I was awoken by Lisa shaking my foot. "You said we would have breakfast. Let's go."

We spent a great morning together. That night, Wednesday, we slept together, but didn't have sex. I respected that.

On Thursday, we consummated the deal and it was incredible. I was glad we waited the two days!

The girls hanging with us had ex-boyfriends who showed up on Friday. We were playing our last set and they threatened to kick our asses when we finished. A couple of the girls called the police.

We were playing *Can't You See* by The Marshall Tucker Band.

And we kept playing and playing and playing that song, hoping the cops would show up and escort us off stage.

We must have played that song for twenty minutes before ending it. Nothing happened, but those cowboys scared the hell out of us.

On Saturday, I had a bad headache and hung out with Lisa all day.

She soaked a bandana in cold water and tied it tight around my head. She combed my hair and let me relax. We read books together. It seemed like a very cowboy, country existence. It was comfortable and I imagined living a life with her. I did that when on the road – imagining what life would be like in various locations with different girls.

Some of our friends drove up from Ogden. One of them hit on Lisa as we tore down our gear at the club. I watched them and figured if she gave him any response then I knew she wasn't for me. But she didn't. Lisa told him to get lost and we spent the night together.

It turned out to be a good thing I spent the night away from the trailer. Those who stayed there got crabs, another STD common in the 1970s much like scabies.

We stayed in town two extra days since the band now had "girlfriends."

Tuesday rolled around and the girls had to get back to work and we had to get back to Ogden. We all had overly long, dramatic good-byes which you're prone to at that age.

Then we drove home and never gave them another thought.

Back in Ogden, I couldn't stay any longer with our maternal coke dealer.

We'd been there a couple weeks except while on the road and the cocaine scene was getting too heavy, making me nervous. Every night, I worried about a bust or a drug rip. Jimmy said I was paranoid, but I didn't care. I wanted to move on but didn't have a place to crash.

The owners of The Public Affair let me stay in the basement of the bar. At that time, they weren't using the basement for a lounge and, instead, were using it for storage. Someone lent me a blanket and a pillow.

I would frequently wake up with cockroaches walking on me.

It still makes my skin crawl thinking of that today. It was a truly horrible experience.

One morning I woke to the sound of someone vacuuming.

It was completely dark in the basement so I thought it was the middle of the night. When I came upstairs, I saw light outside. It was about 11 a.m.

I had been sleeping in my clothes. My hair was dirty and I had put on my dumpy looking cowboy hat. I was a scrawny 130 pounds and totally hung over.

Alone in the middle of the bar, with her back towards me, was the cute blonde waitress with the great ass, Becky Brewer. She wore white pants and a sky-blue French-cut t-shirt.

I stood there, staring at her. I must have looked like a complete hoodlum.

She turned around and saw me. She jumped back, startled. She grabbed a steak knife, set her jaw and demanded, "Who the fuck are you?"

Those were the first real words she ever said to me.

"I'm Billy Bancroft. I'm the new drummer for Clear Sky. We met the other night."

Still pointing the knife, she said, "Oh. I heard they got a new drummer. Where did you come from?"

I was totally bummed. She didn't remember me. "I was sleeping in the basement."

"Do the owners know?"

"They're the ones who let me."

She watched me for a moment, the knife still pointed in my direction. "Want some coffee?"

"Yeah."

She backed around the counter, still pointing the knife in my direction. Until I was sipping coffee, she kept the knife in her hand.

We had some polite conversation after that.

Sher, a friend of Chuck Montes, had a new place for Jimmy and me to crash for a bit.

We stayed in her three-level apartment for several weeks. She had a couple day beds and a couch. She slept in her own bedroom.

We had a good set-up there. Jimmy was off chasing his groupies most of the time and I was chasing mine. Sher tried to live her life the best she could with a couple derelicts sleeping on her couches.

"The Herm" was legendary to the guys in the band and we were scheduled for a six-week gig, playing Tuesday through Saturday, five nights a week. It was a big deal.

Twelfth Street wound up the mountain through Ogden Canyon to reveal The Hermitage. How more people didn't get killed getting off that hill, as drunk as they were, is still a mystery.

In front of The Herm was a small building that housed Bear's Canyon Grocery Store. A basic American food restaurant sat to the side. There was a big parking lot out front. The Gray Cliff Lodge was just up the hill.

The Hermitage was a roadhouse establishment with a big stage. Customers entered through the front door and a railing directed them left or right. There was a large, stone fireplace to the left and the kitchen and bar were to the right. There was lava rock and dark wood everywhere.

Straight ahead was the stage that was highlighted by a huge archway. My drums sat underneath the arch. A big dance floor lay in front of the stage.

Beer signs lined the walls. Smelly, stained, gold carpet was everywhere except the wooden dance floor.

On Tuesday night, I was greeted with a sight I would quickly become accustomed to but would still send shivers of excitement through me. As we rounded the curves, there were cars lined alongside the road. The parking lot was packed. I had never seen anything like this before. The club allowed the band to stage our vans behind the building in the loading zone.

We could hear the full club. There was a lot of noise and energy from people talking and the juke box playing.

The guys grabbed their guitars and I got my sticks. We entered the hallway, passed through the archway and walked on stage. I sat behind my drum kit and the guys plugged in their guitars. The crowd suddenly noticed us and cheered.

After we got our gear ready, we went backstage again. We tried to be nonchalant, but we were too amped. It seemed like we were the right band at the right time in the right place.

I didn't initially agree with Frank on this, but we began the night with *Cinderella* by Firefall.

We played the song a little faster and with more energy than Firefall did. The piece begins with an acoustic guitar before the rest of the band joins in.

The lights were low as Jeff played the first notes of the song. The crowd immediately got loud and moved to the dance floor.

As the acoustic guitar intro ended, the song kicked in and the place erupted. There must have been 300 people on the dance floor. Frank had called it perfectly, and I still get chills telling this story.

That was our opening night at The Hermitage.

Wednesday was the same thing, but it was "Beer Night."

Five dollars got you in the door and then you could drink free beer all night. Wrap your mind around that.

Back then, you could carry a bottle of Jack Daniels or vodka or whatever hard liquor was your choice into a bar with you. You could then spend $3 for a coke and be set for the night.

For those of us who drank our alcohol straight it was great. I proceeded to drink a whole lot of whiskey over those six weeks.

Speaking of which, we performed *Whiskey* by The Charlie Daniels Band and I sang lead. While we were at The Hermitage, I become synonymous with that song.

I took it upon myself to be the King of Jack Daniels. I always had a fifth or a pint sitting on my drum riser.

When we played *Whiskey*, I'd ask the crowd, "Are you ready to drink some Jack Daniels?" The crowd would go wild and someone would pass a bottle of J.D. on stage. I'd take a long pull from the bottle and we'd have a great time with the song.

I sang *Whiskey* in Raven but it never went over that well in a rock band.

In my down time, I was on the phone and writing letters to some of my pen pals. I would occasionally write to Lexie in Lewiston, even though she had dumped me.

I still had the immense hots for The Public Affair waitress, Becky Brewer, but she wouldn't give me the time of day.

I tried to tip Becky large amounts of money whenever I ate there – 50¢, 75¢, or even $1.00.

The girl who introduced me to cocaine came to The Hermitage and brought along her roommate, Melissa. I immediately focused on the roommate and we eventually went home together.

Melissa and I began spending most nights together. Even if she couldn't go to the show, she would get me after her job ended, drive me to the gig and then pick me up afterwards about 3 a.m.

The first time I went back to Melissa's house, she paid a babysitter as soon as we got there. I couldn't believe it. She had two boys – a five-year-old and a baby that was a year at most. It turns out she had a messy divorce and was now a single mom. It surprised me, since she was so tiny and looked young.

Most of my nights were spent with Melissa. One night, however, she didn't come to The Herm and I met this stunningly beautiful girl from an affluent part of Ogden.

It was the first time I snorted cocaine through a $100 bill. We went into her bedroom as moonlight shone through the curtains. She got undressed and lay on the bed, completely posed. She was beautiful.

Unfortunately, it was the worst sex I'd ever had in my life. She didn't know how to kiss and, worse, she didn't like to kiss.

When things got going, she just laid back on the bed. It was like screwing a mannequin.

I was no expert at sex, but this girl left me feeling empty.

Apparently, E.J. slept with her six months later and said the same thing.

I was glad it wasn't only me.

The normal routine during our time at The Herm went something like this…

I'd get up and Sher would already be off to work.

Jimmy and I would then go to Chick's Cafe for a late breakfast. Afterwards, we'd head back to Sher's and kill some time playing Frisbee in the nearby park, watch TV or read books until we could go back to The Public Affair in the afternoon. We'd run into our friends or make some new ones.

We were local celebrities. There's no other word for it.

Melissa worked at a local blood bank as a phlebotomist. I asked her to lunch one afternoon and she brought one of her friends. They wanted to go to The Public Affair and Becky waited on us.

That was the first day Becky was ever friendly to me, other than offering me coffee while she held me at knifepoint. I had tried to hit on her previously, but she would never turn my way.

Becky noticing me put wind in my sails because she always felt out of my reach.

As lunch continued, Becky's old boyfriend walked in. She sat next to him and they held hands. When she stood to go back to work, they kissed. I couldn't help staring.

The wind quickly went out of my sails. Obviously, I didn't have a chance. He was a big, tall, good-looking guy with family money.

I resolved to forget about Becky.

Clear Sky packed the house every night at The Hermitage.

After the gigs, we would often party in the parking lot. Many times, I was given head from some girl in, around or on top of a car.

Jimmy once overheard a girl outside the restrooms say, "That drummer can make me drop my shorts anytime." I immediately went over to her and we found our way to the parking lot.

I wore only satin shorts to play in. Only. Nothing else. One night, a female fan caught me in the hallway and yanked my shorts to my bare feet.

I stood completely naked in that hallway and laughed.

The world is different for guys in a band.

The first time I invited Melissa over to Sher's house, we watched a Chevy Chase movie while she combed my hair. At that moment, I felt I wanted an apartment of my own and maybe even a steady girlfriend.

Some of the girls from Cody notified us that they were going to come see us. Frank's girl wasn't going to make it which was good for his marriage since he was putting it back together.

Lisa was expected to make the trip.

I phoned her and said it wasn't a good idea that she come. I think I broke her heart when I told her to stay there.

The other girls eventually came and never left.

They became Ogden girls.

One night at The Herm, Melissa said, "I guess I'm not going to see you for a couple weeks."

"Why?"

"Because your girlfriend is coming down from Cody."

"There's a bunch of girls coming," I said, "but I asked Lisa not to come."

"Why?" Melissa looked confused.

"Because I'm seeing you."

Tears welled in her eyes.

I may have been down to only Melissa, but I still had Becky Brewer on my brain.

She was the most captivating woman I had ever met. Occasionally, I would find myself imagining her name with mine – Becky Bancroft. She was the only girl I'd ever done that with. I quickly pushed it out of my mind, the musings of a naïve kid.

I stopped by The P.A. to grab lunch during our final week at The Herm. We'd soon be going on tour.

The establishment had a ramp that led from the billiards room in the lower level. A little girl laughed loudly while she sprinted up the ramp. She didn't pay attention as she ran and hit her head on the edge of table. She fell and immediately shrieked.

I bolted out of the booth to help the girl, but another guy beat me to her. He rubbed her back and said, "It's okay. It's okay." He lifted the girl and handed her across the bar to Becky.

I watched in confusion as Becky consoled the girl, quickly calming her. *Was she babysitting this kid?*

I asked, "Is she okay?"

"Yeah, she'll be fine."

"She sure is cute. Is she yours?"

"Yes, this is my daughter, Erin."

This was my first introduction to Erin Marie Brewer.

Becky continued to work and help people as she consoled Erin.

I was impressed with how she did it all.

Not long after that, her shift ended and she bundled up Erin. She brought her orange 10-speed bicycle out from the back of the bar. Becky didn't own a car.

I helped her get the bike to the curb. She put Erin in the little seat on the back and pedaled off.

She was a twenty-six-year-old woman raising a daughter on her own. She didn't have a phone or a car, but she had money and she had her stuff together.

That meant she was really out of my league.

As we neared the end of our six-week stint at The Hermitage, we were booked for a three-week tour in Victor, MT, Moscow, ID and finally in Eugene, OR.

We had big, tearful good-byes that final night at The Hermitage. Some fans brought a cake to wish us well. The crowd was great on our last night.

A picture after the gig shows Melissa and me sitting on my drum cases. I was convinced that she and I could be together.

Becky wasn't giving me any time and I'd stopped thinking of Lexie and had broken off contact with Lisa.

In the late spring, we played Victor's Barn in Victor, Montana which is roughly forty miles south of Missoula. Jimmy's sister, who I'd gone to high school with, joined us on this trip.

Victor's Barn was particularly notable because its stage was in the rafters. We had to haul our gear up a steep set of stairs to get there. If you were in the crowd, you could barely see the band. When you got close to the bar, we were above your head.

Clear Sky only had a two-night gig at the Barn. Both nights were dead. Nobody knew we were there. They were uneventful shows, but it was a cool looking place.

Our next gig was in Moscow which due to the odd shape of Idaho would mean a stop in Spokane.

In St. Regis, ID, we stopped for snack food. Chicken, cupcakes and other junk food rounded out our purchases.

E.J., Frank and Chuck were in the red van. I was in the black van along with Jimmy, Jeff and Jeff's sister.

As we drove, someone in the lead van threw a chicken bone out a window and it bounced off our windshield. We took that as a challenge, sped ahead and threw some garbage out of our van at them.

This launched a food fight between two vans traveling fifty-five miles per hour. Cheetos, marshmallows, chicken skin and other food stuff was thrown at each other.

I didn't participate much because I was hungry and trying to keep weight on my frame.

The red van pulled alongside and opened the side door. Frank was driving. E.J. and Chuck dropped their pants and mooned us. Then they turned around and gave us the 'ol' chicken wing.'

The chicken wing was achieved by grabbing your balls in one hand and your dick in the other and pulling in opposite directions. A couple other times they pressed it against the windows which earned the nickname 'chicken wing under glass.'

We pulled off at a rest stop between Coeur d'Alene and Post Falls. The vans were covered with sticky crap and chicken skin. It was disgusting.

When we arrived in Spokane the band dropped me off at mom's house while they cleaned the rigs and gassed them up. This allowed me some time to see my family.

I visited with mom and my brother, but it was clear to them I was totally wrapped up in myself.

We moved on to Moscow and played The Capricorn Lounge again.

This time the club was under new ownership and they had a better crowd. I contacted Lexie prior to arriving. She drove up from Lewiston to see us play. Then she came to the hotel, the same one we stayed in as Raven. We drank some beers and talked. I made my pitch that I was still a decent guy. I know I just said I thought Melissa and I could be together, but I was also twenty-one and full of myself.

That night Lexie and I slept together but we stayed fully clothed. I never attempted anything. She slept on top of the covers while I was underneath.

In the morning, we had breakfast and chatted some more. When we finished eating, she said, "I'm thinking about buying a new swimming suit. Do you want to go?"

We went to two or three places and she tried on several bikinis. Each time she came out and modeled them. She looked fantastic every damn time, but she never bought one.

I was too naïve to see what she was doing.

Afterwards, she drove me back to my hotel.

When we stopped, I asked, "Is there any chance for us or have I completely blown it?"

She didn't answer my question. "Let's stay in touch."

I gave her Sher's address and phone number.

I got out of her Datsun and walked around to her side. She never got out. I leaned in to kiss her goodbye. She turned her head and drove away.

As she faded it into the distance, I was sad.

That was the last time I ever saw her.

The sadness I felt turned into hurt, then into anger. I got even with Lexie by having sex with some girl who I don't even remember.

Yeah, it sure felt like I got even.

Our next gig was in Eugene, Oregon at Grand Illusions.

One afternoon at the hotel, I sat out on the patio, underneath the sun, my body smeared in baby oil. I read a book and napped occasionally, totally enjoying myself. Throughout the afternoon I drank only water and soda. I sat there for three hours without ever turning over or moving into the shade.

When I got up, I was completely sunburned. My skin was bright red and felt brittle. Thankfully, it was only on the front part of my body.

I was in so much pain I could barely play that evening. I managed to get through the gig but had to keep my shirt unbuttoned. It was fucking horrible. I don't think I've ever been that sunburned before or after.

On the return trip to Ogden, I was literally sick.

I laid in the van and was miserable.

When we got back to Ogden we had some time off.

Jimmy, Jeff and I decided to drive back to Spokane. Seeing my family for a few minutes on the previous tour made me want to head home. Jeff was from Ione, Washington so he drove the extra eighty-five miles after dropping us off. Jimmy stayed at his family's house in Spokane and I went to mom's. I hung out with my brother and didn't try to reach out to any old girlfriends.

While I was back, I saw Raven's new line-up. Steve Hanna and Dave Low were the only band members left. Dan Murphy was still running sound and Rick Wise was on lights. I partied with my old friends and the new Raven guys.

As a side-note, while we were in Raven, we always thought it was weird that in a band full of man-whores, Dan never got laid.

In the mid '90s, Dan moved to Denver. Occasionally, he would come back to Spokane and we would see each other. He sent me an email many years later telling me he was gay. "Did you really think I couldn't find a wife all these years?" he asked.

I told Dan I realized the truth later in life. Then he told me about his partner whom he later married. I was really happy for him. I'm glad we got to be part of something special together when we were younger and became lifelong friends.

Easter came while visiting my family, so I sent a bouquet of flowers to Becky. She was being friendly but nothing more than that. I wanted her to think of me and I figured flowers would do the trick.

The card was supposed to read, *Happy Easter, Becky and Erin – Thinking of You.*

That didn't happen. Instead, the florist screwed up and wrote *Happy Easter, Erin – Thinking of you.*

This offended Becky because she thought I sent it to her daughter.

I also sent Melissa an Easter card and one to Lisa in Casper as I felt bad about how things ended.

On Easter, I went to church with mom.

Clear Sky was a hard-partying band and a big fish in a small pond. I was having the time of my life but coming back to Spokane was a nice and much needed break.

The night we were going to leave, Jeff, Jimmy and I drove over to see Jeannie Carter. We got high with her for an hour then drove over to a local pizza parlor. We drank beer, played pool and pinball before starting the thirteen-hour drive back to Ogden.

It was about 9 p.m. when we decided to head out. We arrived in Ogden in the morning as the sun was rising.

I was in the passenger seat and leaned out the window to yell, "Clear Sky is home!"

It felt good to be back.

The Public Affair decided to re-open their basement lounge so we could play and practice. After some needed cleaning, it turned into quite the party spot.

We played in the basement and the place packed out. Frank, Chuck, E.J. and Jeff were popular guys.

E.J. Bell, who was a few steps left of center, would occasionally come to rehearsal in his dirty, maroon bathrobe with his hair all fucked up. He'd walk through the front door totally spaced out.

We were always embarrassed when he did that, but that was E.J.

By mid-May we began our next stint at The Hermitage.

It wasn't as crazy as our first time, but it was the typical Herm gig – big crowds and good shows.

I was trying to spend more time around Becky even though I couldn't win her over. Except for spending time with Melissa, I quit chasing any other girls. I had my heart set on Becky. I think part of it was who she was, but if I'm honest, it was because she wouldn't give me the time of day. I just wasn't used to that treatment. I could never get her to notice me as anything other than a nice guy.

Then one night at The Herm, Becky came with some friends. Afterwards, she asked if I wanted to join her and her girlfriends at The Swamp Root.

Of course, I said, "You bet."

She was with her best friend. Sher and Robert Petty were also there. Robert was one of the 'circle of friends.' He'd known the guys in the band for years and was a like a big brother to Becky.

When we arrived at The Swamp Root, Becky ditched me and went off to talk with some other people. I was disappointed at the lack of attention from her.

After a bit, only Sher and I were seated at a table. Sher leaned over, "Are you going to go home with Becky Brewer tonight?"

"I don't know. I hope so."

"Don't do it. I'll take you home and fuck your lights out, if that's all you want."

Sher was like a sister so this shocked the shit out of me.

The after-hours party was ending when Becky came back. Becky sat and nonchalantly looked at me. "Are you going to come home with me?"

I tried to be disinterested, but I couldn't say no.

At her place, she was sleeping in her living room on a hide-a-bed couch. She pulled out the bed. On the stereo, she started Gino Vannelli's <u>Brother to Brother</u> album. We made love as *Appaloosa* played.

The next morning, I left Becky to shoot skeet in western Ogden with Robert Petty and his friend. It was the first time I'd ever done it. Robert gave me some tips on shooting and I had a great time. When we ran out of skeet, we shot at fence posts, jack rabbits and even seagulls flying over. I never got a rabbit or a seagull.

"Man, that's the state bird," Robert said. "You get caught shooting one of those and you'll go to jail."

I didn't believe him and kept firing. He finally convinced me that what he was saying was true and I stopped. In case you're wondering, the California Gull, commonly known as the seagull, is in fact Utah's state bird.

When we were finished and storing the guns, I leaned over to Robert and said, "Check this out. I went home with that Brewer chick last night." I felt cocky when those words tumbled out of my mouth.

Robert grabbed me by the shoulder and put his finger in my face. He knew my reputation as a slut. "Don't you ever talk about her like that. She's a good friend of mine. She's a good person. Don't you hurt her. If you get her to fall in love with you and you hurt her, I'll kick your ass."

I shrugged it off because I liked her and had feelings for her.

I didn't give a thought to hurting her. Hell, I was more worried she'd break my heart.

I was still seeing Melissa and going home with her, too, but every chance I got I would also see Becky, which wasn't that often.

One afternoon, Jimmy and I were hanging out with Sher when Marcy, a friend of Sher's came over.

She was a cute Italian girl with long black hair and a great figure. The four of us were watching T.V., drinking beer and smoking weed. Sher took off to run some errands. When she left, Jimmy and I stepped outside for a conversation about Marcy since we were both interested in her.

Now, I know that I said I had feelings for Becky and I was dating Melissa and sleeping with them both. Nevertheless, I was still twenty-one and I didn't know if Becky would ever give me more. With Melissa, I wasn't sure if I wanted more. I wanted to see what Marcy had to offer.

Jimmy wasn't happy.

"Billy, I love you. But you prick, you've got them coming out of your ears. You got to let me have this one."

Looking back at the conversation, we were a couple of young jerks talking about her like she was a piece of cake or something.

We came back in, had another beer and I made a graceful exit. I walked to The Public Affair. I chatted with Becky while she worked. She took a break and we went for a walk.

"I need to talk to you."

My heart quickened. I thought she was getting feelings and wanted to share them.

"If we're going to spend time together," she said, "really spend time together, you're going to have to give me more."

I didn't understand what she meant and she looked at me like I was a complete idiot.

"In bed," she said. "You're not giving me enough in bed. You have your fun and then you roll over and go to sleep."

My mouth opened and I didn't know what to say. It was like the air being let out of a balloon. I was absolutely deflated.

She was dead-on, I knew. I had slept with all sorts of girls and they never asked for "more" or required any finesse – they just came back for more. I was young and self-absorbed and she took my inflated ego down a notch.

"I've got to get back to work," Becky said.

She turned and left me speechless on the sidewalk.

I was embarrassed. Then I got angry.

I walked around Ogden for a couple hours then went back to Sher's apartment. Jimmy and Marcy were in bed having a great time.

I felt sorry for myself.

Jimmy and I soon wore out our welcome with Sher.

One night, she wanted to have her boyfriend over to her house. Jimmy and I were lounging in her living room when they came home. We didn't take the hint to make ourselves scarce.

She finally asked us to leave, for good.

We were terrible house guests.

We moved out and another female friend, Cora, let us move in into her apartment. Cora tended bar at The Public Affair. She was going to Phoenix for a month and said we could house sit her two-story apartment in north Ogden while she was gone. Jimmy and I jumped at the opportunity.

"All I need is for you to keep the plants alive," Cora said.
Of course, we failed miserably at that.

On June 1st, I went over to Becky's for Erin's birthday party. I had bought a little stuffed dog for Erin. Not only did I want to make Erin happy, but I wanted to show Becky that I was paying attention. When I showed up, Becky told me Erin's birthday was the 21st, not the first. I had somehow confused the dates.

Embarrassed, I went home to Cora's apartment. She had gotten home by that time, but she said we could stay for a few more days. I had been staying in Cora's room so I dozed on her bed after reading my book.

She came into the room, wearing her underwear and tank top. Water ran in the bathtub.

"I'm sorry," I said and moved to leave.

"Don't worry about it," Cora said. "Do you want to take a bath with me?"

I stammered, not knowing what to say.

"Come on what's a bath between friends?" she said.

She peeled off her clothes and stood in front of me completely naked. She looked amazing.

"I'm getting in the tub," she said from the bathroom.

I took my clothes off. I was to my underwear and ready to go. I walked toward the bathroom but suddenly stopped. I don't know why I hesitated but I did. I turned around to get out of there.

Cora called my name so I poked my head into the bathroom. The lights were off and candles were burning. She looked beautiful.

"Are you coming?"

"No," I said. "I don't think so."

"Get in here and we can take care of that."

"I can't," I said.

I got dressed and took a long walk.

The next day, Cora was embarrassed and we apologized to each other.

I don't know why I stopped. I liked her, but I couldn't go through with it.

I took Melissa to the Firefall concert when they came through town.

Before I picked her up, I stopped by Becky's place. She knew I was taking Melissa to the show.

"I wish I could go," Becky said.

I remember thinking *she's really starting to like me*, but I had this date scheduled with Melissa for a long time and I couldn't brush her off. We met over at Jeff and his wife's house before the show. There's a picture of Melissa and me sitting on their couch. My thoughts were elsewhere and Melissa looked concerned as she could feel the distance growing between us.

Our latest stint at The Hermitage was coming to an end. Most of the band wanted to move towards a more southern rock band in the style of The Outlaws, April Wine, and Molly Hatchet.

As much as we tried, we couldn't get Jeff Benson to move in this direction. Jeff always played acoustic guitar. We thought it be would a great move for the band to get him an electric guitar and have a three-guitar attack like Molly Hatchet.

To add fuel to that fire, Gayle Allred entered the picture through her friendship with Chuck Montes. She claimed she was an heir to the Singer fortune and incredibly wealthy. She had a couple million dollars at her disposal. She was one of the strangest people I'd ever met. She decided she wanted to finance Clear Sky and take us to the next level by recording an album.

We knew the money would come in from Gayle if we agreed to her proposition. That meant a salary for everyone and an opportunity to record an album. It was an exciting proposition.

Chuck Montes called a band meeting at The Public Affair. When we realized Jeff Benson wasn't there, we immediately knew what was going on.

Chuck said, "My old buddy, Dave Love, is available." We all knew about Dave. He was originally from Ogden, but had been living in Los Angeles, playing in the reformed Iron Butterfly, the group famous for the song *In A Gadda Da Vidda*. The guy came with a built-in reputation.

Chuck continued, "He wants to come back to Ogden."

We talked about the pros and cons before we took a vote. I was the lone holdout on keeping Jeff. I liked him, and we had become good friends. In the end, I was outvoted and went along with the band. I didn't want to miss out on the financial backing and the chance to record an album.

The band fired Jeff Benson.

It was an ugly break-up. Frank fired Jeff over the phone. Crushed and hurt, Jeff completely flipped out. He quickly recovered, though, and claimed the Clear Sky name. "You guys can't use it. If you do, I'll fucking sue."

Clear Sky was country-rock in the vein of The Marshall Tucker Band, Firefall, and Pure Prairie League. We wanted to move in a new direction – a mix of harder-edged country and current rock and roll.

The band let Jeff have the name.

It was our way of saying, "We're moving on."

UTAH: THE GROUP 1979

*(L-R) E.J. Bell, Chuck Montes, James McElwain,
Me, Dave Love, and Frank Hewitt*

We needed a new name and Frank came up with it – Utah: The Group.

I thought it sucked. I mean Kansas, the band with the huge hit *Carry on Wayward Son*, was just that – Kansas. It was enough, right? They weren't Kansas: The Group. Can you imagine The Beatles: The Group achieving the level of success that The Beatles did? No, it sounds weird. Simpler is better. I'm still shaking my head at that name – Utah: The Group. Sometimes you take one for the team, though.

The line-up for the band was essentially the same except Dave Love replaced Jeff Benson on guitar.

After we secured the deal with Gayle Allred, she brought in Jerry "Buck" Buxton to manage the band on her behalf. This shocked the shit out of us because earlier in the year, Buck was the drunk at the end of the bar during the Super Bowl.

Gayle had taken up with Buck. She was a woman with millions in the bank and he was a down-on-his-luck derelict. Suddenly, he was our manager and our soundman. Gayle gave him check writing authority on the account she established for the band.

He didn't exactly get sober, but he tried to act respectable. He wasn't as incoherent as he had been.

About fifteen years later, he would drink himself to death.

Each band member was scheduled to get a $200/week salary which was damn good back then. Dave Love, due to his pedigree, was going to get $250/week. The rest of us were pissed at the extra money he was given.

Gayle rented the band a huge warehouse in West Ogden. It was roughly 10,000 square feet with a small lobby inside the front door. There were offices to each side of the lobby. The carpeted office was our hang-out. The other office had a fridge so that's where we kept our beer.

We put carpet throughout the rest of the warehouse.

I don't know who found it, but someone hung a World War II parachute from the ceiling. It was the type of parachute that the Army used to drop equipment so the thing was huge.

Gayle bought us a new P.A. system for the warehouse. She also kept us stocked with cocaine and marijuana.

The plan was to spend the next five or six weeks practicing, writing songs and preparing for an album.

Who needed to play gigs when we had Gayle backing us?

While we set up the warehouse, we still had a few gigs that were previously booked as Clear Sky. One of them was in The Public Affair's basement lounge. We were still bringing Dave Love up to speed on our catalog of songs. We hadn't even worked on any original music.

Melissa came to watch me play. Becky was there working.

After the gig, I walked Melissa outside. We got in her car and I told her I was breaking it off. I said a bunch of bullshit about the band going back on the road and it wasn't fair to her for us to be together.

Tears filled her eyes. "Can't we have one more night together?" she asked.

"No. I don't want to be tied down with anyone."

I left her car and went back inside. Becky found me and sat on my lap. We partied through the night.

Jimmy later left the bar and found Melissa in the parking lot across the street. She was watching Becky and me through the windows. She told Jimmy she was mad because I dumped her for Becky.

She said I was a lying sack of shit. I couldn't deny it.

One afternoon at The Public Affair, Becky walked in with her younger sister and her best friend.

The four of us played pool together. When it wasn't my turn, Becky sat on my lap. I was in heaven. We'd slept together a few times by now but it was still new.

I'd gotten past the initial embarrassment of her telling me that I wasn't a very good lover.

We liked each other, but the relationship was totally insecure. There were no commitments. Becky had guys hanging around her all the time which made me jealous. I worried about other guys taking her away.

I had to let her know how I felt.

Dave Love and his wife moved into a basement apartment.

They had a spare bedroom and an extra couch. Jimmy and I, the vagabonds, moved in there and slept on their floor.

Jimmy was seeing Marcy and I was seeing Becky.

By now, the Cody girls had faded from our scene. They hung occasionally with Chuck Montes, but mostly they had moved on from us.

Becky and a couple friends planned to drive to Jackson Hole to see Becky's other sister. I spent the night with Becky before she left. In the morning, she said I could stay at her place while she was out of town.

That night, the band played another gig at The Public Affair. By now Marcy and Jimmy were fighting constantly.

Marcy came to the bar. "Where's Becky?"

"She's in Jackson Hole visiting her sister."

"How's it going with you two?"

"Ok, I guess."

"Are you guys an item?"

"To a point. We're not in love with each other."

We laughed about that.

Marcy told me about a party at a mutual friend's house. "Are you going to come?"

"Hell yeah, I wouldn't miss it."

Later, at the party, I saw Marcy, but didn't see my friend. "Where's Jimmy?" I asked.

"Forget him. Let's talk about us."

"Us?"

"Yeah, us. I've wanted you since the day I met you."

My head spun. She was sexy, but I was with Becky now.

Then the phone rang. Someone answered it and then looked my way. "It's Jimmy," they said.

"Hello?" I said into the phone.

Jimmy said, "How come I wasn't told there was a party?"

"Now, Jimmy, don't get mad." I don't know why I said it that way.

"Mad? Why would I get mad?"

"I don't know. I just stumbled onto the party."

I hung up the phone and drank harder.

In short order, I was in Marcy's sports car, heading to her house.

I spent the night with Marcy, my friend and bandmate's girl, who we had previously discussed and agreed that I would keep away from. I let my friend down, myself down and I can't believe what I did to Becky. Even though she didn't know, I knew.

At 6 a.m., Marcy drove me to Dave's house. She stopped her car a block away so no one would see me get out. I usually slept on the floor while Jimmy slept on the couch. The unwritten rule was that whoever got home first would get the couch. This time I snuck into the spare bedroom and slept on the hardwood floor.

I was ashamed and embarrassed of what had happened.

Jimmy didn't say anything that day, although I'm sure he suspected. He let things remain normal.

Becky came back to town and there was a new distance between us. Maybe she did know something or maybe it was just women's intuition. Whatever it was, it felt like she was thinking about not getting too attached and I knew I was thinking the same thing.

There was an off-night party that Sher told me about.

"It's near my apartment. I'll be there with Marcy. She's hoping you'll stop by."

"I'll do my best to get there," I said and I meant it, because despite all my self-loathing, I wanted to have sex with Marcy again.

I was at a different party with Jimmy and told him I needed to take off to see Becky. He said he had a date set up with a girl we both knew wasn't Marcy.

That was all the justification I needed. I walked several blocks over to the party Sher mentioned. I was there for half an hour before Marcy and I split for her house to spend the night together.

In the morning, Jimmy asked, "How's Becky?"

"Fine," I said, feeling like an asshole. The sting of regret and self-loathing was becoming more pronounced than ever.

When the warehouse was finally done, the initial plan was to rehearse five days a week from 9 a.m. until 5 p.m. The music was so loud that the neighboring businesses on each side of us complained.

We defused the situation by moving our rehearsals to the evening. This only gave us more excuses to party late.

If we would have been smart we would have rehearsed at a lower volume and gotten some actual work done.

Instead, the warehouse became party central.

At The Swamp Root one night, Marcy came over.

In front of Jimmy, she asked with a smile, "Want to go for a ride?"

When I didn't answer, Marcy walked away.

Jimmy leaned in. "Billy, I love you. You're my friend. Please don't do this. Don't flaunt it in my face. Hide it from me. I can't stand to see it."

He had tears in his eyes. I hurt him bad and it felt so shitty.

When Marcy came back, I told her, "No." This time, I really meant it.

We never saw each other again.

Years later, I told Becky about my liaisons with Marcy. She responded by saying, "Duh."

Things were getting crowded at Dave's house.

It was mid-summer and we had some time on our hands so Jimmy and I decided to take a vacation back to Spokane. I brought Becky with me while Erin stayed with her father. We were growing closer and I thought it would be nice to take her home. The three of us headed north.

Gayle and our new manager, Buck, were being generous and they gave us a pound of dope for the trip. As a result, it made the whole van smell terrible. We worried about getting stopped by some overly eager state trooper.

It didn't matter since the dope was no good. You could smoke fifteen joints and get nary a buzz. What a waste.

In Spokane, Jimmy stayed with his parents.

Becky and I stayed with mom and my brother. One night the four of us went out for dinner at Clinkerdaggers, a high-end restaurant overlooking the Spokane River.

Becky looked beautiful in a long, pink, slinky dress.

I wore my rock clothes – black slacks, platform shoes, beige long-sleeve shirt, and suede vest. My afro looked sharp.

After dinner, Becky and I held hands and walked through Riverfront Park.

It was a nice evening.

At mom's house, Becky and I slept in different rooms as per the house rules.

That didn't stop us from having sex in the garage out back. Or in the car when we stopped once at the Idaho state line. We were young and having fun with each other.

I was starting to feel that she could be the one.

166

The fourth day of our trip, we drove to Coeur d'Alene and spent the afternoon on the west beach near the river. We had an ice chest full of beer with us. Lying on the beach, she was in a foul mood which put me in a bad place. I didn't know it then, but she thought she might be pregnant.

Afterwards we went to The Rathskellers where Raven previously played.

We shot a couple games of pool and she kicked my butt. After that we played some air hockey and she beat me at that, too.

I can't remember what I said, but she replied, "You're just mad because I keep beating you."

That provoked an argument that continued all the way back to mom's house.

We hardly spoke to each other that night.

The return to Ogden wasn't bad. Becky and I got over our fight but there was a slight undercurrent of resentment.

When we got home, Jimmy moved in with a new girl.

Now, I had no place to go. I had some stuff at Becky's, but the rest of my stuff was at Dave's.

The next day back, Becky caught a ride to work and left me to hang out at her apartment. There was a knock on the door. I looked like hell as I had been sleeping. I opened the door to see a young woman studying me with disgust.

"Yes?" I said.

"Is Becky here?"

"No. Who are you?"

"I'm her sister. Who are you?"

"I'm Billy Bancroft."

"You're not living here, are you?"

I was shocked by her question and I didn't like how it made me feel. "No, I'm not. I'll let Becky know that you stopped by."

After she left, I grabbed Becky's 10-speed and rode over to Dave's.

I had to get away from that humiliation.

"You can stay at my apartment," Becky said later.

She had warmed up, but she never truly invited me to move in with her. Little Erin Marie reminded me often that I wasn't the boss of her and that she didn't have to listen to me. I had a tough time with the situation.

Becky quit working at The Public Affair and got a job at The Balcony on top of The Ben Lomond Motel. I couldn't stand Becky's boss. I was convinced they were having an affair. I don't think that now, but it created a strain back then.

Even though I was staying at Becky's, I would occasionally stay at Dave's house to get away. For both of us, it was too much, too fast.

One afternoon after rehearsal, I had the band's black van and, as usual, Becky had taken her bike to work.

I drove over to her house and knocked on the door. I wasn't allowed to have a key.

Becky said she would meet me there at 4 p.m. I sat on the front porch and heard the telephone ring.

When it stopped, it would immediately start ringing again.

This continued for almost an hour without Becky coming home.

Finally, I had enough and found a window to climb through.

Once in the house, I answered the phone.

Becky had been in an accident with Erin on the back of the bicycle. She had gone off the side of the road, into some gravel and wrecked. She and Erin were at the hospital.

I drove like a crazy man. When cars were in the way, I swerved around them. I even drove on the sidewalk in one area to get by some stopped cars.

At the hospital, I went to the emergency room. Erin lay on a gurney, her forehead bruised. She had some other minor bumps.

Becky was in a nearby room, screaming in pain. She was badly scraped up. As I leaned to comfort her she held onto me tightly.

I cried seeing those two liked that. I discovered how much I loved them both. Not the immature hopes of love I had when with other girls, but the love you have when you care deeply for someone.

When word got out about the accident, Erin's father came to the hospital and took her to his house.

Because she had a concussion, the hospital kept Becky overnight.

I went back to Becky's apartment and sat alone in her living room. I saw my albums in the corner and my books on the coffee table.

This is home, I thought.

It was around this time when Becky shared a story about how during the previous year she had gone to The Silver Cloud in Salt Lake City with her sister and some friends to see a rock band from Spokane. She couldn't remember the name of the group, though. All the girls went to the band's hotel room in The Capitol Motel to party with them. Nothing happened and the girls quickly took off.

I told her I was in that band.

She didn't believe me.

I told her about Raven playing that club and staying in that hotel. I told her about a group of girls from Ogden who came to our room, drank our beer and then left. I described a blonde girl who wouldn't have anything to do with us.

I also shared how that aloof girl took my breath away and left me wondering what ever happened to her for months afterwards.

She believed me then.

A couple weeks went by and Utah: The Band continued to rehearse and write new material. It was some good, complicated stuff.

We even hired a female back-up singer to add some depth to our sound. She was an attractive blonde girl with a good voice. We paid her a full cut.

The band still had its internal strife.

Jimmy carried with him the hurt of my dalliances with Marcy. It came out in a couple of the songs he wrote including one called *Against the Grain* about a cheating friend.

All of us contributed to the song writing process. While some guys wrote, the others would smoke dope or go to the National Tavern to play pinball. This was our creative process. It was an interesting time because everyone around the music circuit knew we had changed our name to Utah: The Group. The band was evolving, and our friends and fans were waiting to see the result.

We had reached a different level of decadence than Clear Sky – we were now salaried and we weren't playing any gigs. Our job was essentially rehearsing and getting stoned. We were no longer hungry.

We had plenty of get-togethers as a band in Dave's backyard. We'd barbeque steaks, drink grape Kool-Aid and sip Miller Beer. For some reason, we weren't drinking as hard as we previously had.

On the weekends, when our friends with regular jobs could join us, we'd go to the Pine View Dam. Some friends brought their boats.

There was usually a large group there. Becky and I were the only ones with a child. We were having a great time. We were well-known, making money and hanging out. For a while no one was screwing each other's girls and things were going well.

We spent most of July, August and early September practicing in the warehouse. Previously being a road band, we quickly got bored. We only produced nine songs in that period.

Our boredom led to more partying in the warehouse as other local musicians showed up to see what we were working on.

The band was going to lose their vans back to Clear Sky's original financier. He was based out of Kalispell and loaded with dough. I met him only once shortly after I joined the band. He wanted his vans back now that we had dropped him for Gayle Allred.

Frank and E.J. made a deal with him. Frank bought the black van. E.J. bought the red van. Therefore, I couldn't use the vans anymore and winter was approaching.

I called my sister, Carol, who was now living in California with her husband.

She'd had my Pontiac for over a year and was disappointed that I wanted it back. After talking about it for a bit, I arranged to go get it.

I bought a one-way airline ticket with $200 that Gayle lent me.

My brother Chris and his wife were living in Santa Maria. They joined Carol, her husband and me for dinner. The next afternoon, I headed out of Santa Maria in my Pontiac.

I drove straight through and was exhausted during the last stretch going through Salt Lake City. When I got home, Becky and Erin were happy to see me. I was definitely glad to see them.

The band was pissed since I had missed a rehearsal.

A friend of the band, Robert Petty, held a bachelor party at his house. Most of the guys in our circle of friends were invited.

Someone hired a stripper who went totally naked. She did some impressive things with a beer bottle. She reminded me of "the Bud Girl" in Rossland, B.C. from my Raven days.

While she danced, some of the guys would lie on the floor and taste what she had to offer.

She continued to dance and eventually came my way. When she straddled me, I was uncomfortable.

In the old days, I would have enjoyed her attention. Despite her encouragement, I wasn't going to put something in her, be it a bottle, a finger, or a tongue. That night, I was embarrassed.

As the night wore on, she asked if I could drive her home because she was too drunk to drive. She promised it would be "worth my while."

"No. I'm not going to do it," I said. "I'm going home."

The next day, I told Becky how nasty things got. I laid it all out for her. I tried to show how true my feelings were and how she could trust me.

Becky exploded. She was furious. After she yelled at me for being around a stripper, she called Dave and Robert's wives to vent. It turned out those guys lied to their women by saying there were only porn movies. This got Dave and Robert pissed at me.

Becky and I fought over how out-of-proportion she had blown the matter. I stomped out and spent the next couple nights sleeping at Jimmy's house.

One of those nights, one of the Cody girls came over to Jimmy's.

She hung with Jimmy, his new girl, and me, drinking and snorting coke. She made a hard play. "If you lay with me once, you'll never regret it."

The girl had a perfect body.

I shook my head. "No. I'm not going to do it."

About 3 a.m., Jimmy and his girl moved into their room and made all sorts of noise. The Cody girl rubbed my shoulders and did her best to get me excited.

I had to get out of there. I stood. "I'm not going to do this. I've got to go."

I walked out of the house and started the long walk to Becky's house.

She ran outside and yelled as I walked into the alley. "You screwed Lisa and forgot her. You screwed Melissa and forgot her, too. All for that bitch Becky. It's a good thing I never screwed you!"

I walked across Ogden to get to her apartment. It was an hour later when I arrived. I knocked on the door and said, "Let me in."

Becky opened the door and wrapped her arms around me.

In early October, Utah: The Group was going to debut our original material.

The warehouse rent was getting expensive so it was time to move on and start earning.

We played The Hermitage on Halloween. Becky dressed as a witch and was totally unrecognizable. She dressed me as the Wolfman. I had on overalls, a blue shirt and fur all over my exposed skin. It was a fantastic costume.

No one recognized us at the club. As we played, I pounded the drums as I normally did, but the fur flew off my hands. Behind the drums, it reportedly looked like a cat and dog fighting.

We were booked at The Herm for a couple weeks. It wasn't like the Clear Sky days but it was still good. The band rocked.

We had a two-week gig at Reggie's Rockin' R in Salt Lake City. We were finally breaking into the big city to the south.

While the crowd liked us at Reggie's, we weren't bookable anywhere else. Utah: The Group wasn't hard enough like Raven so we couldn't get into the clubs I'd previously played with them. We weren't country-rock so we couldn't play the other clubs we played as Clear Sky.

Suddenly, we found ourselves with nowhere to play.

We had spent three months out of the circuit while writing our own material. Any groundwork we laid as Clear Sky was gone.

Looking back, we never tried to send our demo tapes to record companies or agents. We created something and just expected success to find its way to us.

With no work came discontentment and Gayle soon pulled her money.

We had a meeting at Chick's Cafe. We immediately told our back-up singer that we had to cut her pay in half. She responded with a "fuck you" and "I'm out of here."

I don't blame her. Even though she was only singing background, we promised her an equal cut.

The band bickered over this and other things.

We went from being an idealistic, financially up-and-coming band to a suddenly broke group of guys.

I had to find a real job. I now had a girlfriend with a child.

I got a job with Robert Petty installing marble counter tops, showers, and other such things. It was a construction gig, but it let me learn new things. Winter was coming, so I knew it was only going to be for a few weeks before things slowed and I would have to go find something else.

Dave Love took a job at Powder Mountain Ski Resort to supplement his income.

The band secured a gig in Logan, Utah. Instead of tearing down the gear at the end of the night, the guys wanted to go out and party. They had decided to return to Logan the next day and get the gear. I had to work in the morning and wanted to head home.

When I said I wouldn't help, Chuck Montes, said, "We've got to fine Bill since he's not going to load the gear."

"What am I supposed to do? I've got drum payments to make and a family to support."

Jimmy then pulled me aside. "I can never see you having a music career being with Becky Brewer. I can see you having one with Lisa. But if you get with Becky, you might as well kiss your career good-bye. You two will never last."

That was the general attitude among our circle of friends.

After we moved out of the warehouse, in the late fall of 1979, we recorded our album at Mountain Meadows Recording Studios in Ogden. It didn't come out as clean as we hoped, but the songs were now on tape. It was a great accomplishment.

When we played Reggie's we would do a set of covers, then our originals, and finish with another set of covers. The crowds always responded well.

In the end, we had been spoiled by a summer of easy money and low expectations. The abrupt reality of having it taken away was hard to fathom.

We weren't ready to step back to the Clear Sky days and go earn it again.

Unexpectedly, Utah: The Group wasn't that important anymore.

Supertramps, the place we originally practiced when it was Sweetwater Station, booked live music again.

After a gig one night in November, I was on the sidewalk about to head home, when Melissa stepped out of the shadows.

"Can we talk?"

"About?"

"I know you're living with Becky, but I need to speak with you." She appeared upset so I agreed to talk.

I didn't want anyone to see us together so I snuck off with her. I had no intention of doing anything. I just didn't want any rumors to get back to Becky.

We walked over to her car and she offered to give me a ride home since Jimmy had given me a lift to the club that night.

"You'll have to drop me off several blocks from my house. I don't need the aggravation of anyone seeing us."

She was hurt by that.

While she drove, she said her piece. She had been pregnant and said it was mine. I was the only one she had been with.

That hit me hard.

She wanted to keep the baby, but since I wasn't going to be around she was forced with a decision. She already had two young boys and couldn't raise another on her own. Therefore, she had had an abortion. She didn't ask me for anything. She just thought I should know.

She dropped me off and I walked twelve blocks home, dazed by her revelation.

Christmas was coming and I wanted to buy presents for Becky and Erin.

Covered in marble dust one afternoon from a construction job, Robert and I decided to stop and have a beer. While we were drinking, Robert said, "When are you going to marry that girl and make her an honest woman?"

"I don't know if she would marry me."

Robert nodded. "Oh, I know she would."

This conversation went on for a couple weeks until we went to a local jewelry store. Robert co-signed on a quick loan for $120 so I could buy a ring.

I'd set my mind to it. I was going to ask her to marry me on Christmas Eve.

On the afternoon of Christmas Eve 1979, Becky was upstairs with a friend while I was in the basement putting together Erin's Christmas presents – a chalkboard desk and little brown table. They were simple things, but the process took me a couple hours.

Becky kept bringing me another cold Miller beer. She encouraged me and kept Erin away from seeing her presents.

All this time, I had her diamond ring hidden.

My family had a Christmas Eve tradition of turning off the lights, sitting around the tree and reading bible verses. These traditions aligned nicely with Becky's as well.

As the evening wore on, I snuck the ring in and put it behind the couch. That night we watched a holiday movie, *The Gift of the Magi*. Afterwards, we put Erin to bed. We then sipped some wine and listened to Christmas music.

I said, "So…, do you want to get married?" I handed her the ring.

She put it on and cried.

"Well, do you?"

"I put it on, didn't I? Of course, I will."

That was one of the happiest moments of my life.

It was our first Christmas together.

Utah: The Group wasn't going anywhere.

The band continually fought and we weren't performing much. We didn't have the drive to get our originals out. Dave

Love and I grew increasingly frustrated with the group. After talking, we decided to quit.

It was sad since we both had had high expectations. Dave's focus had changed as had mine.

I was looking to settle down with my family. I had been on the road for more than four years.

My life was full of chaos and I was ready for a break.

Dave and I announced to the band that we were quitting.
Chuck barely spoke.
Frank shrugged his shoulders.
E.J., as usual, was out in left field. "Too bad," he said.
Jimmy was hurt and disappointed.

We played our final gig on New Year's Eve at Supertramps. The place was packed. Becky and I, along with Dave and his wife, partied hard. We got ugly drunk as some pictures will prove.

That was my last time with Utah: The Group.

I continued working construction with Robert Petty while looking for a better job. The 7-Up/Dr. Pepper Company hired me to drive a truck. Their warehouse was across from the location where Utah: The Group had previously practiced.

I had to cut off my hair, but I did it willingly to support Becky and Erin.

I laid low although I did a few gigs with some older guys in their forties and fifties. They were based out of Brigham City and I filled in for them when they played at the local Eagles club.

Becky and I planned to get married in the summer of 1980.
I didn't miss my music career much.

And my ego was fed by the fact that the band fell apart after Dave and I left.

They did another gig at The Hermitage with a couple other guys, but it didn't work. Clear Sky/Utah: The Group had lost its momentum.

January, February and March 1980 passed by slowly. That three-month period seems long when you're young.

Becky and I weren't doing so well. The idea of marriage scared her.

One night I played in Brigham City with that older group and got home around 2:30 a.m. to find she wasn't there. I thought it was odd but went to bed. At 5 a.m., she walked in and I was upset. I rolled over in bed and pretended to sleep. She said, "Hi," but I ignored her. She knew I wasn't asleep.

"That's the way it's going to be?" She left the bedroom and slept on the couch.

We were fighting all the time.

I feared marriage, too.

Even though we made plans for me to move out, Becky and I never said that we were calling off the marriage. She remained my fiancé.

We had to get apart from each other and think about things. I planned on moving into a friend's spare bedroom. Becky was against it because it was a well-known party house.

That didn't stop me as I was bound and determined to get some space and pay my own way. I had a good job driving a truck and was making decent money. It wasn't enough to get my own apartment, but it was enough to share a place.

I was also thinking I would try dating girls as a normal guy and not as a musician. I only had one, maybe two dates, in high school.

After that, every girl I had met was through a band which gives you a warped perspective of how things are supposed to be.

I enjoyed my job as a Dr. Pepper truck driver.

One day during my route, I went by the house of a friend of Melissa and knocked on the front door. When she opened the door, the girl didn't recognize me.

She hadn't seen me since I cut off my hair.

"Wow," she said. I looked so straight-laced.

We chatted for a bit and discovered many things had occurred since we last saw each other. I asked about Melissa since they were friends and said it would be great to see her.

"Melissa's been carrying a huge torch for you. She was devastated when you left her."

"My route takes me by here next Friday. Will you call Melissa and see if she can come by about this time?"

I figured I would say hello to her and see if there were some sparks still there.

I was despondent that Becky and I weren't working out even though I was in love with her and loved little Erin. I feared marriage and didn't want to get into something if we were always fighting.

And I will admit I still harbored feelings for Melissa.

Since my friend was still cleaning out his spare room, I hadn't moved out of Becky's house yet. Our daily communication was stilted. Becky still wore my engagement ring, but I was now wondering if I should ask for it back. There were so many conflicting emotions in my head.

On Sunday night, while Becky was in bed, the phone rang around 11 p.m. I answered it.

"Bill, it's Eric."

Eric Lindstrom was the bassist for Stone Johnny Mountain Band.

"Eric, how are you doing?"

"I'm good. I've got Jeannie on the phone."

"Hi, Bill."

Jeannie Carter, my former agent from Raven, was on another phone extension.

"Hi, Jeannie. What's going on?"

The phone clicked as another line was picked up. "Hey, Bill, it's Rick."

Rick Roadman was the lead guitarist and vocalist for Stone Johnny.

"What's going on guys?" I said, confused.

"Dave Dieter quit the band," Eric said. Dave was the drummer for Stone Johnny Mountain Band. "It's your gig if you want it."

I was speechless.

Stone Johnny Mountain Band was an unattainable goal. They were working road hogs, playing cities like Las Vegas and Reno. They made $3,500-$4,000/week and were on a salary through Jeannie.

They were a top-notch organization. They had a step-van with murals on the side. They had great gear and were booked all the time. Stone Johnny had direction. They played original songs. They had a sense of purpose.

They were on a higher level than Clear Sky or Utah: The Group.

Becky came out to the living room. She had a concerned look on her face, the kind that you get when someone calls that late at night. She also heard me saying things like, "I can't believe it" and "You're kidding me."

I talked to the band, ignoring Becky. This irritated her because she didn't know what was going on. I covered the phone to explain and we got into a fight.

Eric said, "Obviously, this isn't a good time."

I got back on the phone. "I know we can't talk now, but how soon do you need me?"

"You need to be here by Sunday night. We've got a gig the following Friday. We're playing a wedding in north Spokane. You've got to be here for a couple rehearsals before that."

I didn't say anything.

"After the wedding gig," Eric continued, "we go to the Million Dollar Cowboy Bar in Jackson Hole. That's a huge gig. We've got to be tight for that. We'll have to rehearse all day Sunday and Monday, then drive to Jackson Hole on Monday night to be ready to play on Tuesday."

My head spun.

"I need some time. Give me until tomorrow to think about it."

They agreed and we ended the phone call.

I explained the situation to Becky.

"I've got to move back to Spokane to join the band. Will you and Erin come with me?"

"I don't know," she said.

"You don't know?"

"No, I don't know. You've got to give me time to think about this."

For the first time in a long while, Becky and I held each other as we lay in bed. However, I didn't sleep a wink that night.

If I left without Becky to join Stone Johnny there was a good chance I would never see her again.

As I lay in bed, I made my decision.

I wanted Becky and Erin to join me and I wouldn't give up on our relationship. However, I was a musician, and this was my career. I was going to join Stone Johnny Mountain Band.

Maybe it was young, ignorant and selfish thinking.

I was twenty-two years old and my life was ahead of me. I wanted to chase my dream, but I hoped Becky and Erin would come along.

On Monday morning, I told Becky I was taking the gig.

"I was already moving out to get some space. Maybe this is what we needed."

"Living nearby with a friend is one thing," she said. "Living thirteen hours away is another."

"You're right," I said, but I was going nonetheless.

We were confused, but I loved her. I told her I still wanted her with me.

"You're going to have to give me time to think," she said.

The next couple days were tense around the house as I prepared for my move.

On Wednesday, Becky finally said, "Ok, I'm going with you."

To this day, I get chills about how happy that one statement made me.

1968 – Age 12
My dad bought me my first
drum kit, a Majestic.
Photo taken by Laurie (Bancroft) Hopkins

Dave Low and I rocking out in Cold Smoke.
Dave was decked out in satin and stars.
Photo taken by my friend, Jack Dial.

*Behind the drum kit during my Organized Crime
days. We were at the Golden Drift for this
picture. Check out the insulation that was blown
on the ceiling to make it look like rock.*

*Raven after we were burned out by the Loose Cabooze fire.
Steve Hanna, Randy Peterson, Dave Low, Dan Murphy, and me.
I have no idea who the woman is in the background.*

Clear Sky playing The Bronze Boot (Cody, WY).
E.J. Bell, Jimmy McElwain, Frank Hewitt, me, Jeff Benson, and Chuck Montes.

Prepping for the camera with Utah: The Group.
Dave Love, Jimmy McElwain, Chuck Montes, me, E.J. Bell, and Frank Hewitt.

Last night with the Stone Johnny Mountain Band.
Dave Griffith, Rick Roadman, Eric Lindstrom, Paul Elliot
and Mark Douty. I'm standing in the back.

Secrets in a rare promo shot.
Top - Darren Robinette, Blue (never did know his real name)
Bottom - Jimmy McElwain, me, Chuck Montes, Mike Medeiros

187

A band photo from the Hotspurz promo pack.
Me, Al Bevan, Doug Artist, Greg Clary and Terry Morris.

Too Slim and the Taildraggers in action.
Tim "Too Slim" Langford, Greg Pendleton, me, and Tom Brimm

Wind Chill just hanging out.
(L-R) Greg Clary, Joe Webber,
Ted Dussor, Blake Gardner and me.

Becky and I hanging out at a show.

Ty Green was a fantastic singer and had a promising future ahead of him. Unfortunately for him (and us), he was sold a bill of goods by his producer.

Picture credit –
Ty Green's promotional photo

A Café Blue promo shot.
(L-R) Me, Chuck Swanson, Russ Hoffer, Pat Coast, Mike Lenke (in tuxedo), Keith Lewis, and Tom Brewster
Photo by Richard Heinzen Photography

A Christmas picture of the family.
Becky, Erin, me, Cory, and Casey.

Photo from individual promo pack - 1989

Erin and me

Cory and me

Casey and me

My new group – The Bobby Patterson Band.
Randy Knowles, Tom Norton, Bobby Patterson and me
Photo by Andy McAlpin.

Sue and I on our wedding day.
Photo by Kelcey Boyce Photography

STONE JOHNNY
MOUNTAIN BAND
1980

(L-R) Eric Lindstrom, Marc Douty, Paul Elliott,
Cowboy John, random guy in the middle,
Dave Griffith, Rick Roadman, and me

On Wednesday, we rented a U-Haul truck. We backed it up to the house and loaded it as fast as we could with all of Becky's stuff, Erin's toys and bed, my drums and few possessions.

I quit my job at Dr. Pepper. They were upset that I didn't give them two weeks' notice. They didn't have anyone to cover my route. I should have handled it better, but I was just given my dream gig and nothing was going to stand in my way.

I thought briefly about my plans to meet Melissa on Friday afternoon. They simply evaporated.

The plan was for Becky and Erin to stay a little longer in Ogden while I drove the U-Haul back to Spokane. Becky would meet me in Jackson Hole where Stone Johnny was set to play and where her sister lived. After that show, Becky would travel to Spokane to set up our new home.

I arrived in Spokane on Sunday, April 20th after thirteen hours on the road. I drove past the exit for my mom's house and continued toward Jeannie Carter's house.

I pulled into the circular driveway of her house. I wore cut-off jean shorts and no shirt while I drove. Before I went in, I pulled on a pair of jeans over the cut-offs and slipped on a t-shirt. I walked in barefoot with my cowboy hat. I had the typical Stone Johnny look from day one.

Stone Johnny Mountain Band was there partying with Jeannie. Paul Elliot, the band's fiddle player, was the first guy out of the house. He gave me a big hug. The rest of the band came out and we hugged, laughed and reintroduced ourselves. We drank a couple beers and smoked some dope.

Then I drove back to mom's. My brother, Chuck, and sister, Carol, were there. It felt good to be home. I took the stuff out of the U-Haul and unloaded it in mom's garage.

Stone Johnny practiced through Thursday, cramming the material into my head. It wasn't easy stuff to learn. We played the wedding party on Friday evening in a north Spokane barn. I struggled through it, but by then I was a decent enough drummer to fake the parts I couldn't remember.

Along with original material, Stone Johnny played songs by Merle Haggard, Vassar Clements, Pure Prairie League, and Little Feat. We were bluegrass with hints of jazz. We were also known for our Texas Swing.

The Stone Johnny Mountain Band was made up of Eric Lindstrom on bass guitar and Rick Roadman on lead guitar. Paul Elliot handled the fiddle while Dave Griffith handled every instrument in-between. Eric sang lead vocals and Rick backed him up. Mark Douty was the soundman for the band.

Dave Griffith was later nicknamed as 'Mr. Wonderful' because he played everything – guitar, steel guitar, mandolin, banjo, and flute.

We, his bandmates, privately referred to Dave as 'Mr. Wonderful' because he was massively endowed.

Soon, Stone Johnny Mountain Band hit the road for Jackson Hole, Wyoming where Becky and Erin were waiting. We were booked to play a week at The Million Dollar Cowboy Bar.

Inside the club, a dance floor sat off to the right as the band faced the tables. The bar was to the left of the stage.

The bar stools were saddles which look great until you get caught in the stirrups when you're drunk. If you fell off, the crowd would yell in delight, "Bucked off!" Trust me – it's not funny when it happens to you.

It was a great gig. The band kicked ass and the crowd responded to us. We were big country boys who dressed in t-shirts and blue jeans and we were musically talented.

We were housed at The Elk Refuge Inn which was managed by Becky's sister and her husband. It was a roadside hotel on the highway outside of Jackson Hole. Across the highway was a refuge where we'd see elk roaming in the morning. Antlers and western themed paraphernalia hung around the hotel in the same way as The Million Dollar Cowboy Bar.

Becky's sister had recently been in San Francisco and brought home a case of king crab legs. One afternoon, we boiled crab legs, barbequed big steaks, drank beer, and smoked dope. I ate so much I felt sick. I had to sleep it off before playing the gig.

At the end of the week, the band went on to an uneventful week-long gig in Laramie while Becky and Erin went home to Spokane.

Becky related on many occasions about how special that trip was to Spokane. She was both nervous and excited about our new life together. She said she fell more in love with me as each mile rolled by and she got closer to Spokane.

Our next stop in Breckenridge, Colorado was Shamus O'Toole's Roadhouse Saloon which marketed itself as being friendly to bikers everywhere.

The band stayed across the street in a two-story house that leaned badly. Prior to our arrival, it was nicknamed The Chateau Ghetto. It was a complete piece of shit. The upper floor didn't even have electricity.

The rumor was our management contact at the Saloon was a member of a local biker gang. He wore a leather vest with a bunch of patches so I'm not going to dispute that claim. I can't remember if he was the owner or the manager, so let's call him our contact.

On Friday night, the Saloon was packed and the crowd was digging us. We were in the middle of a song when our contact waved at us as he approached the stage.

"Shut it down," he yelled. "Shut it down."

Confused, we looked at each other.

A waitress appeared with a circular server's tray in her hand. On the tray were five shots of whiskey and ten lines of cocaine.

"You guys do this," the manager said, pointing at the server's tray, "and then play *Take a Whiff.*"

Take a Whiff on Me is an old folk song made famous by Lead Belly and has been covered by everyone from The Byrds to The Flying Burrito Brothers. It was originally written before cocaine was illegal. It's a fast song and one we'd never played before. We all knew it, of course. You don't go through the '70s drug scene and not know the song *Take a Whiff.*

Now, when you're in a biker bar with a management contact saying drink this and snort that, you do what you're told, not that any of us needed persuading.

Under the bright lights of the stage and in front of a raucous crowd, each band member did their shot of whisky and snorted two lines of wickedly good coke. The crowd cheered as each of us took a turn bending our heads over the server's tray.

We set about playing the song, did our best, and the crowd went nuts for it.

We had so much fun that when we finished, we played it once again.

That night the bar celebrated our management contact's birthday.

A group of his friends brought his gift to the club. They rolled a brand-new Harley Davidson in and started it on the dance floor.

It was definitely a biker-friendly joint.

After our gig, we had a party at The Chateau Ghetto.

Our fiddle player, Paul Elliot, was one of the smartest guys I'd ever met. He was hammered and got into a philosophical conversation with some guy from the bar on the front porch of the house. I stood nearby and listened to them wax philosophical.

While he spoke, Paul stopped mid-sentence, turned his head and barfed over the railing. He turned back to the guy he was talking with and continued his theoretical answer without missing a beat.

This conversation continued, with Paul turning his head to barf three more times, each time in mid-sentence. He then finished his thoughts without ever skipping stride.

We were all so amped and drunk it didn't seem odd in anyway.

The next night, Eric Lindstrom and I found where that cocaine came from. We had to get another taste because it was so incredibly good.

During a set, we ran across the parking lot to The Chateau Ghetto and met the source. He gave us a ½ gram. We didn't even have to pay for it.

"I dig your music," our source said.

We were super excited and appreciative of our new fan.

"Now, don't do it all," he said. "This is some good shit and should last you a couple days."

We shined him on said we'd be careful with it. Of course, as soon as he left, we took the whole ½ gram and made four very fat lines.

Eric and I snorted two lines apiece, each essentially snorting a ¼ gram of high quality coke.

We ran back into the Saloon and jumped on stage. The kick was immediate. It didn't take long before I put my cowboy hat on one drumstick and spun it around in circles while playing with only one hand and my bare feet. Yeehaw!

In the middle of a song, Eric turned around and focused on me. He yelled, "Am I doing okay? Do I suck? I'm really fucked up!"

At the break, I almost leapt off the stage.

Our next gig was a one-night only concert at The Little Bear in Evergreen, Colorado, in the mountains east of Denver. It was Sunday, May 18th, 1980. We opened for a popular regional band. I wish I could remember their name.

We finished about 10 p.m. and then partied our brains out. Afterwards, we drove toward our hotel in Denver. Along the way, we stopped at a bar, as if we needed one more drink.

A rough biker chick was there. She had to put her finger over a hole in her throat to talk. I think she had her larynx removed. Like I said, a rough woman. Anyway, she took a liking to Rick Roadman something fierce.

She asked him, in a harsh gravelly voice, "Want to take a ride on my motorcycle?"

Rick didn't know what to say.

We all lost it at that point.

There was no hurry when I rolled out of bed the next morning around noon. We had a couple days to kill before our next gig in Fort Collins. After a shower, I walked to a nearby grocery store. I bought some donuts, a cup of coffee and a newspaper without looking at the headlines.

I walked back to the hotel, sipping coffee and thinking about life. On the hotel's patio, I sat in a lawn chair and opened the paper. The newspaper's headline said that Mount St. Helens had erupted.

A smaller article said Spokane was a disaster area.

To say I experienced a pucker factor would be an understatement. I jumped, ran to our room, turned on the TV and saw the eruption on the news. I rousted the other guys. I told them lava was running through Spokane.

I hadn't actually read the newspaper article nor listened to the news reports.

I was Chicken Little and the sky was falling.

When I tried calling home, the phone lines were busy. It was the same result all day.

After we were finally able to get through to our families, we learned everyone was fine.

My family was hunkered down at mom's house. Becky told me that Erin had fallen asleep in the middle of the day because the sky had gotten so dark from the ash.

Our next gig at Panama Reds in Fort Collins was uneventful.

I don't remember much except we played Tuesday through Saturday. It was a typical country club with low ceilings and a lot of wood.

Was it a good gig? I guess.

Did we have fun? I suppose.

Did we drink beer? Duh.

Mount St. Helens was on our minds and everything else was secondary. We finished the gig at Fort Collins and moved on as the stress of the week wore off.

Before we left Fort Collins, we bought a shit load of beer for the five-hour trip to Rock Springs, Wyoming. We were drinking and driving, listening to music and arguing. Most of the bickering was between me and Mr. Wonderful, Dave Griffith. He and I simply didn't get along.

One thing I quickly learned was that the Stone Johnny boys could drink beer better than anyone I'd ever met. They had bladders the size of garbage cans. As for me, I had the bladder the size of a Dixie cup. They nicknamed me 'peanut bladder.'

Like a fool, I tried to drink with them while we were driving. At first, they kept pulling over to let me out. That stopped when we were barreling along I-80 and Mark Douty was driving. I had to go bad and he wouldn't pull over.

Twenty miles passed and my body hurt.

"You either pull over," I said, "or I'm going to piss down your neck."

"Fuck you, Billy," Mark shot back, smiling. "We're only a hundred miles from Rock Springs."

"Fine," I said and stepped into the back of the van.

Stone Jonny travelled in a step van with two seats in front and enough room in the back that you could stand and walk around.

I stood behind Mark and unzipped my pants. I pissed on his cowboy hat and neck. It was a beautiful arc and it felt great to relieve the pressure.

Mark damn near rolled the truck pulling it over to the side of the road. I barely got my pants up before he turned around and grabbed me.

We tumbled out the side door and landed on the ground. Mark shook me and roughed me up while I kept yelling, "I told you! I told you!"

The rest of the guys came out of the truck laughing and broke up the fight. Mark and I were both pissed but laughing.

It was remarkable after that incident how quickly the truck pulled over whenever I had to pee.

Our gig in Rock Springs was for two weeks at The Silver Dollar Bar. We were tired when we arrived after driving and drinking all day.

As much as I drank with Raven and Clear Sky, it was nothing compared to these guys. They were hardcore. They started early and kept going.

The first night we sat around my hotel room, drinking and watching TV. Mark and Rick wrestled and knocked each other into my bed. That would jostle my beer and piss me off a little more each time. I kept yelling at them to "Stop it" or "Knock it off."

I finally reached my limit with them and jumped off the bed. I held my beer bottle by the neck and broke it on the end table, shattering it. Holding a jagged weapon in my hand, I flipped out and screamed, "Stop it, you motherfuckers, or I'm going to stab every one of you."

"Calm down, Billy. Just calm down," Rick said.

When I mellowed out, everyone left me alone, even Paul Elliot who shared my room on that trip.

I cleaned up the broken bottle and went to bed for the night.

Eric Lindstrom had walked in earlier as I blew-up.

When we first got to the hotel, we drank in the bar for a while. In his words, Eric latched on to "the ugliest barmaid ever" after the rest of us left. He got into, again his words, "an inseparable lip lock with her." They hooked up while the events leading to the fight were brewing.

When he was finished, he came to my room in time to see the Billy Bancroft blow-up.

The owner of the hotel was on vacation for those two weeks. That's like leaving the fox to guard the hen house.

Every night after we finished playing, we would stay in the bar and drink, of course. Near the end of the night, the bar manager would say to his crew, "Grab a bottle. Let's go to the band's room and party."

I'm not sure if he meant for all of us to grab bottle, but we did.

After the two-week stint, Eric and I walked out of there with over $600 worth of booze. Each. I filled my suitcase with liquor taken from the bar.

To make room for the stolen hooch, I put my clothes in a pillow case which I had also pilfered.

One of the bouncers at the club was supposedly the brother of Jack Lambert of the Pittsburgh Steelers. He was a large guy with no teeth who loved to wear a big ol' cowboy hat.

He befriended Rick so we had him on stage mid-week. He sang The Rolling Stones' *Honky Tonk Women* with us. He introduced us as "Mick Jagger and the Rolling Papers" before he sang.

One of the nights we stayed in the bar all night and drank.

Rick Roadman needed some help back to his room since he was so drunk. At 6'0, I was a little guy compared to him, but I did my best to assist him.

Our rooms were on the second floor and they all opened to an exterior walkway.

Supporting most of his weight, I helped Rick up a flight of stairs. His right foot never touched the ground.

As we slowly worked our way up the stairs, I realized I was getting wet.

From the top of the stairs, Mark Douty pissed on Rick and me.

That woke Rick up. I won't say it sobered him, but he definitely got his legs under him. He ran those stairs and tackled Mark.

I continued climbing the stairs and stepped over them as they struggled on the ground. Rick got most of the piss so I figured he could take out his revenge on Mark without my help.

I went back to my room.

Two months before Becky and I were to marry, I wanted to have one final dalliance as a single man.

There was a waitress who liked me. She was short and full-bodied with great tits. She had long dishwater blonde hair and a round face. She wore a purple string top and turquoise jewelry.

I invited her back to my room and grabbed a bottle of scotch. We sat on the edge of the bed, passing the bottle back and forth. I was bound and determined to go to bed with her.

Finally, she stood and undressed with the lights on.

I thought *this is going to be the last one ever* when I suddenly stopped her.

"What?"

"I don't think we're going to do this," I said.

"Why?"

"I'm getting married in a couple weeks."

"Yeah, I know you are."

Since Becky and I had gotten back together to move to Spokane, I hadn't messed around.

The girl took her bra off and was wearing only panties. She grabbed me through my pants.

I was drunk and turned on by it, but I stood my ground.

"I can't do it," I said. "If you want to stay here, you can and I'll take you home in the morning, but I'll sleep in Paul's bed."

Paul was off with some girl he had met and wouldn't be home. She laid on my bed. I laid on Paul's bed, trying to ignore her. She pulled her panties off and was now completely naked. She spent the next few minutes saying, "Bill," softly and encouragingly.

Finally, I got so agitated that I couldn't take it anymore.

I left the room and went for a long walk. When I returned, she was sitting on the edge of the bed, fully clothed.

"You need to take me home," she said.

The next day, she was behind the bar when I saw her. She gave me the cold shoulder, but I didn't care. In fact, I was rather pleased with myself.

I'm comfortable with this, I thought. *I'm marrying the woman I love.*

We were going to have a family.

Why should I waste my time with other women?

Early in the first week, Eric latched on to a ninety pound cutie nicknamed Smiley. She was a blonde-haired waitress from the bar.

Eric was a big man at 6'5 and 240 pounds so we were worried that he might hurt the poor girl.

When he rolled in the next morning, he had a John Wayne walk and a pained expression.

"How was Smiley?" we all asked.

"She's into ...," he said pausing for the precise word, "devices."

Eric said it was fine as long as she used them on herself. It was a different story when she used them on him.

"She made me bleed," he said.

Of course, that didn't stop Eric from spending the next two weeks with Smiley.

Our second week continued in the same fashion as the first, which is to say complete debauchery.

I don't know how they could afford to provide us free meals. We'd get breakfast, lunch and dinner *for free*. In the evening, we'd order a steak dinner with a shrimp dinner on the side. We ate so much there. It was all free so we didn't try to contain ourselves one bit.

Dave Griffiths had brought along his Dachshund on the road. I felt bad for that dog during this stay. We brought him scraps non-stop. In those two weeks, that dog must have gained ten pounds. That poor, old dog got so fat. His belly touched the ground and we could easily roll him over.

The night before we left, we packed our gear.

As I mentioned before, the band members grabbed a different bottle every night when we came back to the room to party with the hotel staff. Eric and I each had a suitcase full of booze. There were full bottles of Grand Marnier, scotch, Jack Daniels, Tanqueray, Kahlua, and on and on.

In the morning, Eric went to the kitchen and broiled a dozen T-bone steaks and wrapped them in tin foil for the trip.

"Time to go, boys," he said as he carried a sack full of great smelling steaks.

To make matters worse, we took three cases of beer for the road.

And the club still paid us in full.

We hit the road back to Spokane.

While we drove, we ate the T-bones by hand and drank the beers.

When the boss finally came back from his trip, he immediately discontinued the free dinners and booze and blamed it on Stone Johnny for abusing it.

Is it any wonder?

We had fully hijacked their system.

Stone Johnny made it back to Spokane in mid-June 1980.

When Becky first arrived in town, she found a house on the north side. While she was out one afternoon, some teenagers broke in and stole our stereo, vacuum, and Erin's toys.

During the getaway, they rolled their truck which destroyed the stereo. It also got them caught by the police. We would eventually get restitution for the theft after the police arranged it.

Later, one of the teenagers and his father pulled up in front of mom's place. They never even got out of their car. The father handed me a check for $200. The kid wasn't as contrite as I would have expected. My first instinct was to punch the teenager for the trouble he had caused. Still, I was happy for the $200.

The break-in scared Becky enough that she didn't want to live on the north side of town. She found a house in the valley closer to my family.

Stone Johnny was booked to play Washboard Willies, a bar previously known as The Smoke Shop. Stone Johnny played there whenever we were in town.

We were off the road for one week but playing a local club every night.

When we finished that gig, we immediately hit the road.

The new routine was not sitting well with my family.

Stone Johnny was booked to play a week in Esterhazy, Saskatchewan. It was an uneventful gig.

We played and the folks liked us but there's nothing interesting to share.

We went to an after-hours party in the backyard of some fans. The folks were appreciative that we were there. Live music was still special. They didn't kiss our ass or anything, but they were very nice.

I do remember the water from the hotel tap was brown. Eww.

At the end of June, we arrived in Moose Jaw, Saskatchewan for our next gig. Chrissy's Disco was basically a big room and a converted disco. No one was there on the first night.

What a horrible period this was for music clubs. Former discos were quickly changing to country clubs to try and pick-up on the *Urban Cowboy* trend. There were still disco balls and flashing lights while we played country music in blue jeans and t-shirts.

At Chrissy's, we played to almost non-existent crowds, but the pub next door was completely packed. They had a deal where for five bucks you could get ten beers. The Stone Johnny crew filled our table with beers and drank daily.

We played the shows and found people to party with. It was a decent enough time, but not a great gig.

On those nights when we would play for almost empty houses, I'd psyche myself up by imagining cameras focused on me as I played for 60,000 fans.

In retelling my Stone Johnny stories, I haven't mentioned Paul Elliot much. He was the very best fiddle player I worked with in my career. He was also an intelligent, nice, fun guy who got laid a lot.

He just didn't do weird shit so there aren't many stories to tell about him. I bet he's happy about that now.

For the July 4th weekend, Stone Johnny Mountain Band returned to Priest River, Idaho where they originated from to play the Rainer Beer Fest.

What started off years before as a barbeque with a bunch of friends had grown into a large outdoor concert held over two days. Five bands were there for the weekend with Stone Johnny as the headliner. Tickets were sold to the Rainer Beer sponsored event. It was big deal for the area. Several hundred people showed up for the concert.

We performed well which was important since we were recorded live for an upcoming album we were working on. Mountain Fresh was going to be the title and we were tightening up the songs for a future recording date in the studio.

After a couple shows in Calgary, Alberta and Coram, Montana, we had a Friday and Saturday night gig scheduled at King Cole's in Colville, Washington, ninety minutes north of Spokane. My sister, Laurie, and her husband owned some property in Loon Lake which is on the way to Colville. Becky and I were to stay in Loon Lake for the weekend while I would perform the shows on those nights. My mom agreed to watch Erin for the weekend.

I dropped Becky off at the lake and did the Friday night gig.

We were expecting a close friend of the band to show up at one of the shows. Big Bump was a notorious cocaine dealer in this town and a fan of our music. He was a big man with a pronounced limp. Bump always hung around the band and gave us free dope. When Bump was nearby, people wanted to party. The band had a saying, "When Big Bump is around, you're going to have the top of your head blown off."

He didn't show up on Friday night.

On Saturday, I spent a relaxing day with Becky at the lake. We sat on the porch, drinking beers and smoking weed.

The evening snuck up on me and I was going to be late for the show if I didn't haul ass to Colville.

I grabbed three beers for the road, jumped in my car and sped away toward Loon Lake.

The Pontiac was pushing eighty as I whipped passed a Stevens County Sheriff's car going in the opposite direction. Immediately, the car whipped around and activated its emergency lights.

"Fuck!" I yelled.

I was high and had plenty of beer in my system by then. Plus, two of the road beers I brought with me were now empty carcasses in the back seat.

When I pulled over, the Sheriff's deputy walked to my window. He noticed the empties in the backseat.

"Why don't you step out of the car?"

I was screwed. I figured my only ploy was to do what he asked and be as polite as possible. As I climbed out, a second deputy's car pulled up. My heart sank a little more.

"Lean against the trunk," the first officer told me.

I did as directed.

"Where were you going in such a hurry?"

"I'm a musician and I'm playing a gig tonight at King Cole's in Colville. I'm in the Stone Johnny Mountain Band."

The moment the band's name came out of my mouth, their demeanor changed. The two deputies looked at each other for a moment. "Wait here," one said and they walked to the back of the second car and talked for several minutes.

When they came back, the first deputy said, "Pour out the last of your beer and keep it under the speed limit."

Dumbfounded, I stood there, not moving until they turned and headed to their cars.

As I drove toward King Cole's, several miles under the speed limit, I tried to calm down. I convinced myself that I was a lucky son of a bitch and that maybe the deputies were Stone Johnny fans.

When I arrived, I was late and the guys were worried.

"Where were you?" Rick Roadman asked as I hurried inside.

"I'll tell you on break," I said as I took my place behind my drum kit.

While we played that first set, Big Bump walked in with five women. It was going to be a party tonight.

On the first break, the guys gathered around and I told them what happened.

"That's crazy!"

"How'd you get away?"

I was so freaked out re-telling the story, I didn't feel like drinking. I ordered a Coca-Cola from the bar.

"Let's go outside and do some coke with Bump," Eric said.

"Okay. Let me take a piss and I'll be right there."

"Meet you outside," Mark said.

I sat my glass of soda on the hallway ledge and went into the restroom. When I came back out, I stared at my glass. Multi-colored lights were flashing in it. I stared at it for a moment before opening the hallway door to the parking lot.

Outside, cop cars swarmed the parking lot. There must have been eight sheriff's cars there with their lights flashing.

Bump and his entourage were lined up in front of the cops. So were Eric Lindstrom and Mark Douty. I closed the hallway door and went back inside.

I found Rick Roadman and said, "We've got problems."

Eric and Mark went to jail that night along with Big Bump and his group.

The rest of us, Rick, Dave, Paul and I finished the night without our bassist and soundman. Rick moved to bass.

The rest of the night was subdued. An hour went by before we took the stage again. We played another forty minutes before the night was over and we got out of there.

My weak bladder saved me that evening.

In retelling the story, it's my theory now that the deputies didn't arrest me because they had a bust ready to go for Big Bump. Had they busted me for drunk driving, the show might not have happened and their plans would have been for naught. I was extremely lucky in many ways that night.

Unfortunately, a couple of my friends weren't.

After King Coles, we played four nights at the Cotton Club in Hayden, Idaho which had turned country. I previously played there in my Raven days.

We then took off Sunday through Tuesday. I was getting married on Wednesday.

My bachelor party was held at Washboard Willies and there was a big turn-out.

The band didn't want me to get married and was disappointed that I was going through with it. In their minds, I was fucking up our synergy.

I went out to the parking lot with Mark and Eric to snort some cocaine. While we did that, everyone dispersed from the party.

In the end, it was only my brother, Chuck, and me hanging out, shooting pool, and talking. He dropped me off at my house by 1 a.m.

It was nice that my bachelor party was more subdued.

My job was partying. I needed a break.

Becky and I were married on Wednesday afternoon, August 20th, 1980.

We had to pick a Wednesday because the band was heading out for a twelve-week tour.

The wedding ceremony, which was beautiful, was held in mom's backyard. As our wedding present, mom paid for the cake and our wedding rings.

Four-year-old Erin Marie was our flower girl. She didn't want anyone to step on the flowers that she threw.

Becky was so nervous she giggled throughout the ceremony. She didn't like speaking in front of people.

We had a great turn-out for the service. The original Raven guys were there – Steve, Randy, Dave and Dan. Most of my family was there as well. Chuck was my best man and my sister, Carol, was Becky's maid of honor. Not one member of Becky's family came to our wedding.

Afterwards, the reception was also at mom's house. We cut the cake and opened presents. It was nice and low key. I was extremely happy.

We later went to Carol's house for an after-party. The Stone Johnny guys didn't join us. They were their own clan and I suddenly had a different family. I was now the only married member of the band. The guys went to Jeannie Carter's to party.

Becky and I borrowed a cabin on Deer Lake. On the way to the cabin, Becky and I got lost and argued. We yelled at each other. I was drunk and she was driving.

We ended up having a nice time, though. We were there only Wednesday night and Thursday.

It was a day and a half honeymoon.

Stone Johnny Mountain Band hit the road a couple days after we got back from our honeymoon. I'd only been home for a handful of days since the first tour.

The band pulled up in the van to get me. Becky was in the front yard in a skimpy bikini, watering the yard. As I threw my suitcases inside the bus, the guys got out to say hi to her.

I hugged Becky and kissed her good-bye.

When I climbed in the van, Eric Lindstrom smacked me on the back of the head and knocked my cowboy hat off. My ears rung from the hit.

"What are you doing leaving *that* to go on the road with *us*?"

Becky had gotten her message across.

As we were headed to Canada, the band agreed not to bring any dope since we knew we would be searched.

At the border, in our big flashy Stone Johnny truck, the border patrol waved us over. As predicted, they wanted to search our rig. They brought their drug dog in and that pooch went crazy.

There was residual pot smell in pillows, blankets, the seats and the carpet. Hell, we probably had the smell in our clothes and hair.

The border patrol made us unload every ounce of equipment and tear it all apart. I had to take the heads off my drums. We pulled the backs off our speakers with screwdrivers.

Eric Lindstrom, who was normally "Mr. Don't-Take-Shit-From-Anyone", was downright helpful to the border guards.

"Come on, guys. The sooner we get this stuff opened up, the sooner we are out of here."

The guards took us inside and patted us down. They made us drop our pants and our drawers to make sure we weren't smuggling dope in our asses.

We were there for three hours.

After we reloaded the truck and crossed the border, we were five miles into Canada before Eric pulled up his pants and yanked a bag out of his boot. Inside was a solid 5 grams of hash.

We all wanted to hurt him, but instead we smoked his dope.

Our first stop was a wedding reception gig in Calgary, Alberta for a couple that were huge Stone Johnny fans. Afterwards we had a week-long gig in a venue that was an old disco.

They housed us on the top floor in a former banquet room. They put beds up there to make it the band's apartment. The sink and bathroom were also lined along the wall. It was essentially a big dorm room.

I was reading *The Stand* by Stephen King during the day which pissed the other guys off. They wanted me to sightsee on our time off. They couldn't understand that I was engulfed in a book and harassed me for being different. I didn't live completely for the moment any more.

When I had some quiet time, I would sit in the room with a view over Calgary and reflect on *The Stand*. I would imagine that happening and how I would get home to Becky and Erin.

We next arrived in Vernon, B.C. to play a two-week gig at The Village Green, a club with a sunken dance floor in front of the stage.

It was the first time I ever saw a mechanical bull.

A local television news station came in and filmed us while we were on. Just because John Travolta put a cowboy hat on in a movie, the media now thought we were trendy. We had a chip on our shoulder because of the latest fad.

One night after the bar closed we stayed and drank. I got hammered and climbed on the mechanical bull. It threw me in less than two seconds, thereby kicking the shit out of me.

On a different night, someone broke into Rick and Dave's room during our show and started a fire. Their mattresses were burned and the place smelled like smoke, but none of their clothes were torched. We never found out who did it. Maybe a crazy groupie did it. Who knows?

That was the highlight of the week.

In September, we headed to Vancouver, B.C. and played two weeks at The Cowboy.

It was a long, miserable two weeks.

As with many places, the club had recently been a disco. The girls arriving for our shows wore shiny disco dresses and silly, little cowboy hats. *Urban Cowboy* may have been the latest trend, but the Canadians were still trying to figure out how to pull off the look.

The stage was on one floor that was essentially an atrium. The crowd was either above us or below us. It was weird and made for a shitty band-to-crowd experience. We were essentially a juke box.

My birthday, September 8th, was while we were there. As usual, I drank a bottle of Jack Daniels to celebrate.

During this stay, the Greater Vancouver Brewery Strike was in progress which made beer tough to get. On an off-night, the band drove to Blaine, Washington which sits on the Canadian Border to get beer.

We parked the truck on the Canadian side of the border so we wouldn't have to worry about the possibility of an inspection again. We walked across the border to a convenience store and each of us bought a case. As we walked back, rain poured. The cardboard boxes were wet and strained to hold our beers. We made it through customs and back to our hotel rooms in Vancouver.

While there, my former bandmate, Steve Hanna, called. It took some work for him to track me down.

After Dave Low and I left, Raven continued for a bit. A while later, Randy Peterson quit, leaving Steve as the sole remaining member of Raven. With essentially a new band, he rebranded as Dogface and relocated to the Seattle area.

They were losing their drummer and Steve asked if I would like to join him. I was surprised because he vowed there'd never be another return for me. I would later meet with him to discuss the possibility. I don't think I ever considered it because I was married with a child and I was not going to relocate to Seattle. I guess I enjoyed the invitation.

I respectfully declined and things were good again with Steve.

To this day, Steve is one of my best friends.

Stone Johnny had been on the road for five weeks by now and finished our last show at The Cowboy on Saturday night. We were scheduled to open Monday night in Reno, Nevada at the Shy Clown Casino. It was a helluva long drive down I-5 and across CA-20. It took us twenty hours in our truck to get there.

Jeannie Carter's tour routing skills were legendary and often praised as having "sucked."

In Reno, we headlined The Shy Clown Casino for two-weeks. The opening band, Family Portrait, was a local favorite and heavily into cocaine. They not only loved it, but they had a ton of it. Since we were also cocaine fueled, it was a hard two weeks of partying.

At the end of our first week, we had Sunday off. We went to the woods outside of Reno. Family Portrait brought along a group of twenty people consisting of their band members and actual family.

Of course, we didn't go to the campgrounds for a picnic. We went to eat mushrooms and trip.

I ate them, too, even though I promised myself I wouldn't do a hallucinogenic ever again after the purple microdot incident. No one pressured me, but I wanted to fit in with the Stone Johnny guys.

After we ate our mushrooms, each of us wandered off in a different direction to trip in our own way.

I sat at a picnic table and didn't move for hours. I mumbled repeatedly that the table was moving at eighty miles per hour. The only thing that kept me grounded was thinking about Becky and Erin. I reminded myself that I was Erin's father and Becky's husband and I shouldn't be there stoned on mushrooms.

I wiggled my feet back and forth, digging the heels of my boots in the dirt. It was eight inches deep when I saw it later. People walked by and hollered at me.

Finally, I regained enough of my senses to walk to the restroom. I had to go, but I was constipated as hell. The restroom had a metal roof. It was a one-man john and members of our group threw stones on the roof. The noise was horrible. It sounded like giant boulders falling on top of me. The rocks hit and caused dust to fall from the ceiling. I freaked out and screamed. There were laughs from outside the restroom. This went on for an eternity but was probably only five minutes. People yelled, "Billy, have you shat yet?"

I couldn't go and had to get out of there.

I wandered around the woods until I found Rick Roadman observing ants fornicating on his knee. He also told me about a raging river he couldn't cross.

It was two feet wide and six inches deep.

Still tripping on the mushrooms, we followed the guys in Family Portrait to a party at a fancy house. There was a group of younger guys there. One guy said he didn't like Marshall Tucker and I went after him. I was going to kill him. The shrooms were messing with my head. The band had to pull me off him.

I then meandered around the three-story house until I was on the balcony. I figured it was a perfect opportunity to take a piss. I arced it off the balcony onto the patio where the crowd stood.

That was it. Everyone had enough of my act by then. They wanted me to leave but the band had abandoned me by leaving the party earlier.

I got a ride from the drummer of Family Portrait who was also drunk and stoned.

By then, I was so messed up that I was freaking out, afraid that I wouldn't find the band and would never escape Reno.

The other drummer got us back to the hotel early in the morning.

I slept until 4 p.m. the next day.

The next week was subdued after the mushroom experience.
We played the shows.
We stayed up late.
We drank a ton.
We snorted a lot of cocaine.
Like I said, subdued.

Our next tour stop was the Whiskey River in downtown Boise. The club was essentially a huge room with a big stage and dance floor.

On our final night, we opened for Commander Cody with Johnny Vernazza on guitar.

Johnny V was the lead guitarist for Elvin Bishop and was playing a guest spot with Commander Cody.

After the Commander Cody show, Norton Buffalo came on and Commander Cody backed him. That whole night was a great show.

At the end of the Norton Buffalo show, Stone Johnny was invited on stage and we all jammed together. I played the cowbell.

Norton Buffalo (whose given name was Philip Jackson) and Commander Cody (whose real name is George Frayne IV) were jerks, but Johnny V was cool.

After the show, Johnny V and I had a beer together and chatted about our families. I talked about being a new husband and father.

Johnny said, "I wish you luck, Bill. One or the other is going to have to give. You're not going to be able to have both."

That stuck with me.

At that moment, I felt out of place with both my wife *and* my band.

On the way out of town, we stopped at an older couple's house that knew Stone Johnny before I joined them.

They were a sweet couple and they feed us deer and elk for lunch. They loved Dave Dieter, the previous drummer for the band, but they treated me nice. They were almost parental to us.

After lunch, the guys grabbed their acoustic guitars to play some songs for them. I pulled out my brushes and used a pie pan as a drum head. We jammed in their living room for a good hour.

Eric was in a sour mood and kept trying to get us on the road. I appreciated his concern as it was a twelve-hour drive.

Still, it was a nice moment.

We rolled back into Spokane early Monday morning.

I had been gone for twelve weeks. Becky had moved us to a single wide trailer. As I walked silently around my new house, I thought, *This is it.* I had reached a point where I didn't want to constantly be on the road. I still wanted to play but being in a band that was on the road for months on end held no allure for me. In fact, it was the exact opposite.

I crawled into bed with Becky and held her.

It was then I wanted to leave the music business.

I didn't say anything to the guys because we still had a couple road trips, and this was my job. We had a four-week gig scheduled that would take us through Canada. It would mean missing Thanksgiving with my new family.

But I knew it would only be two short trips.

Stone Johnny was in Spokane for a couple weeks before our next tour. We played Washboard Willies a few times and, as always, it was fun. During one of these shows, we were recorded live for a second time in support of the upcoming album.

The bar had an underground lair which was accessed by a trap door near the front of the bar. In this hide-out were couches, chairs, and old lamps. Guys would go down there to snort cocaine, smoke weed, and have sex with groupies. I'd go into the den for the drugs.

One night after a gig, I went into the hide-out and snorted a bunch of coke and partied with the guys.

I came upstairs later and the sun was out. I was totally disoriented.

Holy fuck, I thought and ran to my car.

I got home at about 9 a.m.

Becky was pissed, oh man, was she pissed! She wasn't worried I was screwing around. She was worried I had been arrested or been in an accident.

It's still a mystery how Becky ever endured shit like that.

Stone Johnny hit the road again in the fall. After a week at the Bend Woolen Mill, we landed at The Grand Allusion in Eugene, Oregon.

The notable thing about this venue was that part of the crowd sat off to the left of the band.

I'd played there before with Clear Sky which was more country-rock than Stone Johnny. That's what this crowd wanted. They would holler "Play some Skynyrd" during our songs.

There was a drunk woman off to my left who shouted her comments through the show. "You guys suck," she yelled repeatedly. "Play some rock and roll." Her boyfriend, seated at the table with her, laughed along with her comments.

Finally, I had enough. During a break between two songs, I turned to her and bellowed, "Hey, bitch, I don't stand next to your bed and heckle you while you work."

Her boyfriend jumped out of his seat and came toward the stage.

Eric Lindstrom, the beast of a man he was, moved in between me and the embarrassed boyfriend.

Eric said, "Now, you don't want to do that."

The boyfriend studied Eric for a moment before sheepishly going back to his chair and sitting down.

Score one for the band.

Maclean's, the Canadian equivalent of Time magazine published an article on the *Urban Cowboy* fad and we were mentioned in it. It came out in the October 13th, 1980 issue. The article was titled *Ridin' High* and was written by Thomas Hopkins. Basically, it said everything we hated about the craze. How young men and women were flocking to stores to buy western wear to go out to clubs. I can say it now because we aren't playing shows like this anymore, but our Canadian fans looked ridiculous.

Man, I hated that fad.

We took a week off before we were to begin a two-week stint at Washboard Willies. We went to the bar and rehearsed. Jeannie Carter stopped by. She said she needed the band to stop by her new house in the country to get promo pictures taken.

I followed her outside.

"You better hold off on the pictures, Jeannie."

"Why?"

"I'm quitting the band."

Jeannie wasn't happy about my news and we talked for a few minutes. Finally, she accepted my decision and left.

In retrospect, I wish I would have gotten a picture done with the guys. With all the miles we put on that season, I would have loved to have had a professional picture with them.

I told the band about my decision to leave.

Eric said, "Man…, fucker…, don't do this."

Rick said, "I understand, man," and gave me a hug.

Paul said, "I'm sorry, man. Good luck."

Dave Griffith didn't give a shit.

With that said, I must let you know that Dave and I are friends now. Maturity and life made all the bullshit between us fade away.

Stone Johnny was opening for Hoyt Axton on Wednesday, November 5th, at the Spokane Opera House. This was a big deal.

Before the show, Jeannie gave everyone $200 to go buy new clothes. Except me. She didn't give me anything since I was leaving the band.

While the rest of the guys showed up to the gig looking put together, I looked ratty in comparison. Jeannie reluctantly peeled off $20 for me to go buy new jeans. Becky and I raced out to get a new pair.

The night of the show we played our hearts out.

The next day we were kicked in the nuts by <u>Spokesman-Review</u> staff writer Rick Bonino's review of the concert – *The Hoyt of Entertainment.*

> If you were there early, you caught the warmup act, the Stone Johnny Mountain Band, five immensely likeable, long-haired country boys from Spokane who won immediate points by playing all-original material.
>
> Their talent and enthusiasm cut through a poor sound mix. Stone Johnny is probably better off in their natural environment, the bar circuit, where they're closer to the audience and more in control of their own product.

After a week at the King Eddie in Calgary, we played a week at the Paddock in Regina, the capital of Saskatchewan.

The club had a big stage, nice lights, great staff, good sound and free beer for the band. In other words, it was fantastic! The club was packed every night.

The stage was extremely tall. On top of my drum riser, I sat near the ceiling.

Eric, Dave and Paul each found girls there.

I missed my first Thanksgiving with Becky and Erin.

Our next gig was at the North 40 Club in Saskatoon, Saskatchewan.

When we first arrived in town, the band found a bar to do some drinking. We were sitting around a table when a girl hit on me. I showed her my wedding ring to scare her away.

"That doesn't matter," she said.

"Yeah, that doesn't matter, Bill," said Dave Griffiths, laughing.

I got indignant with the band. I grabbed my beer and moved to another table. This got me in trouble with the bartender.

Back then in Saskatchewan, you couldn't move your beer from table to table. A staff member had to move it for you. That was an odd law.

After the North 40 Club, we were the headliner for a one-night gig.

The venue billed us as having been on tour with The Charlie Daniels Band and The Marshall Tucker Band. It was complete bullshit, but it was sponsored by a radio station and part of their winter festival.

The show was in a big auditorium. They led us to the stage by flashlight. The place was packed and the crowd responded to us well. Every silly thing Eric said got a laugh. When Paul walked to the edge of the stage with his fiddle, the crowd went wild.

In the dressing room were bottles of scotch and Jack Daniels. They'd also stocked plenty of our favorite beer.

After the show, the radio station rented several suites in a downtown hotel. They filled the bathtubs full of ice and beer.

It was an incredible taste of stardom.

The drive back to Spokane was eighteen hours. It was normally a long trip, but it was made longer due to a heavy snow that was falling. It was a brutal drive.

We arrived back in Spokane County late at night. Since I lived on the edge of the county, I was the first one dropped off.

When the guys drove away, I stood in the street and watched the truck. As the brake lights brightened prior to the corner, my chest tightened.

This is it, I thought. *I'm done.*

That was my last road trip ever.

Stone Johnny began a one-week stint at Washboard Willies and, during the day, the band auditioned replacement drummers. In a short time, the guys found Eston Way as my replacement.

After I left the band, they recorded the album, <u>Mountain Fresh</u>, in 1981.

As I mentioned earlier, in preparation for the album, we were recorded live in 1980 at Priest River on the 4th of July and at Washboard Willies. None of the live music made it on the album. I feel like I had a hand in helping them to get that point and was happy for them. However, I was also sad, because I wanted to be a part of the album. I just couldn't do it anymore.

I played my last night with the Stone Johnny Mountain Band at Washboard Willies on December 13th. It was a good night at the venue. There was a full house as always. We drank beer, snorted a bunch of coke, and smoked a bit of dope. A typical Stone Johnny gig.

Jeannie Carter and her husband, Tom Lapsansky, didn't come to the show. I'll admit I was hurt by that.

The band and our fans gave me a big send-off as this was the end of music for Billy Bancroft. People came to say good-bye and good luck.

After the show, I went home to our trailer. I crawled into bed and held my wife.

I didn't have any money. I didn't have a job. I was no longer in a band.

I was scared to death.

SECRETS
1982

(Top L-R) Blue, me, Darren Robinette
(Bottom L-R) Rob DiPietro, Mike Medeiros, Chuck Montes

After leaving Stone Johnny, I needed a job.

I spent my time driving around, looking for work, hoping to land a baking gig.

Eventually, I got a job at Duff's Restaurant as a dishwasher. My salary was $175 every two weeks. I felt defeated accepting this position.

Becky went back to school at Spokane Community.

We barely scratched by.

I looked for a local band to join, but not one that toured. I found one in town searching for a replacement drummer. They invited me over and we jammed. They were a New Wave/Punk band. It was 1981, remember?

They called themselves The Zipperz and to fit in with their look, they wanted me to shave and get A Flock of Seagulls style haircut. In retrospect, I probably should have done it to get the job.

I was too proud to get rid of the beard and long hair I'd grown with Stone Johnny after cutting it previously for my truck driving job with Dr. Pepper.

I grabbed a one-off gig at Eastern Washington University.

Rob Conway, who was in Cold Smoke early on, was recording an all-original project and needed a session drummer.

In exchange for my work, I was offered royalties off the sale of the album, but I declined. I'd like to say I was smart enough to say, "No, thanks," but the reality was I needed immediate cash. I made $75 for the gig and had a fleeting thought that maybe I could make a living as a studio musician.

In February, Becky learned she was pregnant. I couldn't be more excited, but suddenly the struggle for money took on more urgency. As money got tighter, I thought I should take another look back at Utah.

I contacted my previous employer, 7-Up/Dr. Pepper. They gave me a job, albeit as a junior driver which was a lower position than when I had left. I couldn't blame them with how abruptly I took off a year prior.

The pay of $175/week was double what I was making as a dishwasher.

Out of financial desperation, Becky and I returned to Ogden. We moved in with Robert Petty and his wife for a short time. I am forever grateful for their generosity. We stayed there until we saved enough money to rent a house of our own.

It didn't take long to hook up with a local band. I did a few gigs with The Kap Brothers, Robbie and Richie. They used me as a double drummer to compliment Jay Lee. We had two complete drum kits set up. It was a neat sound and was fun for a few bucks here and there.

The night Becky went into labor, I was so excited, nervous, and scared, that I put on three pairs of socks. Yes, three. I don't know where my head was.

We dropped Erin off with Becky's sister and headed for McKay-Dee Hospital. Becky was in labor from 3 a.m. October 26th until 4:40 p.m. the next day.

Our son, Cory John, was born October 27th, 1981.

Watching the birth of my first-born and experiencing the euphoria of it all still ranks right up there with the best moments of my life. When I held him in my arms for the first time, it was like nothing I'd ever experienced. I walked down the hallway to the maternity center to show friends and family on the other side of the window. I pointed at Cory and mouthed, "It's a boy!"

They all clapped.

I returned Cory to his mother's arms and watched them together. What I was feeling was beyond description.

While driving for 7-Up/Dr. Pepper and unloading cases of soda pop bottles, I hurt my back. The glass bottles back then were heavy as hell. This would affect me for years.

I was off work for a couple days. While reading the newspaper, I saw an ad in the newspaper that Weber State College was looking for a baker.

I applied and got the job. It wasn't as much money, but it had better insurance benefits.

It was tough work. I was responsible for two bakeries on campus and I hadn't baked for a while.

I was quickly in over my head.

During this same period, I reunited with Chuck Montes, one of my former bandmates from Clear Sky/Utah: The Group. We were going to reform the band as best we could.

It turned out Gayle Allred was still around and would back the band, but not to the level she previously did with Utah: The Group.

We pulled together a new band. Chuck Montes would play bass. Rob DiPietro would play lead guitar as would a guy named Blue. We had two guys singing lead. Mike Medeiros would sing the low to mid-range stuff and Darren Robinette would sing the high vocals while playing acoustic guitar. A guy named Ray handled the lighting for the band.

We flew in Randy Peterson from my Raven days to possibly join us. He sounded good, but we couldn't put it together with him.

I came up with the band's new name, Secrets, and Becky's dad drew the logo.

I booked our shows and coordinated all business and marketing aspects. Along with drumming, I was management. Therefore, I thought of Secrets as *my* band.

As our backer, Gayle provided us with a new P.A. system.

We got quite a bit of work at the start. We grabbed local gigs like The Hermitage and others in Salt Lake City.

Mike Medeiros cut an interesting figure for a lead singer. He was 5'8 and roughly 300 pounds.

Along with Ray on lights, we had a crew of "hangers-on" who acted as sound and light assistants. I can't remember any of their names. We had an entourage of about fifteen unpaid people. It was fun, but we weren't making much money.

One of our lead guitarists, Blue, was an asshole to the rest of us. He repeatedly said, "Covers are nowhere, man. Only originals are worth our time."

We were at The Herm for rehearsal and Blue was totally spaced out. He said, "Guys, you are all going to die."

"What?" I asked.

"You're going to play other people's music and die."

Blue was also fucking Gayle Allred which none of us could comprehend. Gayle resembled the Wicked Witch of the West, only not as pretty.

In the end, it didn't work with Blue.

We fired him.

Not long after, Rob DiPietro quit the band. He never gave a reason and I never heard from him again. He simply stopped coming.

To replace Rob, we hired Jimmy McElwain, my former bandmate in Clear Sky/Utah: The Group. He had just returned from southern Utah after working with a mining company. For Blue's replacement, we hired Cordell Baird after he left a band known as Hotspurz.

When the band began, I burned the proverbial candle at both ends with the bakery. To keep myself going, I snorted a fair amount of cocaine. Becky had a friend who was selling it and I saw how well she was doing. I told her I wanted to give it a try. She spotted me an 8-ball for $400. She said, "Whatever you can make above that is yours."

An 8-ball is 1/8 of an ounce or roughly 3.5 grams (which is equal to about seven small paperclips in weight). It can be divided into fourteen 1/4 grams. I sold each 1/4 gram for $80 and was cleaned out in a couple days.

When I gave her the money I owed her, she was surprised. "Want to do it again?"

"Hell, yeah," I said. It was fast, easy money.

Unfortunately, my clientele was mostly my bandmates.

As a band, we played five to six nights a week and made about $1,500, which sounds great until you divide it up seven ways ($215/week).

The guys would want me to front them their drugs. I had a ledger book and kept detailed notes. Talk about incriminating evidence! It's a wonder I was never arrested.

Every time the band would get paid, I'd bring out the ledger and clear their accounts. For some of the guys, I would pocket their pay to wipe out their debt. Other guys were in the hole for the next week. Some of the guys would get $10 for a week of performing.

One time, Jimmy wanted to buy a quarter gram from me. The only thing I had on me was a "taster" gram, one that I had let a couple guys take snorts from to test the quality of the dope. When Jimmy saw what I was trying to sell him, he said, "Geez, Billy, this seems a little light."

"Don't buy it then," I said. I was an asshole to my own bandmates when it came to dope dealing.

Jimmy bought it, of course, and paid full price.

When I started selling, my own coke use plummeted. For whatever reason, the business angle excited me and I got focused.

I made decent money, but it was on the backs of my bandmates. It took me six months to see how wrong it was.

The final straw was a late-night phone call from a close friend.

Becky and I were in bed. My kids were asleep in the other room.

"Billy," my friend said, over the phone, "are you holding?"

"Maybe," I said, in answer to his question about having cocaine.

After some back and forth, he said, "I've got a good party going on over here and I can't leave. My wife has my car."

"Promise me that if I come over no one will see me."

I was paranoid. I was married with two kids and I didn't want anyone knowing I sold drugs.

I drove over to meet my friend. Once there, I waited, but he wouldn't come outside. I should have left him stranded for dope, but I walked up to the house and knocked.

My friend threw open the front door. "Billy!"

Everyone stared at me, expectantly. The drug dealer had arrived.

My buddy grabbed my arm and pulled me into another room with a couple other guys. I was pissed.

The three of them tasted about $80 worth of cocaine. I lost my mind.

"Are you going to buy this or what?"

They bought my entire stash, cleaning me out.

My friend walked me out of his house and back to my car.

I said, "If you fuck me on this, I will kill you."

I was scared because he had exposed me to a room full of strangers.

Then I went home and told Becky I was done selling cocaine.

"It's stupid," I said.

"Yes, it is," she agreed.

The next day, I gave the borrowed scales back to Becky's friend and told her I was done.

It's unbelievable that I had my kids, Erin and Cory, in the house with that shit.

I can't explain the level of shame I feel in reliving that moment of my life.

The schedule of the bakery and the band finally caught up with me.

I would get into the bakery at Weber State at 3 a.m.

When my shift was over at 1 p.m., I'd race to band rehearsal.

When that was over, I would run home to have dinner with Becky and the kids.

After dinner, I'd head out to whatever venue we were playing that night.

I'd get home around 1 a.m., take a shower and return to the bakery.

Living this schedule finally took its toll on me.

Secrets played a Saturday night gig at Supertramps. At the end of the night, I did some cocaine to keep me awake. It didn't work. I passed out in the doorway of the restroom. I was rushed to the ER and treated like I had overdosed.

On Monday, Becky took me to the doctor's office to get checked. I had dropped a bunch of weight and was now weighing 119 pounds. I had a urinary tract infection and was suffering from exhaustion and dehydration. The doctor told me, "You either go to the hospital now or she'll take you to the funeral home tomorrow."

When Becky cried, I figured I had no choice but to check into the hospital.

When I was released, I quit the bakery and took a job at the Powder Mountain Ski Resort to work in their kitchen and ski shop. Becky was already working there at the ticket office.

In our off time, we became ski bums.

Playing in Secrets was no longer fun.

Becky and I were living beyond our means and making bad financial decisions.

On our own, we were thrifty individuals. Together, we weren't financially sound. We were always buying things we thought would make the other person happy.

We received a Nordstrom credit card in the mail. It had a $700 credit limit and we maxed it out in two days.

We bought a new vehicle, a Toyota Tercel, on credit. We were barely scraping by and we added more debt without really considering the consequences, like so many other things in our lives.

To make matters worse, when I quit selling cocaine, I started using it more frequently. At times, Becky did the drugs with me, but she was always in control. She was the first one to say, "Enough."

When I got the job at Powder Mountain, the band faded. Secrets focused on current hard rock music like the Scorpions, Sammy Hagar, and Aldo Nova. It was fun to play, but places to perform that type of music were drying up in the Ogden/Salt Lake City area.

The final nail in the coffin of Secrets was a phone call from my friend, Greg Clary.

He was in Hotspurz and they had fired their drummer and wanted me.

Our lead guitarist, Cordell Baird, had played with Hotspurz previously but they had fired him for his cocaine problem.

Hotspurz was a country-rock band that had recently won the Wrangler Star Search competition for the state of Utah. The year before, Hotspurz went to Nashville and competed in a national Star Search competition but didn't win.

When Greg made the offer to join Hotspurz, I jumped on it.

Secrets had worn out its purpose, so I dissolved the band. This pissed off the guys, especially Jimmy. He thought I betrayed him.

After Secrets broke up, someone called claiming to be a member of the Ghost Riders motorcycle gang. He said he was associated with Gayle and that I needed to return the P.A.

system she provided the band. She had never come for it nor called about it. The call was totally weird, but after everything else I'd gone through, I was happy to give the damn thing back.

HOTSPURZ
1982-1984

*(L-R) Terry Morris, Doug Artist, Alan Bevan,
me, and Greg Clary*

I joined Hotspurz in January 1982.

Hotspurz was as popular in Ogden as Clear Sky was in 1979. I was extremely lucky to be in two bands with that level of local popularity.

When I first joined Hotspurz, Al Bevan handled rhythm guitar and Doug Artist played guitar and pedal steel. Greg Clary was the bassist and Terry Morris was on piano. Al sang lead vocals and everyone sang back-up.

We were going on the road almost immediately so I quit the job at Powder Mountain Ski Resort.

Hotspurz had a green school bus fixed up nice inside with tables, chairs, couches, and bunks.

A little more than a year prior, I'd left the Stone Johnny Mountain Band due to their touring schedule so I could be with my family. Now, I had joined a band that was soon going to make that schedule look easy. I didn't understand it at that moment, of course, because I might have made a different decision. Or perhaps not, if I'm honest. The reality is that Hotspurz was on the edge of something special and even if it might have caused hardship with my wife, I know I would have stepped onto that bus to chase my dream.

Our first stop was in Evanston, Wyoming at Billy's Country Music Emporium for a one-week gig.

In Hotspurz, Greg Clary was notorious for farting. It was gross and childish, but the guy took pride in it. During a show, he would dance his way near my drums and fart, exactly like Eric Lindstrom of Stone Johnny. *What's up with bass players and farts?*

On Wednesday night, during the middle of our second set, Greg stood at the front of the stage playing his bass. He wore tight, light colored blue jeans. Suddenly, Greg danced backwards toward my drum kit. I knew what was coming and there was nowhere to go. I had to sit and wait for it to happen.

Greg stopped in front of my drum kit and farted. He immediately froze. A big, brown spot appeared in the seat of his light, blue pants.

He shit his pants!

I laughed out loud and missed a beat, causing the other guys to look in my direction. Greg stood frozen but continued to play. He couldn't leave the stage. The others figured out what happened between Greg's rigid stance and my laughing. The remainder of that set was a pure delight for the rest of us.

We finished the last song of that set and Greg waddled off-stage to the dressing room.

Who said rock and roll isn't glamorous?

On Friday night while in Evanston, we opened for Johnny Duncan.

He had several number one hits in the late '70s, including *She Can Put Her Shoes Under My Bed (Anytime)* and a couple with Janie Fricke. He arrived in a big tour bus which impressed me.

Johnny was a nice guy who had a real cowboy way about him. We all had long hair and beards. We assured him we were country all the way after he asked why the Emporium had a rock band opening for him.

When we opened for him we only had to play half as long as our normal nights. Then we went up front to watch Johnny's show Afterwards, we partied in the dressing room with him and his band. There were pitchers of Kamikazes amid scores of other liquors. We snorted a bunch of cocaine and generally had a good time.

Johnny was staying at the same hotel as we were. At the end of the night, I jumped on their bus and rode with them to the hotel. It was my first exposure to a nice tour bus. It blew me away. It solidified the fact that I wanted to make it with Hotspurz.

When we got off the bus, fans clamored for autographs.

I signed some since they thought I was with Johnny Duncan's band.

On Saturday night, it was a much smaller crowd.

The Emporium held 1,200 people at full capacity and there were only about 400 people that night. It was still a great crowd, but it felt empty.

On one of our breaks, we were in the dressing room reclining on couches around a coffee table with a big ashtray sitting in the middle of it. The in-house soundman, a crazy bastard from New York, joined us. We were laughing and retelling the story about how Greg had shit himself earlier in the week.

The soundman interrupted the laughter and said, "Want to see something you'll never see again, but you'll talk about forever?"

We all looked at each other and collectively said, "Ok."

The soundman jumped on the table, pulled down his pants and shat in the ash tray.

For several moments, we sat there in stunned disbelief.

Shit. Was. In. The. Ashtray.

We sprinted out of the room.

He was right, though. I'm still talking about it all these years later.

About this time, The Hermitage closed.

It might have been sad as it had been the center of my musical universe for several years, but I was on my way to becoming a star so I didn't give it much thought.

In Ogden, we were booked to play a new club, Bigfoot's. We weren't the official house band, but we were there all the time. Basically, it was huge room that seated roughly 250 people. Becky got a job waitressing there. We were playing five nights a week, with Sundays and Mondays off.

We were making good money now so Becky and I moved into a three-story apartment.

Behind the scenes, Ann Van Meeteron financed the band.

The rumor was that she was a trust fund baby. Regardless of how she got it, she had money – lots of it. She didn't put the band on a salary like Gayle Allred did with Clear Sky, but she paid for the promo packs and our P.A. system. She would also bring giant shrimp cocktails, booze and cocaine on the bus whenever she'd join us on a trip.

We never paid her back and didn't even think about doing so. The return on her investment was getting to hang out with us. That might sound callous now, but we didn't think so then.

The entire music industry is built upon the concept of reflected glory. Hell, much of the world is built upon it, whether it is entertainment, sports, or politics.

Reflected glory is when a person feels illuminated by standing near an individual directly under a spotlight.

This is what happens with groupies. Some of them give out sex to have a moment of glory reflected upon them. They get to tell their friends what they did or brag that their boyfriend was in a band.

Some female fans might not have slept with us, but they fed us, housed us, clothed us, and performed all sorts of other motherly duties. They did this to have the light shine on them when they were around the band.

Reflected glory happened with the hangers-on, as well. The guys who hauled the band's gear from place to place without monetary compensation. Their pay was in the form of telling some willing girl, "I'm with the band," and getting a blowjob in the parking lot.

The drug dealers got in on the action, too. They provided us with free narcotics to be around the party. We loved those guys, because they kept us touching the stratosphere, but they were there to catch a piece of our spotlight, our moment of glory.

As for the band, we wanted to get paid, get high and get laid by the fans who were looking for that reflection as well.

It's the law of rock and roll.

Or country-rock as the case may be.

We were going to record an album but couldn't afford an effort that large so we recorded two songs for a 45 record.

We recorded *Walkin' Shoes* written by Al and *A Whole Lotta Time on My Hands* written by Greg. *Walkin' Shoes* was a beautiful slow song while *A Whole Lotta Time* was a country-rocker.

The songs were recorded at the studios of KUTV in Salt Lake City. *Walkin' Shoes* took me three takes and *A Whole Lot of Time on My Hands* took me two. I nailed them.

Locally, *Walkin' Shoes* got some airplay.

I was driving to rehearsal one day when it came on the radio. It was the first time I heard myself on the airwaves.

The song was on juke boxes around town and fans could buy the 45 at record stores.

It was a heady experience.

Hotspurz was a five-piece band with sound and lights so we needed a road unit. The former lead singer of Secrets, Mike Medeiros, became our soundman. Ray, who was the light guy for Secrets, also came aboard.

Truth be told, Mike Medeiros wasn't really cut out to assist us.

During a gig at Gentle Ben's in Boise, Idaho, Mike was invited to sing with the band during an encore. He sang *Dreams* by The Allman Brothers Band and he sounded good. When he was done singing, he spoke to the crowd like he was the band's leader. "Thank you, ladies and gentlemen. Hotspurz is…" and he introduced the rest of the guys.

Al chewed him out after the show. "You're acting like it's your band, Mike, but you're just the soundman."

When we got back to Ogden, Mike quit.

In March '83, we had a two-week gig in Jackson Hole, Wyoming at The Million Dollar Cowboy Bar where I had previously played with The Stone Johnny Mountain Band.

Mid-week, an older guy with white hair approached the stage during our first set and asked us if we would play Willie Nelson's *On the Road Again*.

That wasn't part of our song list and we had never rehearsed it. We told him no.

"I'll give you $100 if you play it," he said.

Of course, we did it.

Al knew the words enough to fake his way through it.

The old guy came back during the second set and asked if we'd play *On the Road Again* once more.

"Yeah, but it will cost you another $100," Al said.

All told, the old guy came up five times during four sets and paid us $100 each time. We made $500 extra dollars playing a song which we'd never practiced once.

Finally, the old guy's wife dragged him away.

At the end of the night, instead of each band member pocketing an extra $100 and being smart, we spent it on cocaine.

$500 worth of coke.

Near the end of the second week in Jackson Hole, Ray got married.

His fiancé drove in from Ogden to be with him at the show.

We had hired Chad Gardner as our soundman after Mike Medeiros quit. He was a friend of the band and didn't know shit about sound, but back in the '60s, Chad was an ordained minister. Therefore, he presided over Ray's wedding. I acted as Ray's best man.

They were married on the stage of The Million Dollar Cowboy Bar during the day.

Becky and Terry's wife came up for the ceremony.

For their wedding picture, the group went to one of those "old time" photography studios and dressed in vintage clothing. I'd love to see that picture again.

After our tour, an important competition occurred in Salt Lake City. There were two big country clubs in Salt Lake City then – the Western Star and the Westerner.

The Western Star was a big venue and they had a "showcase" where the upper-echelon bands from the surrounding areas were invited to play. For the event, they brought in radio folks, promoters and record company representatives.

The venue had two stages. While one band played, another could get ready.

As we prepared on our stage, a solo act performed on the other. To prove what an asshole he was, Doug Artist, our lead guitarist, sat on stage tuning his guitar. He could have done it silently, through a tuner. Instead, he plunked the notes through his amplifier. It wasn't loud enough to disturb the guy on the other stage, but it affected the folks in the audience near us. An audience member yelled at Doug, "Hey, can you stop? We're trying to listen."

Doug stood, in front of promoters and record folks, and shouted at him to shut the fuck up.

Embarrassed by Doug's antics, we all freaked out.

In the end, it didn't matter. Our performance sounded solid. We nailed it.

We were one of the bands picked by the record folks to go to Muscle Shoals, Alabama and cut tracks for a possible album.

This is it, I thought, *we are going to make it.*

Terry Morris's wife threatened to leave him if he went on the road again. If we were going to make it, we'd be on the road regularly and she wouldn't stand for it. Therefore, he quit.

We hired Tommy Taylor to replace Terry.

We also knew that we had to fire Doug. He was a loose cannon.

I convinced the band into hiring Dave Love from Clear Sky/Utah: The Group. We were sneaky about adding Dave to the mix while Doug was still in the band. We did it under the guise of having two lead guitar players.

One night at the end of a gig in Logan, Al and Greg fired Doug. He blew a gasket and kicked a couple chairs. As a band, we didn't handle his firing like professionals, and he was right to be angry.

A few weeks had passed since Dave Love joined the band and he didn't sound good. He was regressing from when he first arrived. I'm not sure what was occurring in his life. Al and Greg were worried that I would quit if they fired Dave. They came over to my house and explained the situation. I made the decision to stay with the band while agreeing to fire Dave. We had a record contract pending. It hurt my relationship with Dave for years to come.

Bob Parsons out of Logan was hired to replace Dave.

Even though we signed the contract for the album in Muscle Shoals, we were a little disappointed that we weren't going to Nashville. We understood the great history of Muscle Shoals, but Nashville was our goal. That's where all the big country acts came through.

Before we left, we signed Richard Obits as our manager. He also managed Don McLean of *American Pie* fame. We then signed an exclusive contract with Mike Sullivan as our booking agent. Mike was out of Salt Lake City.

Ten percent was the average pay to management. That sounds like a lot until you realize we were paying ten percent to Mike *and* ten percent to Richard for a combined twenty percent.

That was tough, but it seemed worth it as we were booking gigs with better money.

We were booked to open for Freddy Fender in Muskogee, Oklahoma then we would back him on stage. To prepare for the gig, Freddy's people sent us rehearsal tapes so we could learn the music beforehand.

After we signed the various contracts, our benefactor, Ann Van Meeteron, took us to the Ogden City Country Club.

Ann insisted our wives and girlfriends couldn't come. While it irked us, we all wanted to see the country club which was a high-end affair.

"These are my boys," Ann said, bragging to her wealthy friends.

I ordered blue cheese steak. I think the entire band did, as well. It was the first time I had it and it appeared like a top shelf thing to order. There were bottles of champagne on the table.

We lived it up at dinner.

When the bus dropped me off at home, I got an earful from Becky. She was hurt about not being included and I couldn't blame her.

At the start of the tour, the band met in the Bigfoot's parking lot.

We had a series of gigs booked on the way to Muscle Shoals.

The rehearsal tapes from Freddy Fender were in Al's suitcase. We loaded our gear and packed our suitcases.

The last person on was Tommy Taylor. He didn't close the luggage door after he loaded his suitcases. We circled the Bigfoot's parking lot and headed to the freeway. Someone honked at us excitedly before we got on the interstate, signaling us that there was a problem. We pulled off to the side of the road to discover the luggage door was open.

We didn't hang around long enough to see if anything was missing. We shut the door and headed out. In Pocatello, we found Al's suitcase was missing along with Freddy Fender's rehearsal tapes.

Al's wife, Jeannie, drove to Pocatello and brought him new clothes, but the tapes were lost.

We arrived in Pocatello, Idaho to play The Green Triangle. The second night there, a couple large ladies, one white and one black, decided they wanted to double team me. Each of the gals had to weigh 300 pounds while I barely hit 145 on the scale.

They gave me some coke to get me involved in a conversation.

Their shtick had a bunch of 'white boy' references along with the sexual favors they promised to deliver.

I told them I'd go home with them if they got me a ½ gram more of coke. They left after that and I thought I was safe. Shortly after we finished playing for the night, they returned with that ½ gram.

I told them a deal was a deal and took the coke. "I'll be back," I said and headed for the restroom. Then I snuck out the back and left the club.

I'm lucky they didn't come back another night and kick my ass.

Becky drove up from Utah with our son, Cory. Erin was at her grandma's house.

We celebrated Becky's birthday at a local park. We had a picnic and watched Cory play. The three of us napped on a blanket in the sun. I was going to be gone for a few weeks so we tried to connect as much as we could in that short amount of time. It was a great three hours.

Back at the club, I kissed Becky goodbye before she drove away towards Ogden. Cory strained to turn around in his car seat to wave good-bye.

That moment hurt.

After the Saturday night gig in Pocatello, we packed our gear and drove straight through to Alabama, stopping only for gas. We had to be in Muscle Shoals on Monday afternoon.

It was August and the entire band was crammed into a bus for twenty-nine hours without air-conditioning. We were on our way to the hot and humid south.

As you can imagine, that bus was in some sad and funky shape by the time we got there.

Before the recording session, the album's producer brought in some studio guys on stand-by in case the rest of the band wasn't good enough. The producer knew they liked Al's voice, but the rest of the band was a wild card.

We set up in the studio and started playing. A bit later, the producer came by and said, "Okay, I've told the studio guys we don't need them. You guys are good enough."

This was a big deal to us. It meant we belonged there.

We recorded all our originals in three days.

After we recorded our songs, we went to Muskogee to play the show with Freddy Fender.

On August 20th, we pulled into the hotel, signed into our rooms and started unpacking. A few minutes later, Greg walked in.

"Pack up. They've got rooms for us with Freddy."

We had been booked into a nicer hotel, the Holiday Inn, along with our headliner, Freddy fucking Fender! The marquee sign read, *Welcome Freddy Fender and band, Hotspurz.*

Our collective dread was now palpable since we had never gotten the rehearsal tapes to prepare for Freddy.

The next morning, we headed to the Muskogee Civic Auditorium. The auditorium held 10,000 people and the show was sold out. It was by far the largest audience I had ever played for to date. It was also my third wedding anniversary with Becky.

Right before show time, Freddy Fender arrived.

Supposedly, he had plane trouble. We told him we never got his tapes which displeased him. Freddy was a professional and took it in stride. He laid out the song list and broke them all down. He told us the key every song was in.

He said to me, "Drummer, I want you to do this on this song," and explained how I was to play. He wanted to start with *Got My Mojo Working*, an old Muddy Waters tune.

It was ten minutes of sheer cramming.

We hit the stage as Hotspurz.

There was a big curtain at the front of the stage. It opened and the spotlight hit me. I stood and clicked my sticks with Al on rhythm guitar. The crowd roared and their energy flooded over me. We opened with *The Highway Home* by Earl Thomas Conley.

Our opening set was killer. We did some of our original stuff as well as some covers. We played for ninety minutes. That gave Freddy plenty of time to snort some cocaine and drink some Miller Lite, his favorite beer. When the curtain closed, we hurried off the stage.

We thought they were going to introduce Freddy by himself, but they wanted us back on stage. We started playing, then Freddy came out and we rolled into the set list.

I'll tell you that guy could play guitar. He was really good. Al sang backup to him.

We did a good show. We finished with *Wasted Days and Wasted Nights*. I don't think anyone in the crowd ever realized that we hadn't rehearsed.

When the show was over, Freddy immediately left. He wasn't that friendly of a guy.

Afterwards, we hung around and signed autographs at the edge of the stage.

In the dressing room, a promoter asked us, "Do you guys have what you need? Do you need some drugs? Want girls? Want boys? Anything you want, we'll get it for you."

He looked my way. I said, "I've got Jack Daniels and beer, I'm good."

We hung in the dressing room and did some interviews for the local paper.

Freddy's management stopped by the dressing room. "Freddy liked you. What's better is Freddy's wife liked you."

We looked at each other and smiled.

"You guys might get some more gigs out of this."

Back at the hotel, a country band played in the bar. When we walked in, the place went silent. The poor band on stage practically froze. Everyone knew we were Freddy Fender's band and that night we were big time.

We took a table and the bar gave us free drinks. Later, the band asked us to play with them. They were decent musicians and it turned into a nice jam session.

We hung there the rest of the night until the bar closed.

Afterwards, the hotel moved our party into the pool area and closed it off for "Fender's band and friends." There was a pass-through window from the bar so they continued service after hours. Many people hung around – promoters, coliseum workers, and, of course, women. I never went near the women.

Greg Clary wore snake skin boots along with a big, fancy watch. He got so drunk that he dove, completely clothed, off the diving board into the pool. It ruined his watch, but he didn't care. We were having the time of our lives.

In the morning, the check for our performance was supposed to be delivered to the hotel, but it didn't arrive. We phoned the promoters and were told they couldn't get the money to us until the next day. They comp'd us another night at the hotel, but by then the "rock star in a small town" act wasn't as fun.

Bob Parsons, Greg Clary and I walked across the parking lot and saw a movie. When we came back from the movie, we saw that someone had written on the back of our dirty tour bus window, *Muskogee wants to get in Hotspurz pants.*

The second morning, we got the check and headed to our next gig at the 40 & Plum Club. It was a shitty club and couldn't compare to playing a coliseum with Freddy Fender.

We stopped in Tulsa, Oklahoma to see Randy Gibson, the original pedal steel player for Hotspurz. He was doing some session work at Long Branch Studios.

While we were there, Stuart Copeland of The Police was recording the movie soundtrack for *Rumble Fish*. After introductions, he came off as an asshole, but in fairness he was preoccupied and didn't know us. We were simply an interruption to his work.

We moved on, working our way home by performing different gigs.

The Ogden Standard-Examiner, the local paper, wrote an article about us. Basically, it was "hometown boys make good" type of stuff.

Mike Sullivan, our booking agent, called us to his office for a scheduled a call with Richard Obits, our manager.

The band crowded around Mike's desk as he put Richard on the speaker phone.

"I think you boys did a good job for us," Richard said. "Freddy really liked you."

We all murmured some bullshit and Richard continued.

"You're going to get more shows backing Freddy. I'm going to let Mike handle the details. Keep up the good work."

Click. The call went dead.

We looked at each other and then to Mike.

And like that, we were playing with Freddy Fender.

We were in Boise for a gig when we met Maureen.

She was an interesting chick, in that she liked everybody in the band. She offered to give me a blowjob, but I declined.

Later, I walked into one of our rooms and saw her sandwiched between a couple guys. One guy was taking her from behind and the other was on his knees, getting a blowjob from her. They both had a beer in one hand and a cigar in the other.

I said, "I'll be back" and ran to get my camera. When I returned, they didn't stop.

One of them told her to "hold still" and they both put their beers on her back. They posed for the camera, blowing smoke to the ceiling. All three of them laughed after I took the picture. I left them to their business and returned to my room.

After it was developed, I quickly got rid of that picture.

I never wanted it discovered by Becky, or anyone else for that matter.

Outside Odessa, Texas, our bus met up with Willie Nelson's tour buses. We, as Freddy Fender's band, were going to open for Willie in Austin.

Quickly, all the buses pulled over and golf clubs were hauled out. Greg, Al, Bob and I were golfers and had brought our clubs along on the tour.

Willie led the group in hitting golf balls into the scrub brush. While some of the guys hit, the others smoked joints and drank beer. It was a great time on the side of the road. Eventually, everyone took a break from swinging clubs.

Willie sat on a lawn chair next to his bus, covered by the shade. I was a few people away from Willie.

Ray, our light man, suddenly ran off to shag the golf balls. Those balls were 200 to 300 yards out in the scrub grass.

Willie yelled, "Son! Son!" Not getting a response from Ray, Willie looked at me. "What's his name?"

"Ray," I said.

Willie yelled, "Ray! Ray! Son, you don't want to be doing that."

Ray finally stopped and listened to Willie.

"Son, there are snakes out there."

We all laughed.

Ray was frozen from fear. He couldn't move.

How did we come to his rescue?

We hit golf balls at him, of course.

Ray was forced to dodge balls and snakes as he ran back to the safety of the buses. He was pissed when he made it to the asphalt, but we probably saved his life. Texas is home to eleven different types of venomous snakes.

Back on the road, the antics of our keyboardist, Tommy Taylor, were wearing thin on the band.

He always tried to play practical jokes on Al, who was a jumpy son of a bitch. If someone dropped a book on a floor, Al would jump and raise his fists, ready to fight. He was real twitchy.

In October of '83, while we were in Bozeman, Montana, Tommy spent an afternoon wiring some firecrackers underneath the driver's seat of the band's bus. He wired the firecrackers into the ignition switch so when the key turned, they would light off. Al was our normal driver.

"Knock it off, Tommy," I said. "You'll give Al a heart attack."

He ignored my warning, so I got the rest of the band in on it. "If you don't tell Al, we will, and he'll kick your ass" was the general message.

Before we left for the next gig, Tommy got in the driver's seat and set the fireworks off, revealing his prank to Al.

"You are *so* lucky," Al said, "I'll break your face if you do something like that again."

We arrived for our next gig in Evergreen, Colorado the night before Halloween.

The club we were playing was having a costume party. None of us dressed up except Tommy. He wore a complete ninja outfit. I think that strange duck wanted to be one.

Tommy sat at the bar all night. He didn't drink. He didn't talk to girls. He just played ninja.

Heading back to the bus, Tommy made the announcement, "I'm going to find my own way back." We watched in disbelief as that 5'6 ninja snuck off into the darkness of a Colorado night.

I had to share a room with Tommy at this time because he and I were the only non-smokers. That crazy bastard put nunchucks above his bed and practiced how quickly he could jump out of bed and start swinging those things.

One afternoon, I woke from a nap to a strange, swooshing sound.

Tommy had drawn a target on a piece of paper and taped it to the wall. He was on the other side of his bed, with a blow gun, shooting darts across my bed, above my sleeping body.

After every gig that week in Evergreen, he'd come back to the room, put on his ninja outfit and disappear into the night.

Like I said, he was strange.

On Halloween night, the band kicked ass and the crowd dug us.

During our break, a square looking guy brought up this big, dorky jock. He was in a yellow sweater and Dockers pants.

After he introduced himself, the guy announced his friend as Denver Broncos quarterback John Elway, who was the number one draft pick that year. After a tough start to the season, Elway was benched earlier in the month. Everyone knows where his career went after that.

John Elway wanted to meet the band. He shook our hands, said a few pleasantries, and then moved on. He was polite and seemed nice.

On our last Saturday afternoon there, Tommy found a costume store where he bought a $200 full-head bat mask. Apparently, he was tired of being a ninja.

The mask had big ears and was scary. I couldn't believe the price of it.

Tommy put the mask on, entered Al's room and hid behind the door. Before our gig, Al walked in and Tommy jumped out, scaring him. In frightened response, Al punched Tommy in the face, through the mask. He broke Tommy's nose, causing him to bleed profusely.

"You stupid asshole," Al said, "What did you expect?"

Tommy stuffed toilet paper in his nose to stop the bleeding. He pouted throughout that night's show with his swollen, red nose.

It served him right. Al had threatened to break his face if he continued to pull those antics.

As we packed the gear on the bus, Tommy left the book he was reading, *The Anarchist's Cookbook,* on top of some equipment. I picked it up and flipped through it. It was a book about manufacturing homemade explosives and drugs like LSD. Tommy ran the length of the bus, snatched it from my hands and pushed me away.

"Don't you ever touch this again. This is private property."

The band saw his act. I stared at him in disbelief.

When we got back to Ogden, we immediately fired Tommy and hired Joe Webber out of Grand Junction, Colorado to replace him. He was a nice, mellow guy and the antithesis of Tommy.

Richard Obits received a call from the producers in Muscle Shoals. They didn't feel the songs we recorded were strong enough for an album release. They wanted us back to record some different tunes penned by Nashville songwriters. Of course, we didn't like that idea. They sent Richard some tapes which included a song titled *Band of Gold* to be our single.

In hindsight, we should have been enthusiastic about it, but we weren't. We were naïve.

Our agents lined up a bunch of gigs for us to work our way back to Muscle Shoals.

We were scheduled for two weeks in Longview, Texas at a hotel lounge. After that gig, our next stop would be Muscle Shoals.

One night during the Longview gig, we opened for John Anderson, who was a big act at the time. This was more of a rehearsal gig for him than anything else. John was so drunk he could barely stand. Also, his band didn't give a shit about anything. It was a dysfunctional night. They played poorly and didn't interact with the audience.

We thought he was big stuff back then.

It turned out to be disappointing.

After another show, we all got drunk in our room and then high on hash.

It was a sophomoric tradition in the band to light our farts. We were always doing it.

Al was lounging around in his robe when he decided to light one. He opened his robe, exposing himself to the band. He spread his legs, ignited a lighter below his ass and farted.

Man-scaping wasn't in vogue back then, so his entire crotch went up in flames.

Al jumped off his chair, screaming in pain and slapping at the fire around his man parts.

After the flames were out, Joe Webber calmly filled two glasses at the sink. He walked over and threw the water on Al.

Richard Obits came into Longview to see our show.

He complimented us by saying we sounded great and then dropped a bombshell. "We can get more recording time if we fly."

For a moment, we all got excited.

"But I'm just going to fly Al," Richard said. "We'll use their studio cats for the recording."

Richard could see the confusion on our faces. "It's not because I don't think you boys aren't good, but we can get more recording time in and it's too expensive to fly you all."

It was clear what he wanted. Looking back, Al could have dumped the rest of us and probably gone on his way to fame and fortune.

After the gig in Longview, Al flew to Muscle Shoals and recorded the tapes. The rest of us returned to Utah.

When Al arrived back in Ogden, he said, "This is not working. Richard's not promoting us and the album is never going to happen."

What he was saying was true. All we were getting from Richard were bills.

Our contract expired with Richard and we didn't renew with him.

To Al's credit, he didn't dump us to be famous on his own, which he certainly could have.

The guy was that good.

Financially, Becky and I were still struggling.

Becky was working at Albertson's as a bookkeeper and I was on the road. We were having a tough time making ends meet. We had a discussion and it was decided that she would move to Spokane again. Mom said she'd let Becky move in with the kids. Since I was mostly on the road, I'd stay with my brother in his apartment as he'd recently moved to Ogden. I ended up sleeping on the floor at Chuck's.

Hotspurz got a house gig at the Westerner, playing Tuesday through Saturday. It had a big, movable stage. On weekends, the club rolled the stage back to the dressing room to allow for more seating. Tuesday through Thursday, the club moved the stage forward to make it more intimate.

We were playing a gig at The Westerner when the guys from the band Alabama walked in. The crowd immediately got excited – why wouldn't they? They were huge stars, but we had met them a week prior.

They were on a mid-tour break and had been partying at Bear Lake, just east of Logan, Utah. We had a gig up there and they came into that show. We talked with them that night and invited them to The Westerner, not really thinking they'd show up.

After our gig was over, Mark Herndon, the drummer for Alabama, invited me back to his bus. They were on their "Roll On" tour and each of the bandmates had their own bus. That's success! Several other people were on Mark's bus, but I can't remember if any of the other bandmembers were there. All I remember was how hard we partied.

When the sun finally came up, I stumbled off the bus to see a group of fans still lingering around. I walked across the parking lot, crawled into my car and slept, or at least tried to with the sun baking down on the roof. When I finally gave up, I drove back to Ogden and slept on the floor of my brother's apartment.

Hotspurz took a two-week road trip – one week in Gillette, WY and the second in Rapid City, SD. We played Boot Hill Saloons in both places.

In Gillette, it snowed so hard they closed the club early and announced they weren't going to open the next day.

We were all cranky at the announcement and headed to our rooms. I helped Al carry his guitars off the bus and our soundman, Chad, was behind me carrying Greg's bass.

When I passed through the bus's door, it swung shut on Chad and it pissed him off. He thought I did it on purpose and he bitched at me for it.

As we walked into the band house, a split level, I climbed the stairs to the main level and Chad shoved that bass guitar case into my ass. It hurt like hell. I spun around, put my foot on his chest and shoved him into Greg.

Al was on the main floor and shouted, "You two knock it off."

I got to the top of the stairs, put down Al's guitar and turned around in time for Chad to clear the entryway. I grabbed him by the shoulders and shoved him out of the way.

Chad said, "You think you're bad? Fuck you."

He rushed me and I punched him in the throat. He fell into a chair and it tipped backwards.

Al grabbed me. "Enough!"

Chad stood and rushed me again. I hit him in the forehead and hurt my hand. That took the fight out of both of us and things calmed down.

An hour or so later, we forgave each other and forgot the fight by getting drunk together.

In Rapid City, the Boot Hill Saloon was in a Victorian style venue. The outside was nice, but the inside was a beat-up bar.

Before a gig, my tradition was to call Becky. As was common now, the conversation was stilted.

As our talk ended, I said, "Well, I love you."

Becky didn't reply.

"I need you," I said.

Becky was quiet another moment before I could hear her crying over the phone. "I'm not sure I love you anymore."

That devastated me.

I struggled to end that conversation by saying our good-byes and asking her to give my love to the kids.

The band had already left our hotel for the gig. I ran several blocks to the saloon. I played the show with my sunglasses on, crying periodically through the night.

It was ugly.

Our next show was in Laramie, Wyoming. On one of our breaks, I called Becky. I was in the early stages of strep throat which added to my woes.

Becky and I argued on the phone about the same old shit – money, the distance between us, and being lonely. The conversation put me in a foul mood as I went to the dressing room.

The band was snorting coke and having a great time. All I wanted was to be with Becky and the kids.

I headed to the men's room to be alone. Inside the restroom, five cowboys decided to give me shit. I had long hair and a feathered earring.

The shortest cowboy had the biggest mouth. "Look at the faggot," he said.

I patted him on the cheek and said, "My wife and kids don't think I'm a faggot."

I pushed my way past him to the door. He punched me in the back of the head and I went stumbling out. I turned around as the little guy approached, his fists balled. I had my cowboy boots on and I kicked him in the nuts as hard as I could.

The little cowboy crumbled to the floor.

I ran as his friends came around him. I made it to the front of the main room where the pool tables were. I grabbed a pool cue off a table and wildly swung it around. I hit one of the cowboys in the shoulder and broke the cue. He went to the ground. I reached for a chair and was knocked to the floor by the three other guys. They proceeded to kick the shit out of me.

I covered my head and face. They beat me and yanked my hair.

Someone yelled, "They're killing the drummer!"

Greg and Al, who were big guys, came to my rescue and threw the cowboys off me. When the fight finally ended, the bar kicked the five guys out.

I didn't want to press charges against them. I only wanted to be left alone, but I had to get back on stage and perform. My hair fell out in clumps from the fight. I'd see it on my drums as I played. It was horrible.

On that last night in Laramie, I played four hours, with bruises forming everywhere and my illness increasing in intensity.

I woke the next morning with full blown strep throat. I loaded up on Nyquil and boarded the bus.

I wanted to go home, but I couldn't. We had several more weeks to go on the tour, including many shows with Freddy Fender. I fought through the strep throat and turned to cocaine and booze to help deal with the hurt of Becky saying she didn't love me anymore.

On an earlier trip to visit Becky, we had a particularly rough fight where the conversation turned to our marriage not making it. Becky said no matter what happened to us she would make sure I always had access to the kids. Those words haunted me while on the road.

I wanted Becky and the kids back, but I didn't know how to do it.

The road was my mistress and she kept getting in the way.

As we rolled along Interstate 80, I awoke early one morning on our tour bus. It was quiet as everyone was asleep except our driver. I quietly walked until I got to the front of the bus and eased myself into the "jump" or passenger seat.

Through the large windows of the tour bus, I saw the most remarkable sunset I'd ever seen in my life. There were purples, pinks, yellows, and browns. The front windows of the bus wrapped around us from driver side to passenger side.

"Amazing, huh?" the driver asked.

I nodded and continued studying that wonderful sight.

When we stopped, I phoned Becky, even though we were fighting. "I have to tell you about this sunset I saw."

She was happy for me and listened to how excited I was. I wanted to share that moment with her, even though we were miles apart both geographically and emotionally.

That view is still in my mind all these years later.

In all, we played roughly thirty-five shows backing Freddy Fender. The venues were a mix of large bars, motorcycle shows, county fairs and some concert venues. We played across Texas in cities like Odessa and Austin. We even made it as far east as Alabama. We mixed them in with our own Hotspurz gigs.

Freddy flew directly to where the shows were. He never traveled on the bus with us.

We didn't get paid much for the gigs. To make matters worse, there was 20% off the top for Richard Obits and Mike Sullivan. Even though we had fired him, we still owed Richard his 10% for shows he had previously booked with Mike.

Out of the remaining receipts there were costs of the bus and driver we hired while touring with Freddy.

We were now big time, but we weren't making any money.

We'd roll in, set up our gear, and then do the show.

All the while, I'd do a bunch of coke to keep myself as high as possible. Even though I was broke, there was always cocaine around. I never paid for it. Our hangers-on provided it for us.

I quit taking pictures around this time which is a shame. I previously took a slew of them, wherever we went. This was one of the darkest periods of my life.

I'd like to share some of the more interesting shows with you, but I simply can't remember much.

I do have a random memory of Hotspurz opening for Tammy Wynette during this cocaine phase. All I remember of it is her walking backstage and saying, "My lord, you boys sure have a whole lotta hair, now don't ya?"

Tammy Wynette dropped by to say hi and that's all I can remember. Shit.

I missed my family, but I was in a fog. I communicated less and less with them as I hurt more and more. It was a hellish spiral.

The guys were worried about me since I was amped all the time on cocaine. It was a three-month blur. We finally "made it," but I really don't remember much about those gigs. It's a fucking shame.

After we finished playing with Freddy, we used "Freddy Fender's band" in some promotional materials. We got a call from Freddy's management that we needed to knock it off or they wanted a cut.

We got back to Ogden and had a couple days off. During a phone call home, my little Cory said, "Daddy, I don't like Rick."

When Becky got back on the phone, I said, "Who's Rick?"

"He's just a friend."

I never let myself imagine Becky going out while I wasn't around. I didn't want to go too far down that path then and I still don't know. I never slept with anyone after we were married. I might have partied with them and there was plenty of opportunity, but I never did anything I would regret.

I immediately flew home to Spokane.

I didn't have much money, but I made it happen.

My sister, Carol, picked me up at the airport and took me to mom's house.

Mom said, "Let me fix you something to eat."

"I need to go see Becky."

"At least, have a glass a milk," mom said.

Becky now worked as a machine operator at Keytronic, a manufacturing plant.

I took mom's car and showed up at her work. She was stunned to see me walk in.

"Call me when you get off," I told Becky. "I'll be at mom's house."

I went to Cory's daycare. When he saw me, he stood, walked over, lifted his arms and started crying. I picked him up and cried with him.

We went to Erin's school. When she saw me, she ran over. "Daddy!" she exclaimed and jumped in my arms.

The three of us went to mom's house.

Becky had left a message that she was so upset by my coming to her work that she had gone home for the day.

I drove to north Spokane and the trailer she had moved into. It was a horrible realization that we were living separate lives.

We had it out.

She didn't want us to split and she wanted her husband back.

We weren't sure where it would go, but we wanted to try to keep our family together.

We got the kids from mom and drove back to Becky's place. I left her trailer and sat in the car. I watched Becky and our kids move about inside. I bawled.

In the pursuit of my music career, what had I done?

Had I sacrificed my family and the woman I claimed to love?

I woke in the morning and went back to Utah because we had more gigs scheduled.

Hotspurz continued to play the Westerner for a few weeks.

While that was going on, Becky and I talked on the phone daily. Our conversations were getting warmer. I talked with the kids. I promised her that I would quit Hotspurz and come home. It took five weeks of talking before Becky wanted me to move back in with her.

I was ready to announce I was leaving the band.

The band was at the Westerner for rehearsal.

"Guys, we need to talk," I said.

There were several girls around. Everyone was confused when I said, "I need them to leave," motioning to the girls. The guys hustled their female friends out.

"I need to do it," I said.

Al asked, "You're getting a divorce?"

"No, my family means too much. I'm going back to Spokane. Becky will be here Sunday to drive me home."

The guys were pissed.

Then the girls came back in. A couple of them started crying. One of them said, "The band is breaking up."

We played out the week and the guys brought in drummers to audition. Becky arrived Saturday and came to my final show with Hotspurz. She took pictures of us in the dressing room. No one looked happy in those photos.

After the gig, we loaded the car and headed back to Spokane.

It was sad leaving Hotspurz.

It was the biggest success I had had in my musical career. I loved those guys and we had such high hopes.

It's hard to admit I fucked up my marriage over drugs and the blind pursuit of my music career. It's true that cocaine had a hold on me, but I didn't screw around on Becky. I only partied.

Poor decisions on both Becky's and my parts had led to serious marriage troubles.

TOO SLIM
AND THE
TAILDRAGGERS
1985-1987

(Rear L-R) Tom Brimm, Greg Pendleton, Norm Bellis, me
(Front L-R) Bo Diddley and Tim "Too Slim" Langford

By early spring of '84, Becky and I were back in Spokane.

I cut my hair and went to work for the Off-Broadway Bakery. That was a shitty job.

I worked from 6 a.m.-2 p.m., Monday through Friday for $6/hour. To make matters worse, my baking skills had gone to hell.

Before long an ad caught my eye for a baker in Okanogan, Washington which is three hours north of Spokane and in the middle of the state. In other words, it is Bumfuck, Egypt.

The job was at The Okanogan Food Depot, a supermarket bakery and the starting wage was $11/hour. I answered the ad and got an interview.

The owner of the grocery store took Becky and me to dinner. As an incentive for the job, he offered to pay our moving expenses and buy Becky an appliance of her choice.

I accepted the job offer, figuring it would help us get our marriage together.

Before moving, we went to Sears and Becky bought the most expensive refrigerator she could find.

The job with Food Depot was a bad experience as far as jobs go. The manager was a volatile man. He was an ex-boxer who liked to intimidate his employees. He didn't like me and resented the wage I was paid. I lost a lot of weight due to the long hours and work stress.

Becky and I continued to struggle. We still fought, but we found some happy times together again. We had always loved each other, but we had stopped respecting each other. We worked on that and found our way back as a couple.

On New Year's Eve 1984, Becky and I went to a club in Omak, a small town near Okanogan, to see a rock band out of Spokane. They performed songs by bands like Huey Lewis and the News, The Romantics and Bruce Springsteen. They asked me to get on stage and jam.

One of the members pulled me aside, "We're thinking about hiring a new drummer. Let us know if you come back to Spokane." That got my juices flowing again. I hadn't played since I left Hotspurz.

After some reflection, Becky and I decided to return to Spokane so I could take a job with Pie Time, a start-up pie bakery. Dave Low, my friend and former bandmate from Raven, had referred his younger brother, Dale Low, my direction. Dale had a start-up venture manufacturing and distributing pies. He needed someone to run the operation.

Even though the money was horrible, I wouldn't be baking. I would handle the business side of things.

The band that I played with in Omak broke up before I ever got a chance to join them.

Money was awfully tight again, but we were doing well as a family and that's what I was focusing on.

Sadly, Dale Low drowned while hunting. It was a shame since he had just had a baby girl.

With Dale's passing, Pie Time came under new ownership and they quickly decided I wasn't needed. The final straw was when my brother came to town with his fiancé. We all went to a bar and got obliterated. I had to work the next day but went full throttle through the night.

The next morning, I was so hung-over I laid on my office floor. I reeked of alcohol but told my new employers I had the flu.

Three days later, they let me go.

I didn't have a job or a band.

Things quickly turned around.

My sister, Laurie, and her husband moved to Seattle. They let Becky and me move into their mobile home at a reduced rent.

I then got a job at Music World running their drum department. It was a commission-based job. Some months I made good money while others were tight.

To help make ends meet, I filled in occasionally with a band, Buckshot. They were around when I was in The Stone Johnny Mountain Band. Buckshot had a house gig at the Cotton Club in Hayden, Idaho for two nights a week.

Raz, a Top 40 cover band, put an ad in the newspaper looking for a drummer.

They had a six-week gig at The Pine Shed in Spokane. I had to audition for them, which didn't make me happy, but I got the gig.

It was a five-night a week gig and it paid well. Plus, it allowed me to still work at Music World.

Raz played Top 40 stuff from bands like Billy Ocean and Kenny Loggins. Some of it was fun to play. The guitarist for the band, Mark Gilmore, was very talented.

The Pine Shed's stage was wide, but not deep. My drum kit sat off to one side while the rest of the band was lined up at the front of the stage.

People could climb on the railing of the stage and look into my face as I played. That normally didn't happen at other venues.

A lot of cocaine was used and dealt out of The Pine Shed. It wasn't a secret, by any means. We were all doing it back then.

There was a stout waitress working at The Pine Shed who liked me. She wasn't fat, but she could have played fullback on a high school team. I think she had a thing for drummers. The drummer from the previous band that had played the venue said he was fucking her the entire time they were at the club.

We were playing one Friday night when the waitress asked if I wanted to do some coke.

"My best bud will set us up. He's outside."

I went out to the parking lot with her to meet her friend and dealer. Spokane is a small town at times and her dealer was an old friend of mine from high school. We exchanged some quick pleasantries, did some cocaine, and then I headed back in for the next set.

My old friend later came inside the Pine Shed while we played. He enjoyed our music and I could tell he was having a good time. While we were in the middle of a song, he leaned over the railing, in front of my drum kit, so he could yell into my face.

"Want to do some more?"

"Hell yeah!" I yelled while I pounded my drums.

"Come outside on your next break!"

"Ok!"

He walked out of the club and I continued to play, already thinking about the next bump.

When Raz ended our set, I headed for the exit. I yanked open the door and saw police cars with their lights flashing in the parking lot. My old friend was bent over the hood of a police car with his hands behind his back.

I closed the door and remained inside the club. *Just like Colville*, I thought, realizing I had dodged another bullet.

My old friend would later go to federal prison for five years for trafficking in cocaine.

At the end of the six-week gig, Becky and my sister, Carol, came to The Pine Shed to watch me play.

After the show, I loaded my drum kit into a bandmate's car while Becky and Carol waited nearby in the parking lot.

Ms. Fullback Waitress suddenly burst from The Pine Shed and ran over. She wrapped her arms and a leg around me and planted a kiss on my lips. I turned my head and tried pushing her off, but she had me in a vice-grip.

From a distance, Carol yelled, "Becky, no!" To this day, I still hear that voice.

Becky raced over and yanked the waitress off me. She threw her to the ground, bouncing her head off the pavement.

My lovely wife straddled the waitress and stuck a finger in her face. "If you ever touch my husband again, I will kill you!"

Becky got off her and the waitress stumbled back inside, crying.

We got into Carol's car and Becky gave me an earful.

"Why did you let her kiss you?" she demanded.

"I didn't!"

Carol stayed out of our quarrel as she drove.

Becky was in my ear for the twenty minutes home and then some.

Raz was booked to play a wedding in St. Maries, Idaho.

Mark Gilmore, our guitarist, got lost on his way to the gig and stopped at a tavern to ask directions. Mark, who is African American, was harassed by some of the local rednecks. In an area of the country that was once the headquarters for the Aryan Nations, those assholes scared the shit out of him.

When he arrived at the wedding, he looked shell-shocked.

It really affected him and with good reason.

After we ended our tenure with The Pine Shed, we played at a lounge located inside a Chinese Restaurant in Airway Heights. We had to play quietly due to the restaurant. It was a shitty gig.

Mark wasn't the same following the redneck incident in St. Maries. He was quieter and didn't laugh nearly as much as before.

In the fall of '85, a fellow drummer walked into Music World. With him was a guy in a black leather jacket and a black stocking cap pulled over his ears.

The fellow drummer introduced his friend as Tim Langford who previously played in The Studebakers. The other drummer left quickly after the introduction, leaving Tim and I talking in the middle of the store's drum section.

"I'm putting together a power trio blues-rock band."

Tim said that Eric Lindstrom, my friend from Stone Johnny Mountain Band, was instrumental in putting us together.

"What the hell," I said, "I'll come over and play."

I brought my drums over to Tom Brimm's house who was set to be the bass player for Tim's band. I hauled my gear down to a smelly basement.

A guy stood in the corner who looked familiar.

He introduced himself as Gary Yeoman. We knew each other from high school. He said he played guitar and was an unofficial roadie for Tim and Tom.

We jammed some songs from The Fabulous Thunderbirds and George Thorogood. Then we moved to some original stuff that Tim and Tom had already written. It all clicked.

They decided I would be a good fit.

The problem was that I was still in Raz.

On the next Saturday night, Raz played the lounge and I was hassled about my volume. This was a reoccurring issue. Near me was the blanket I laid over my drums on off-nights.

"Fine," I said, making a scene by putting the blanket over me and my drums. I proceeded to play along with the band. I couldn't see anyone, and it muffled all my cymbals. I was a complete ass.

At the end of that set, I climbed out from under the blanket and said, "That's it. I don't need this shit."

I used that moment as my "excuse" to quit Raz. I chose a chickenshit way out of instead of being a professional.

Too Slim and the Taildraggers started rehearsing in October 1985.

The original line-up was Tim Langford on lead guitar and Tom Brimm on bass. Tim handled the lead vocals.

Tim had named the band from the start. I always thought it sounded more like a country band than a blues band, but what did I know?

Our first gig was at a local bar, The Armadillo, during January '86. We played four weekends in a row.

Then we got additional gigs at Red Lion BBQ and Ahab's Whale.

We also booked some gigs out of town and I had to make a choice.

I was still commission-based at Music World and Too Slim was starting to make a little money. I opted to quit the music store. Becky was working as a bookkeeper at Valley Food Market so we got by.

The band got some decent press when we opened at Ahab's Whale for the famous blue guitarist, Mighty Joe Young.

By then Becky was pregnant with our second son, Casey.

Hotspurz had a "reunion" concert in Salt Lake City at the Westerner.

Al Bevin was retiring and moving to Florida since he and his wife had gotten back together.

Bob Parsons was also retiring. He had always hated being on the road.

After this, the band was retiring the name Hotspurz.

Becky and I flew to Salt Lake City for the show.

Cordell Baird was there. He had played guitar with them before I joined the group, but he had also been in my band, Secrets. Sometimes the music business can be very incestuous.

Randy Gibson, the original pedal steel player for the band, showed up for the event.

I had a chance to meet the drummer who replaced me, Grady Whitfield. He seemed like a decent guy.

With Al and Bob retiring, the remaining guys were going to reassemble under a different name and hire Blake Gardner and Ted Dussor. Both could play and sing well.

I wonder now if it was the right thing to say, but I leaned over to Joe Webber and said, "If you ever need a drummer, you call me. I would love to come back."

It felt so good to be around those guys.

Back in Spokane, Too Slim and the Taildraggers opened for Robert Cray at Ahab's Whale. I wasn't a big fan of Robert's before I met him because he always sounded in control and never let loose. Don't get me wrong, the guy was talented, but he didn't unleash when he played to suit my taste. Upon meeting him, my impression completely changed.

After the show, we went into the bar's office and hung out, drinking beers. Robert liked us and was complimentary.

"I'm excited about the things that are happening for us," he said. He included his band in his success. He was humble and a genuinely nice guy.

Six months later, Robert Cray was on the cover of *Rolling Stone* with the caption, "The Blues are Back and He's the Boss."

Our next notable show was playing with Bo Diddley at Ahab's Whale.

Prior to the show, I had back surgery. My back had been messed up from the days when I worked at 7-Up/Dr. Pepper. For a couple weeks, the band brought in a substitute drummer, but I wasn't going to miss playing with Bo Diddley.

For the show, we brought in Norm Bellis on keyboards.

Bo came straight from the airport to the venue. Prior to the show, we sat around the stage to rehearse. He pulled up a chair and plugged his square guitar into an amplifier. He played a riff and then would point at one of us to play a solo.

We did that for a bit and then he stopped us.

He said, "This is how we are going to end each song." He played a triplet type of chord progression. Bo would end all songs by that signal whenever he got tired or wanted to move on.

Bo also didn't want me to play the "Bo Diddley beat." He wanted me to play a straight 4/4 time and stay off the ride cymbal.

I still had staples in my back from the surgery and was on pain killers. The prescription drugs made me sleepy, so I snorted some cocaine. I had mostly stopped doing coke by this time as the thrill was gone. However, I figured I needed the bump to keep me up for the show.

The gig went great and the venue was packed with people wall-to-wall.

There was some excited talk about Bo taking us to Europe as his back-up band. Due to my age and experience, I was cautious and more mature about conversations like this.

Still, I couldn't shake the thought of returning to a full-time road musician.

There were many drunken nights with Too Slim.

After one night in Missoula, Montana with a particularly dead crowd, Tom Brimm and I were at the bar inventing new drinks. We drank for free, so this is one of those games you play when money isn't an object.

The bar was mostly empty when we invented the Watusi Wombat.

It's one shot of Wild Turkey (my contribution) and Ouzo (Tom's input). We named it the Watusi Wombat because when you taste it, you move fast like you're doing the Watusi and the sound you make when you barf it up is eerily like "wombat."

It was the most disgusting drink I'd ever tasted, so naturally, we had two each.

In the Spring of '86, Too Slim and the Taildraggers returned to The Palace in Winthrop, Washington. They had played there prior to the first Bo Diddly concert without me when I was recovering from my back surgery. By then, we'd added Greg Pendleton, a saxophone player, to the Too Slim mix.

Above The Palace, there was an old hotel. Our room featured one common room with several bedrooms that spread out from there. The stove and sink didn't work in the common room. It was basically a place for us to hang out.

After our show one night, the four of us sat in the common area, drinking beer and snorting cocaine. We were joined by the then-owner of the bar.

We were involved in a rapid-fire discussion that occurs when you're on cocaine.

Someone mentioned the idea of doing a "big jam session" with local blues musicians.

That was followed by "let's put on a show."

The bar owner said he'd sponsor it.

We prattled on about it for a while until we moved on to other ideas.

A couple years later the bar owner sponsored the first blues festival in the area, the Winthrop Blues Festival '88. He would sponsor it for roughly ten years and it has since grown into the Winthrop Rhythm and Blues Festival, still an annual event today.

When Tom Brimm passed out, a cannon firing would not wake him up. One night he made the mistake of not locking his door when he blacked out. We went into his room and literally coated him head to toe in shaving cream. We pulled the covers back and covered him in the white foam.

In the morning he woke up, screaming. "You motherfuckers! You cocksuckers!"

We weren't worried as we'd all locked our doors. Tom banged away on our doors as he ran around yelling, "Don't you ever go to asleep around me, you motherfuckers!"

As a couple, Becky and I were doing much better. We managed the road trips as they were short and infrequent in comparison to previous bands.

I'd only be gone for a week then back home for six weeks.

My second son, Casey William, was born July 26, 1986. He was a great surprise. We did not plan to have another child but we were so glad that Casey came along. When he was born, it was the accumulation of all that I'd hoped for in having a family. My loving wife, my daughter and two sons while playing in a good blues band, brought a sense of contentment that had previously alluded me.

Near the end of July '86, my former manager, Jeannie Carter, died in a car accident after seeing a band play in Coeur d'Alene, Idaho.

Her funeral was the same day Becky was set to come home from the hospital with Casey.

The day was a rollercoaster of emotions.

Jeannie was an incredibly influential person in my life. If it wasn't for her, I wouldn't have moved to Utah and would never have met Becky or had my kids.

I went to her funeral in the morning. There was a laundry list of musicians in attendance, too many to list here. Once the service was done we went to a local restaurant afterwards and toasted Jeannie.

That's when I discovered Long Island Ice Teas. I had three of those suckers.

I later drove buzzed to the Valley Hospital to pick up my wife and newborn son and bring them home. I was reckless and a complete moron. That's what looking back on your life does. It points out these moments of shame.

In August, we had a weekend gig at Fizzie O'Leary's in Priest Lake, Idaho.

We played Thursday night and afterward went to a campground for the night. We drank, smoked dope and played the radio loud in our van until a park ranger told us to turn it off. The four of us bandmates slept in the van after the ranger left.

On Friday, we visited my sister, Cathy, and her husband at their house on the lake. It was a nice, hot day. We spent the day drinking beers and talking about how we were going to be rich and famous. It's crazy how many times I've had that same discussion with various bands.

That night, we played Fizzie's which billed itself as "The Home of the Slammer." Well, we pounded their namesakes during the night and got hammered.

Since Greg had his Cadillac with him, he and I decided to make the two-hour drive back to Spokane after the show.

As we walked to his car, I stepped on a broken beer bottle in my mesh shoes. I cut the shit out of my shoe and my foot. We had to go back inside the venue for a bar towel which we wrapped around my foot. I still have the scar from that cut.

Ten miles outside of Priest Lake, blue lights flashed behind us.

As Greg stopped the car, I opened my door and puked.

"Be cool, Bill," Greg said. "Be cool."

I shut my door and did my best to look sober.

A police officer walked to Greg's door and asked him to get out. A few minutes went by and the cop came to my side of the car and squatted next to my window.

He saw my bloody foot wrapped in the towel.

"We're going to have to take your friend in. Are you okay to drive?"

I nodded and smiled. "I'm great."

The cop shook his head. "No, you're not."

I stared at him. *How could he not see how perfectly okay I was?*

"Mr. Bancroft, you can go to jail with your friend," he said, "or you can go to the Newport hospital."

As drunk as I was, I easily understood my choices.

"I'll take the second option."

At the hospital, the police officer waited as they admitted me.

Trying to make polite conversation, I said, "My brother was going to be a cop, but they found out he smoked pot once."

He looked at me like I had lost my marbles. He left shortly after that and the hospital stitched up my foot.

At about 5:30 a.m., I called Becky.

"I thought you were coming home," she said.

"I was, honey, but here's the situation."

Bless her heart, Becky drove all the way to Newport and got me. Don't get me wrong, she wasn't happy.

I slept most of the day and then she drove me back to Priest Lake for Saturday's gig. Becky kept close tabs on me that night.

Greg walked in at 8:45 p.m. and we started the show. I could barely play drums since my foot was cut so deep.

Becky drove me home immediately afterwards.

There was no partying that night.

In the spring of '87, we were booked to support Bo Diddley again at The Dug-Out in Post Falls, Idaho. Several of our family members came to that show, including my sister, Carol.

Norm Bellis was on keyboards again like the first show at Ahab's.

Unfortunately, Bo's plane was late. Our fans were restless so we got onstage and played without him. Some folks left the show before Bo finally arrived around 10 p.m.

He looked terrible having just flown in from Florida. He was tired and looking old. Unlike his first show, he hardly spoke to the audience. Bo would barely sing before pointing to one of us to do a solo. He didn't do a good performance.

Many fans left in the middle of the show.

I was so disappointed.

One of Greg Pendleton's favorite statements was "I *am* the blues in Spokane."

For a sax player, he was a cocky son of a bitch and he didn't think much of me. Greg always thought I was a rocker. He continually said I didn't know how to play the blues and I generally sucked.

We were playing The Bouquet in Boise, Idaho. It was a great club with a big stage and it was usually fun to play. But this night, the crowd was small and not into us.

Greg partied hard before the show and gave me shit throughout our set. We were doing *I Got You (I Feel Good)* by James Brown when the ending of the song came around. Greg was supposed to mimic James's classic scream while I hit the drum.

Greg was so drunk he missed his cue, forcing us to continue playing. It got to be a clusterfuck of an ending. Finally, the rest of us car crashed the song to its finish.

Greg and I chipped away at each other on stage. By then, I wasn't going to take any more shit from him.

Tim told us both to, "Shut up."

When we got off stage, Greg and I moved near the bar. Greg, who is shorter than me, got in my face. Looking up at me, he said, "You stupid motherfucker. You don't know how to play the blues." He spoke so much and so fast that spittle flew in my face. "I gotta carry this whole fucking band."

"Greg," I said, "Shut up or I'm going to knock you out."

I kept repeating it as he spouted off.

"You know nothing," he said.

I smacked him in the throat and he fell to his back.

Tim immediately tackled me. We landed on a table, breaking it. I swung at him, hitting him in the shoulder. He hit me back and then held me until I regained my composure.

Greg laid on the ground. He wasn't unconscious. He was just out of it.

The bar emptied out and the manager was obviously upset about our fight. Who could blame him? The band had just brawled amongst itself in the middle of a gig.

I was so pissed that I walked the couple miles to our hotel. I didn't speak to Greg that night or the next day. Before the next gig, we shook hands and made up.

I knew that was the beginning of the end for me with Too Slim and the Taildraggers.

My former bandmate in Hotspurz, Joe Webber, called to say Grady Whitfield was leaving to join The Montana Band.

Joe asked if I wanted to rejoin the band which was under a new name, Wind Chill. It was a dorky name, but it was already decided.

Joe sent me some tapes of Wind Chill and I liked what I heard.

Becky and I talked about the opportunity. She had lost her job at Valley Food Center. To make matters worse, my sister, Laurie, and her husband were asking for more rent on the trailer. They'd let us move into it initially at a reduced rent. It was a great help, but we got comfortable with that rate and forgot that someday it might go up. After quitting my job at Music World, I wasn't making as much money as I'd hoped with Too Slim. It seemed like the chance to rejoin the former members of Hotspurz might be what we needed for a fresh start.

We decided we'd make the return trip to Utah.

I played a couple more weeks with Too Slim and the Taildraggers. I stopped by Tim's house and then Tom's and told them about my decision. They were both disappointed in my leaving, but they understood.

Greg didn't give a shit.

My departure came while Too Slim and The Taildraggers was in the process of recording, <u>Swingin' in the Underworld.</u> We'd been in the studio already and had finished about half the album. The band recut my tracks with Carmen Conti. On the album, Tim publicly thanked me for which I'm very grateful.

Too Slim and the Taildraggers went on to great success after I left. Tim and I still talk frequently and exchange emails. He's a good guy and I'm happy as hell for him.

WIND CHILL
1987-1988

(L-R) Greg Clary, Joe Webber, Ted Dussor, Blake Gardner and me

I immediately hit the road with Wind Chill in late spring 1987.

Ted Dussor sang lead vocals and played guitar. Blake Gardner and Joe Webber both played guitar and keyboards, switching duties when the song required. Greg Clary was on bass. We all provided back-up vocals.

The band later sent their bus to Spokane. They picked up Becky, the kids and our furniture and brought them back to the Salt Lake City area. She found us a house in Kearns, just outside of Salt Lake City.

Sometimes the wind changes direction and that's exactly what happened with the band before I joined them.

Things were waning at the Westerner and the guys thought the band felt stale. Greg wanted to learn a Top 40 set list and even one set of '50s music. On Wednesday nights, the band would slick their hair back for one set, put on letterman's jackets and act like a 1950's era band. They had already worked on this shtick before I arrived.

The original music we did as Hotspurz was gone. It was entirely cover music now.

I felt lost.

I thought I was returning to play original music and to stand out from the crowd, but we were firmly in the middle of the Top 40 cover pack.

We took a hotel gig in Roy, Utah which was completely current radio, young crowd territory and nothing reminiscent of a country band.

During our afternoons at the Westerner, we would rehearse Top 40 stuff. The management heard us one day and said, "What the hell are you doing?"

After that, they cancelled a few dates on us. We filled them with gigs at a couple rock clubs in Ogden, which didn't work out well.

We were confusing our fans.

Compared to other Top 40 cover bands, we weren't very good.

On July 5th, 1987, we were home and the band was set to leave that day to Gillette, Wyoming.

Becky woke me and she looked pale.

"Montana's plane crashed and everyone was killed," she said.

I sat up and she filled me in. The Montana Band had finished a 4th of July concert. The band was in a small plane that buzzed over the concert goers as it headed toward its next show. The plane crashed almost immediately in a nearby orchard killing all ten people on board.

Grady Whitfield was on the plane. He was the drummer who replaced me in Hotspurz and who I had replaced in Wind Chill. I had also known most of the guys in Montana.

The leader of our band, Blake Gardner, was especially close to Grady before I joined. I don't know if two words were said on the bus ride from Salt Lake City to Gillette. It was a horrible ride. The guys kept themselves pickled drunk.

We played the gigs which was tough.

After that, the band lost steam.

While on the road, we quit rehearsing during the day to learn new material. The other guys wanted to hang out and self-medicate.

I was sad about the guys in The Montana Band, but I didn't know them as well as my bandmates. I tried to push us to rehearse, but it wasn't well received. The band was just going through the motions.

We took a break after a while.

Joe Webber always wanted to return to Nashville so he continued to cultivate relationships there. He picked up a studio musician gig and invited me to go along. We would be paid $50 an hour to be in the studio regardless if we played. There were a couple days that we played for twelve hours straight and several days where we hung out all day and never played a note.

Musicians would come into the studio to record their demos and hand us sheet music. Joe and I, along with the other musicians, would have only a short time to get familiar with a song and then we'd lay down the track with the artist paying for our time.

We made this journey to and from Nashville several times while Wind Chill had down time.

It was a great opportunity and one I'm lucky to have experienced.

After a bit, we regrouped as a band and scheduled some new gigs. We had shows in Rapid City, SD, Gillette, WY, and Grand Junction, CO.

After our trip to Nashville, Joe and I wanted the band to return to our roots. We pushed for a band meeting while in Rapid City.

I said, "This isn't doing it for me. I quit my other band in Spokane to come back here. I thought we were going to do something original. Instead, we're doing Top 40 covers and a '50s show that we're not very good at. This has to stop."

We did some soul searching and re-dedicated ourselves to being a country band and to writing original songs.

Joe and Ted were great songwriters and we all pitched in on those efforts.

In Grand Junction, we opened for The Forester Sisters. Some folks thought we were national stars when we opened for them as a country act.

Unfortunately, the problems at home started again as the tours stretched longer and longer.

This time Becky was home with three kids. Her family and friends were in Ogden and I was gone all the time. She wanted to go to school and I wasn't around to help.

To make matters worse, the money wasn't as good as it was in the Hotspurz days.

When Wind Chill returned home in mid-August of 1988, Becky and I sat on the front porch of our house in Kearns. We had a conversation about life. She wanted to go back to school, but with three kids and me on the road she couldn't see how she could reach her goal.

She took a big breath, let out a long sigh and sobbed. Years of frustration came out in her tears. "When will it ever be enough?" she asked.

I realized that the band was essentially shuffling along and wasn't what I had dreamt about. The work on the original material had stopped and we were just playing covers again.

I thought, *Fuck it.*

I immediately went looking for work. I found a job with Condies Foods. They packaged and delivered vegetables.

I asked for two weeks before my official start date, but Condies Foods only gave me one. Wind Chill was booked for two weeks in Grand Junction, Colorado.

I promised Becky I would take the job and would leave the band in the middle of the week. I accepted the offer and the one-week lead time. I figured I couldn't tell my new employer I was in a band.

How could I quit Wind Chill?

They had only brought me on the previous year.

This was September 1988. The second week of the gig would be over my birthday.

For a long time, I had foot problems caused by my bunions. I would wrap my feet all the time. At times, it was truly difficult to play, but I would work through it.

On Tuesday night, in the middle of our third set, the pain in my feet was strong, but nothing I hadn't worked through before.

Yet, I pretended like it was much worse. I told the guys I had to stop playing after the set. I finished the songs and the guys helped me off the stage.

The crowd watched us, trying to figure out what the hell happened.

Back stage, I put my foot in a bucket of ice. I really played it up.

One of Ted's friends, a guy named Milt, was in the crowd. He was a drummer from another band. He jumped in and finished the night. Wind Chill had another week to play.

Ted's wife, Victoria, was driving back to Salt Lake City the next day. I rode back with her, crutches and all.

My tenure with Wind Chill had come to a dubious end.

Except to Becky, I have never admitted how I lied to the band that night.

Greg Clary never believed I hurt my foot and he was angry with me. It strained my relationship with him and rightly so. I had made another cowardly excuse to leave a band, and Greg saw right through me. I didn't see any of the guys for a long time. They didn't check on me and I didn't check on them.

It was a weird ending.

I went to work for Condies Foods. I drove a truck for a couple months. It wasn't good money, but at least I was home.

A new Australian bakery, Brumby's, opened in the area and they advertised for a bakery manager. It was an upscale bakery with impressive methods.

I answered the ad and got an interview. They needed someone to learn their procedures and run the crew. They offered me the job and I took it.

Over November and December of 1988, I worked eighty-ninety hours per week. I busted my ass. I would start at 10 p.m. and then be home by noon. I would take a nap before the kids were done with school.

Becky was taking classes to be a medical assistant.

We didn't get to see each other enough, but we were a family and it felt like we were building something. I got a job offer from another company to sell baking equipment. When I told my boss at Brumby's, they offered me more money to stay and I did.

During this time, I went to the Westerner one night with Becky.

I wasn't playing the drums anymore and didn't have the desire to be in a band.

Wind Chill was playing and I received a tepid reception from the guys. I told them my feet were healed. They invited me to play and I jammed with them for a bit. It was fun and all seemed well between us.

The job at Brumby's was killing me.

I moved away from shift work and was now training bakers. I was also a buyer. One day, I would get on a plane and fly to Kansas City to buy a bagel machine. The next day, I was off to California to purchase a different item. On the third day, I'd fly somewhere else to help open a new shop and train some apprentice bakers.

I had been awake for three days straight, flying in and out of Utah, running to the bakery in between flights to pull a shift since our bakers were quitting due to the stress.

While I was working on some rolls, I passed out cold.

After I came to, I called Becky to come get me.

I had burned myself out at my job and my musical bridges in the Utah area were in flames.

It was time to go back to Spokane.

THE TY GREEN BAND
1990

Back (L-R) Ted Dussor, Joe Webber, me, Jay Columb (comedian)
Front (L-R) Duane Becker, Kurt Baumer
Not Pictured - Rick Roadman and Eric Lindstrom

After our previous quick moves, planning a transition seemed the mature thing to do.

Becky had recently earned her Medical Assisting degree, so we decided she would move to Spokane first while I finished at Brumby's.

I rented an apartment closer to the bakery and worked another eight weeks to cover us on money and benefits.

It wasn't the best decision for us to be separated, but we had an end goal. We wanted to be in Spokane and knew that it would be our long-term home.

While in my waning time at Brumby's, I filled in with Smooth Moves, a house band for a Salt Lake City club. They were a Top 40 cover band.

Through the summer of '89, Becky and I felt the old strain of being apart.

Luckily, we recognized it this time. I returned home a couple times during the summer and we promised each other we wouldn't let things get out of hand again.

One night before leaving Utah I drove to Ogden to see The Kap Brothers and say farewell.

Then I dropped in on Greg Clary's new band, Justyn Time, an updated version of Wind Chill.

They had recently recorded a self-titled LP. They said I had inspired them when I left, and they dedicated part of the album to me.

Justyn Time was finishing a set when I arrived. Greg and I hugged each other. The past was over and we were okay.

That was the last time I ever saw him. He passed away from cancer in 2005.

Smooth Moves had a going-away jam session for me and they brought in their new drummer. We had double drums set-up for that show. It was a good time.

On the morning of August 5th, 1989, with my few possessions packed into my Mazda truck, I headed to Spokane.

Back home, I didn't have a job and we were broke, again.

I slipped into depression.

Despite having a degree in medical assisting, Becky went to work in Client Services at Itron. My sister, Carol, worked there as well and helped Becky get the job

I received a call from Joe Scribner, a guy with whom I went to high school. He was playing in The Stetson, a house band for Curley's Alibi, a bar in Lewiston, Idaho. They needed a drummer through the fall of '89. The bass player was also the owner of the bar. He planned to retire soon and close the club. The band didn't know what they would do then.

I took the gig out of necessity.

I would drive two hours down to Lewiston on Tuesday afternoon and stay through Saturday. I stayed in an extra bedroom at the bass player's house. After Saturday night's gig, I would drive back to Spokane about 4 a.m. so I could spend Sunday and Monday with my family.

I was making roughly $300 per week.

One afternoon, I arrived at the bar early to have a beer before the show. On the radio, a corny song started and I listened to the voice of the singer. I asked the bartender, "Hey, who is this singing?"

"Garth Brooks. The song is *If Tomorrow Never Comes*."

We all know now that Garth Brooks is one of the biggest selling recording artists of all time, but back in the fall of '89, *If Tomorrow Never Comes* was his second single and most people still didn't know much about him.

The name of the singer kept bugging me and I had a sneaking suspicion why.

The next day I called Joe Webber, my former bandmate in Hotspurz. After we caught up with each other, I asked my question.

"Joe, have you heard of this Garth Brooks guy on the radio?"

Joe laughed. "Yeah. He's the guy we backed up for a demo."

As soon as he said that, I remembered the guy. He was a dumpy looking guy who came in to record a demo when Joe and I had landed the studio musicians gig in Nashville. It turns out Garth not only recorded demos for himself, but he recorded several demos for other songwriters while he lived in Nashville.

When we were done with a session, Garth complimented all of us studio musicians and said something about whenever he got his record contract, he'd love to have us play with him.

I looked at Joe like the guy had lost his mind. After Garth left the studio, I smirked at Joe with the false bravado of a studio musician. "That guy will never amount to anything."

At Thanksgiving, our bass player retired. Since he also owned the bar, we knew this could spell doom since we were the house band. Fortunately, he sold Curley's Alibi, allowing it to stay open under new management.

The band didn't want to stop playing with the exit of their bass player. They changed their name to Chateau, picked up a new bass guitarist, and asked if I wanted to make it a permanent thing.

I agreed and played with them from December '89 through March '90.

By the end of March, the strain on my marriage had resurfaced again and we were barely making ends meet. It didn't make sense to keep doing it. I announced my departure from Chateau. They were a good band and people loved us there, but I had gotten burned out.

While I was in Lewiston, I met a guy named C. Douglas Smith who ran M. Fabrikant Promotions.

It was a recording studio along with a training program for aspiring country singers. The Nashville-style program covered all sorts of things – diet, grooming, singing lessons, contacts, personal management. Doug was getting some folks in there. He had a phone number based in Nashville that would ring in Lewiston. It seemed shady and I probably should have smelled something rotten. I rationalized away my concerns due to my excitement about being around the music business.

One day I went to his studio which was in the basement of his gift shop. The studio was arranged like a TV show, where he could do interviews and have a studio audience. We became friends and he asked if I would run the lights for his show. I would activate the "applause" signal and turn on the lights for the performers. Doug introduced me to several of the people he was grooming. One of them was a guy named Ty Green.

In April, my sister, Carol, let me know they had an opening in the maintenance department of Itron – the large tech company in Liberty Lake where she and Becky worked.

I interviewed with the facility manager and was hired for $6.75/hour to run their grounds keeping crew. Except for a couple temps now and then, I was the only member of the crew. It was a job with benefits, so I took it.

In mid-summer of 1990, Doug Smith called.

His guy, Ty Green, had an album that was number three on the blue label, or independent charts, which essentially tracked the unsigned acts. His song, *Fool That I Am*, was the first single released from his album I'm Green and was already getting radio air play. Doug had produced the album, along with a financial contribution from Ty, and was pushing it under CDS Records (C. Douglas Smith Records).

Doug was taking Ty on tour through thirty-six cities and financing the whole thing. The tour would go through the Pacific Northwest, head over to Montana then run down through Colorado, New Mexico, and Arizona. He offered me carte blanche to develop the band behind Ty. He and Ty wanted certain instrumentation, but the musicians were my choice.

Ty was going to play concerts, not clubs. Contracts were ready to be signed. Doug basically needed a band to support his performer.

There was some industry chatter about Ty. The September 23rd edition of Music Row Magazine honored him with their DISCovery Award for his first single. Some were claiming him to be the next Garth Brooks or George Straight. He had cowboy looks and swagger. Hell, he'd been a professional bull rider when he was younger. On top of all that, the guy could really sing. He was going somewhere.

Becky and I agreed we'd take one more try at it. This wasn't bar bands anymore. This was a concert level band with a fancy tour bus. We were promised good money plus a per diem.

This was the next step we had suffered so long to achieve. As hard as my career was on the family, Becky always was behind me and supported my dream.

Doug sent me the music to learn and I went about the task of assembling the band.

I reached out to a couple Stone Johnny Mountain Band friends. Rick Roadman came aboard to play guitar and Eric Lindstrom would play bass. Eric took some encouraging since he was now living in Sacramento and had left the music business.

Then I called a couple friends from Hotspurz. Joe Webber agreed to play keyboards and Ted Dussor would play guitar.

I rounded out the band with Kurt Baumer on fiddle and Duane Becker on pedal steel.

Ty Green would handle the lead vocals and play rhythm guitar. We'd have three guitars going with Ty, Rick and Ted. It would sound great.

Doug sent me the contracts. We all signed them and sent them back. We never got his signature on the documents, but it didn't matter to us. He appeared to be a decent guy and things were moving quickly ahead.

I announced my departure from Itron and the whole band assembled in Lewiston for two weeks of rehearsal as The Ty Green Band.

Things were funky from the beginning.

On the first night, we were supposed to have dinner at Doug's house which was a beautiful three-story house in Clarkston, the neighboring city to Lewiston.

It was October so it was chilly, but Doug didn't let us in his house. We had a barbeque outside and drank beers that we brought ourselves. All of us were shivering by night's end.

Doug said, "I'm going to put you guys in the back of the equipment truck. I've got some sleeping bags. It'll be like camping."

We didn't agree with his plan so he took us over to his mother's house. "You guys can sleep in the garage."

Rick and Eric had enough of Doug and went to a hotel. Ted and Joe left as well. A few of us stayed in his mother's house after she finally let us in.

It was weird.

Of course, for those two weeks, Ty stayed in a hotel on Doug's tab.

The rest of us were on our own. Ted Dussor put the hotel rooms on his credit card. We naively thought the program was just disorganized coming out of the gate. We figured it would right itself as time went on.

We rehearsed the songs as we put together a show. We sounded really good.

To be the opening act for our tour, Doug hired Jay Columb, a comedian with a country boy schtick. He was out of nearby Moses Lake, Washington and would walk on stage with a banjo. He'd tell jokes, play a little riff and tell another joke.

Before the tour, we went home for a couple days.

It finally felt like I had made the big time again and I was going to bring home some decent money. I was going to be paid $192.50 per gig as the band leader while the rest of the guys were set to make $175.00 per show. Along with that, our per diem was an additional $128/week.

Before hitting the road, I kissed the kids and my wife good-bye.

Becky whispered in my ear, "I love you. Go fulfill your dream. I'll always be here."

Back in Lewiston, the band waited on the sidewalk for our tour bus. First, the equipment truck arrived and we loaded our gear. Then the tour bus rounded the corner and I can't tell you the rush that went through me. It was the big time again.

Our first gig was at Cordiner Hall on the campus of Whitman College in Walla Walla, Washington. We were so excited. We had performed our sound check earlier and we sounded good. That night, we waited back stage while Jay did his comedy routine, anxious to get playing.

For the tour, I bought new snake skin boots and felt like a million bucks.

Jay ran into the dressing room, looking shocked. "My God, nobody is out there," he said.

We hadn't watched his show so I ran out of the dressing room to get a peek at the audience.

In an auditorium that sat 1,300 people, there were maybe fifty people in the seats.

"Oh, my God, what's going on?" I said.

On October 8th, we played our first show to an empty coliseum.

We next went to the Richland, Washington, but it was the same story as Walla Walla.

Doug Smith was charging $17.50 per ticket, for a performer no one had ever heard of before, and no one was buying. It was crazy.

We kept doing gigs with the same results.

The band stopped in Longview, Washington. We'd been on the road for a week and hadn't gotten our per diem. I chased Doug via telephone.

"You've got to give us our per diem," I begged.

Things were already shaky when a couple shows cancelled.

Jay Columb did not fit in well with the band. He was a comedian riding on a tour bus with a bunch of musicians. He was a smart-ass which pissed off the other guys, especially Joe Webber and Ted Dussor. Rick Roadman and Eric Lindstrom did their best to needle Jay, but Joe and Ted went out of their way to fuck with him.

Our tour bus had stopped at a roadside restaurant for dinner. Afterward, as we boarded the bus, the driver asked, "Everyone aboard?"

Joe and Ted looked at each other with big smiles. "Yup," they said in unison and dropped into their chairs.

The bus lurched away from the restaurant and headed toward the interstate.

The door of the restaurant burst open and Jay sprinted after the bus.

The driver saw Jay waving his arms as he ran. "Is that one of your guys?" he asked, not stopping until he got an answer.

Joe and Ted burst out into laughter.

We headed to Klamath Falls, Oregon to play The Ross Ragland Theater.

A few more people showed up, but it was still a miserable turn-out.

People simply weren't paying that kind of money to see someone they didn't know.

I suggested to Doug that we shrink the band and get rid of the tour bus. I hated to do it, but we needed to do something.

Also, I recommended we get some local bands to open for us. We discussed playing large bars instead of concert halls.

Doug didn't take any of my advice.

The tour took us back to Spokane and the venue changed twice. At first, we were to play at Gonzaga University. Then it was changed to Shadle Park High School's auditorium. We finally landed at the Ferris High School auditorium. A high school auditorium, for shit's sake.

It was embarrassing especially since we had our best crowd to date. About one hundred fifty people came out to see us, mostly friends and family. Many Itron employees were there to show their support.

Afterwards, I signed many autographs for folks with whom I had previously worked.

The Ty Green Band then headed west to Tacoma. It was an okay crowd, but the venue had consolidated two shows into one.

A couple more dates fell out on the tour.

We came back east into Pullman in late October 1990 to play the Beasley Performing Arts Center on the campus of Washington State University. It was easily the best ticket sales we'd had so far.

Ty had gone on ahead and did radio spots and a couple of promotional events at western clothing stores. It was exciting to finally see a good turn-out.

While we were in the dressing room, I overheard the comedian's booking agent arguing with Doug Smith.

"You either pay my guy or he's not going on," she said, loudly.

I walked back to the dressing room and said, "Guys, I think we've got a problem."

None of us had seen our salaries and we had to fight to get our per diem. We decided to confront Doug.

We had an emergency band meeting on the bus and invited Doug.

"Where's our money? If you don't pay us, we don't play," I said.

He said, "There is no money. None."

Just like that, on October 20th, The Ty Green Band came to a screeching halt.

We never played the WSU gig. They immediately announced the cancellation on the radio and on the giant marquee outside the center.

Back inside, while we were stowing our gear, I threw a microphone at Doug.

He was escorted back to Lewiston by the sheriff. He probably thought we were going to kick his ass. He was right.

At that moment, I couldn't be the band leader anymore. I was embarrassed at what had occurred and that I'd led my friends into this mess. I also felt bad for Ty. He could have really hit it big, but Doug Smith screwed him and his career. The guy was bad news.

I phoned Becky and admitted the failure to her. She drove to Pullman to get me. The band dispersed from there.

Becky hugged me tightly and cried, not so much for the tour folding, but she knew of my hurt and disappointment.

We put my drums in the bed of our truck. We stopped in Colfax, grabbed a six pack of Miller, and I sipped beers all the way home.

I had put my heart and soul into the band. I had left my family and a good job for The Ty Green Band. I had put my trust into Doug.

It was devastating, and it broke my heart.

My full-time music career was officially over.

CAFÉ BLUE
&
THE PAT COAST BAND
1993-2011

*(Top L-R) Bob Spitahl, Russ Hoffer, Little
Buzzy Foo Foo, and Pat Coast
(Bottom L-R) Me, Keith Lewis, Tom
Brewster, and Gary Smith
Photo by Denny Leneirt*

Back in Spokane, I put my drums in mom's garage.

A couple days later, I contacted my former boss at Itron. He put me on the maintenance crew again.

On my first day back, we were on the east side of Itron's building constructing a new sidewalk between two of the parking lots.

I was slinging mud when a couple women from the administrative offices walked by. They were nicely dressed. As I worked in the muck, one woman watched me with disdain. She never recognized me, nor grasped that a couple weeks prior she had asked for my autograph when The Ty Green Band had played the Ferris High School auditorium.

It was a disappointing moment.

It reinforced my commitment that I was done pursuing music full-time.

The rollercoaster ride was over.

In many ways, I'm thankful that woman didn't recognize me.

The Ty Green Band debacle had overwhelmed me.

Initially, Joe Webber and Ted Dussor went to Lewiston to negotiate a pay-out out with Doug. They were unsuccessful, but they kept calm about it. Better than I would have done. After Doug failed to pay, we threatened a lawsuit. He settled by giving each of us of a couple thousand dollars.

Jay Columb was pissed that we settled. He had filed a lawsuit and wanted us to join in. We had no plans of joining his legal action.

We all needed the cash.

A few weeks later, Gary Yeoman, the guitarist I met in Tim Langford's basement, called. He was forming a band, Yo and De Cats, with him as the front man. He had Eric Rice on guitar, Slim Medina on bass and they needed a drummer.

I joined them and we played weekends around town. That was fine as I didn't want more than that.

Eric Rice and Slim Medina would soon quit Yo and De Cats. Eric Lindstrom was hired to replace Slim and Gary took on all the guitar playing duties himself.

Back then, Gary was still developing as a guitar player, but we still garnered enough gigs. We played Friday and Saturday nights as well as Sunday afternoons. We even had a regular Monday night gig at the Fort Spokane Brewery.

After several months and a bunch of local gigs, Gary Yeoman wanted to move Yo and De Cats to Portland to go after a bigger market. Eric Lindstrom agreed to go. I didn't. The band moved on without me.

I quickly joined J.R. Boogie, Eric Rice's new band. Ramiro Vijaro was on bass.

We were playing a Tri-Cities hotel and the gig was sponsored by a local radio station. They were promoting the hell out of the it and the band. For the show, we added a harmonica player, D.K. Black, who later became a full-time member.

I packed my Mazda truck for the two-hour drive. This time I loaded it a bit differently than normal. I put the kick drum and its case in last, on top of the drum riser which was perched on the rest of the equipment.

I secured the case and headed south.

I was on Hwy 395, past Ritzville, WA, with a motorhome behind me. The kick drum broke loose and flew off the truck. It hit the highway in front of the motorhome.

That big rig swerved hard and missed the kick drum. I slammed on the brakes and pulled to the side. I still couldn't believe the Winnebago didn't destroy the drum or roll trying to avoid it.

I backed along the highway. I got out and cars honked as I ran into the highway to get the drum. Back at the Mazda, I inspected my drum while cars zipped past. The case was toast, but the drum was intact. I examined it like it was my baby.

The crowd treated us like rock stars and Eric Rice loved it. He thought he was the second coming of Stevie Ray Vaughn and tried to mimic him on stage.

Every J.R. Boogie gig started the same way. Ramiro and I would play a funky groove and Eric would saunter on stage in his trench coat and snake skin boots. He'd grab his Stratocaster and make a show of putting it on before he'd start playing.

Eric was a fine guitar player and a nice guy but come on. I understand showmanship, but he was trying too hard. He was a good guitar player, but he was young and immature.

A future bandmate of mine, Pat Coast, would write a song, *Day Job*, dedicated to Eric. It wasn't flattering as it made fun of some of Eric's youthful antics.

As time passed, I climbed the ranks at Itron, eventually becoming the Facility Manager after my boss left.

Not long after my promotion at Itron, Eric Rice decided he wanted to move J.R. Boogie to Seattle to go after bigger and better things.

I wished him luck and the band moved on without me.

Pat Coast's band, Café Blue, was getting rid of their drummer.

Pat and I had talked previously when I played at the brewery with Yo and De Cats and later J.R. Boogie. I dismissed him initially because he looked like a shoe salesman. He was a straight-looking guy when the rest of us had rocker looks, but when Pat Coast played guitar, holy shit, could that guy *play*.

When he asked me to join, I immediately said yes.

In 1994, the Café Blue line-up was Tom Brewster on bass and Keith Lewis on keyboards. Chuck Swanson and Russ Hoffer both played saxophone and Mike Lenke blew the trumpet. Pat Coast sang lead vocals and played lead guitar.

My initial rehearsal was at Keith Lewis's house. From the first night we played, I loved that band.

We immediately set about gigging. The horn section was funky with a rock edge. We played Chelsea's in Coeur d'Alene and the Fort Spokane Brewery.

The whole band was married which made for a completely different vibe than my previous experiences. When we finished a gig, everybody went home. The band got along well.

We went to record six songs for a demo at Boptech Studio. The technician said the band wouldn't be able to get the work done in our allotted time. He was unaware of how well-rehearsed we were. We did every song in one or two takes. We sounded sharp.

In mid-1995, Becky got sick due to complications from Hepatitis C. It was discovered she had it in the early '90s, but we didn't think it would develop into anything. When it eventually did, we learned she needed a liver transplant.

The band agreed to go on hiatus while Becky and I dealt with her illness.

I still worked at Itron but stayed as close to home whenever possible. Whenever I was forced to leave the house, I carried my pager. It was pre-determined that a "911" page meant a transplant was available and we had to get to Seattle immediately. If it were to ever happen, we had eight hours to get to the University of Washington hospital.

On July 4th, Spokane held its Neighbor Day celebration. It was an annual downtown gathering of music, events and food. The bay area funk band, Tower of Power, was playing an evening show. Becky told me to go and take along our son, Cory. She wanted me to get out of the house and hear some music. I reluctantly went.

I enjoyed the concert and spent some time with my oldest son. After the show, Cory and I walked back to my car, talking easily and reliving the concert. Sitting in the car, I pulled out my pager to discover a weak, yellow glow. The screen faintly read "91." My battery was dying.

I raced home and ran into the house with Cory. Becky was on the couch crying. Half of my family was gathered around her.

"Where were you?" Becky said. "We got the call. We need to go."

When they couldn't reach me, my family had contacted the police who got on stage as the crowd disbursed after the Tower of Power show. They announced my name and told me to call home. Unfortunately, I never heard it.

Becky was freaked out that we weren't going to make it in time.

Thankfully, we had pre-planned for this call so we had emergency bags already packed. We loaded our car with the bags and the three kids. By now, Erin was twenty years old, Cory was fifteen and Casey was ten.

At 10:45 p.m. we headed to Seattle.

I'd already lost three hours in her window of time. I had to make it up on the road.

I made a five-hour trip in less than three hours and fifty minutes.

I was lucky that there were no state patrol officers on the freeway that night.

At the hospital, we got Becky checked in and settled.

My brother, Chuck, was living in Seattle then and had a room pre-arranged at the nearby Residence Inn. Before I took the kids to the hotel, each of them spent time with Becky.

It was a surreal moment. It was never said but it could have been the last time they ever saw their mom. When the kids stepped out of the room, Becky cried and told me, "I just want to live to see my kids grow up." It broke my heart. It was an extremely tough moment for us both.

At 6:30 a.m., I was back with Becky while she waited for the transplant. I lay next to her and we held each other. We spoke about our life, its ups and downs, our kids and our love. We talked about how she was going to be fine and get a new lease on life. An hour and a half later, they wheeled her into surgery.

Twelve hours and twenty minutes later, they brought Becky back out. I was in the waiting room the entire time. She was unconscious and unrecognizable. The body shuts down during that type of surgery and she had a tremendous amount of water weight on her from those twelve hours. It was horrible.

They were unable to wake her for recovery. They tried to bring her out of sedation, but she would get agitated and freak out. They would sedate her again.

This became a pattern that continued for nine days.

At one point, we thought she had a stroke.

Eventually, she woke up in ICU without agitation. I'll never forget her first words. Her lips trembling, she said in a quiet and shaky voice, "I want to go home."

Becky got better over the next few weeks and we finally went home.

We were at the University of Washington hospital from July through August.

Back in Spokane, I met Pat Coast and Keith Lewis for lunch. We talked about putting the band back together.

"How about double drummers?" I suggested.

I listened to some new stuff while in Seattle and liked the sound.

They told me they had been talking with a drummer named Gary Smith in case I didn't come back. We all agreed it sounded like a neat idea.

That's when we added a new level of percussion to the band. I would play instruments like congas, bongos, and shakers. It was the stuff we normally wouldn't get to play with only one guy behind the drum kit.

We put out one album as Café Blue – <u>A Good Night for the Blues</u>.

The Inland Empire Blues Society awarded us the best album, best drummer and best band. We swept the awards that year and I was the first ever recipient of the best drummer award.

Shortly after our album's success, we had a show at Roxy's in Sandpoint, Idaho. We had finished a Saturday night gig when Pat announced he was quitting the band. He felt a calling with his church to be their musical director.

This pissed me off.

Yes, it was completely hypocritical after how many times I've left bandmates for lesser reasons than a higher calling. However, this was the first time someone else's quitting would kill a band that I wanted to survive.

We had recently put out an album and won a bunch of awards.

The initial anger disappeared quickly and turned into disappointment. Pat was a good guy and I supported his search for meaning and happiness.

The weekend after Pat's announcement, a band meeting with the remaining members was held at my house.

We drank a lot as we discussed what to do next.

As the alcohol flowed, I grew dramatic. "How do we continue?" I asked. "How do we measure up to that white-hot light that was Café Blue?"

Like I said, dramatic.

I was also full of myself and drunk, but we were *the* blues band in town.

Mike Lenke and I got into an argument about Pat. I kept saying we couldn't continue without Pat. Mike said we could.

The argument spun out of control and I kicked him out of my house.

Mike got in his car, revved the engine and then spun gravel in my face.

The band ended in the summer of '97

But I didn't let Café Blue breaking-up keep me from playing.

I immediately joined Chip and the Bushwackers. Chip Bush, Eric Lindstrom and Rick Roadman had formed the band before I joined.

For about a year, we played clubs like the Fort Spokane Brewery, West 4 Main, Red Lion BBQ, and Chelsea's in Coeur d'Alene.

The Bushwackers were incredibly popular.

We had a great run, so it was disappointing when Rick Roadman announced that he wanted to move to Portland.

I was so mad at him for breaking up the gang. Again, I was Mr. Hypocrite.

His farewell gig was at the Fort Spokane Brewery. Rick got hammered drunk during the day. At our gig, I have never been so mad before or since at Rick. Eric Lindstrom was pissed at him, too. Too his credit, Rick managed to pull off the gig which is a testament to his professionalism as a musician.

Chip and the Bushwhackers ended after that.

In 1999, Café Blue got back together.

Pat Coast had returned to playing. Much like my personal journey, he couldn't stay away from music, though he tried to walk a different path. He missed it.

Pat had joined another band for a short time after swearing a hundred times he wouldn't. I understood his journey. It was good to see him back in music.

Keith Lewis, Pat and I met to talk about the band. We brought in Gary Smith for the double drums and percussion.

Shortly after that, Chuck Swanson and Mike Lenke went off to join Mumbo Jumbo. We still had Russ Hoffer on saxophone.

We added Bob Spitahl, a professor of music at Gonzaga, on trumpet. We also added a young, cocky trumpet player that we nicknamed Little Buzzy Foo Foo.

His nickname was Buzz and he was an immature punk. It didn't take long for someone to tag him with the demeaning nickname of Little Buzzy Foo Foo. I have no idea of his real name.

Foo Foo was a good-looking kid with a long pony tail. Women liked him for some unexplained reason. He was so full of himself. One night after a gig, he told me, "You've got some good chops for a weekend warrior."

He was a great player, but he didn't have a soul for the instrument.

Foo Foo would get drunk before and during our gigs then fuck up his parts. When that happened, he'd yell, "Yeah!" on stage calling attention to his screw up.

He acted like a complete punk.

On New Year's Eve, 1999-2000, Café Blue played the Shiloh Inn.

After this show, Keith Lewis announced he wanted to quit. That was the tear that would end Café Blue permanently because Pat wanted to get rid of the horn players as well.

In 2000, we renamed as Pat Coast and Out of the Blue. I pushed Pat for the new name since he wrote the material and should have been the focus.

We reformed as a four-piece band. Tom Brewster was still on bass and Jan Danielson was brought in to play piano.

A local musician wanted to try out for piano. We sent him some tapes, but Pat hired Jan before he was given an audition.

This guy came to a Schweitzer Mountain gig and, during a break, walked on stage to hassle Pat.

"I spent two weeks learning your fucking material," he yelled.

I took it upon myself to be Pat's protector. "If it took you two weeks to learn this material, then you're not good enough for this band."

"Fuck you," he said.

I got in his face and repeated his kind words.

This went on for a couple rounds until the guy shoved me. I calmly put my beer down and said, "Now, listen –" before punching him in the throat.

He collapsed like a lump of bricks and I went about my business.

The club ejected the guy after that.

Here's something I've learned about myself in writing this book.

Whenever I'm in a fight, I punch at the throat.

I never like to hit the head, it hurts my hand.

Plus, guys always drop when they get hit in the throat.

From 2000 through 2009, as Pat Coast and Out of the Blue, we played the usual bars as well as the major blues festivals, from Helena to Bellingham to Portland.

We put out another CD (<u>Play Me Something I Can Dance To</u>) and swept the blues awards – best band, best album and best drummer. I won Best Drummer three years in a row and went into the Hall of Fame. We opened for The Fabulous Thunderbirds in Spokane's Riverfront Park. By all accounts, the crowd liked us better.

A couple years later, we opened for John Mayall in River Front Park.

After our show, John Mayall, John-fucking-Mayall, came up and introduced himself to me.

"You can really boogie," he said.

Holy shit, I thought.

That guy is a legend, for Christ's sake.

On a business trip to Chicago, I went into Buddy Guy's bar.

He happened to be there.

I bullshitted my way on stage for the jam by telling him I played with Robert Cray, which in a way, I did. Well, Too Slim and the Taildraggers did open for him a couple times.

Buddy said, "You played with Bobby?"

"Yep, sure did," I said.

He invited me on stage and I played three songs with him and other jammers.

He introduced me as this "shit hot drummer from Spocane." That's how he pronounced it.

It was high praise from a blues legend.

Pat Coast and Out of the Blue opened for others and rode high for several years.

We all kept our day jobs and I refused to consider jumping back to full-time road work.

After a gig at The Wine Cellar in Coeur d'Alene, the band had dinner at a local restaurant. Near the end of the meal, Tom Brewster, our bass player, suddenly went off.

"I've had enough being led around by the nose. It's Pat's band now. I'm out."

He packed his shit and was gone.

It was a complete shock to us as he was always Mister Mellow.

To replace Tom, Pat hired Larry Brown, a remarkable bass player and a raging asshole.

Larry's nickname was, "Frog." He was with the band for about a year before he was fired for bad mouthing me in public, something he had done repeatedly while he was with us.

Frog was a weird fucker.

At the end of a show, Pat would thank the crowd for coming and to check us out on our website, patcoast.com.

Larry would then grab a microphone and say in his deep voice, "And don't forget to check me out on suck my dick dot com." He would cackle loudly as the crowd sat in stunned silence.

We recorded <u>Pat Coast Live!</u> at the Wenatchee Civic Center.

It was the third Out of the Blue album. A couple thousand people were there for the recording.

Chuck Swanson (sax) and Mike Lenke (trumpet) rejoined us for this gig and then stayed with the band.

In 2000, feeling completely burned out by corporate life, I left Itron to take a break. Becky had a bookkeeping job and we had additional money from side work coming in.

Besides playing with Café Blue, we owned a candy vending machine route that I filled weekly. It wasn't a huge money maker or a big-time demand, but it added a few dollars to the bottom line.

Becky and I had also taken over my grandma's old farmstead where my mother had grown up. The house was behind my parent's home. We sold the vegetables we raised at a local farmer's market. Shortly after we took over the farm, we had to tear down the old house. We discovered it had been built around a tent which we discovered in the walls. We put a manufactured home in its place.

When cash started to get tight, I found a consulting gig with the telephone switch company, Telect. I helped them relocate a site in Minneapolis and they liked my work. They then asked me to handle international site selection for new sales offices.

I started off in Mexico City then went to Shanghai, China to find a site for not only a sales office, but a manufacturing warehouse as well.

From China, I was asked to go to South Hampton, England to negotiate an expansion of their sales office.

After England, I was in Wroclaw, Poland to oversee a demo project of an old factory.

My normal schedule was to be home in Spokane for a week and then in another country for a week.

I was in England with a planned hop to Poland to check on the status of the demo when I received a call from the main Telect office. They asked me to come back to Spokane and work on a new project.

They wanted me to create a soup to nuts process for "real estate acquisition and disposition." I set to work on it, happy to be at home for an extended period. When I finished my report, I gave the presentation to my employers.

Not five minutes after the presentation was complete, I was notified that my consulting contract was now terminated. I had been with them for eighteen months.

Even though the end of the Telect contracting gig was unceremonious, I had enjoyed it so much I decided to create my own company: Bancroft Corporate Facilities Services. One of my first accounts was with Software Spectrum whose main office was in the Spokane Valley. They contracted with me to develop and oversee the build-out of their new call center in Eugene, Oregon along with the management of their Liberty Lake site.

I'd handled the account for two years and was onsite in Eugene with the guy who oversaw my contract. He was ten years younger than me and an arrogant jerk. We had lunch and discussed how things were going. It was clear he wasn't listening to me as I answered his questions.

At the end of lunch, he said, "Call me tonight at my hotel room and we'll go over some other things."

"Let's go over them now," I said.

"No," he said, not making eye contact. "Let's go over them later."

That night I called him at his hotel.

After the pleasantries were out of the way, he said my contract was cancelled.

I couldn't find work immediately, so I focused on farming the land we had available. There were two acres with our house and we leased an additional five acres next door.

We grew a variety of crops and I tended them closely.

It was a great experience and I enjoyed it immensely.

The house I grew up in abutted the land I was now farming. My mom would occasionally watch me from her window. She once said it made her happy to watch me turning the soil since no one had done it since "daddy," my grandfather, had worked the land.

There were several peach trees on the property. Occasionally, I'd pull a few peaches off the tree. They'd be warm from the summer sun. I'd take them to mom and she'd cut them up. She'd then place them in a bowl and pour half & half over them. We'd sit together at the buddy bar in the kitchen, eating our peaches and cream, and chat about life.

I treasure those memories of mom.

I soon found a nice consulting gig with Servatron, a spin-off of Itron for twenty hours a week as their facilities manager.

In early fall of '03, I went to a BOMA (Building Owners and Managers) lunch one day and ran into the Facilities Director from Sterling Savings Bank. He mentioned they were looking for a Facilities Manager. I threw my hat in the ring but didn't get a call back for over two months. In December, I was offered the job and joined the Corporate Facilities division of Sterling Savings Bank as a Facilities Manager.

A restructuring occurred at Sterling Savings Bank shortly after I started. The department I worked in was reorganized, renamed as Corporate Property Services and I was put in charge of it.

My mom had a stroke right before Thanksgiving of 2003.

She did get to come home from the hospital for Christmas Eve. The next morning, Christmas day, she suffered another major stroke.

She hung in there as best she could, a fighter all the way.

She passed away on January 30th, 2004.

I happened to be the only one in the room with her at that moment. I remember the last thing I said to her was, "Dad's waiting for you mom, he's jingling his keys." He did that when he was ready to go somewhere or feeling impatient.

She still pined for dad all those years after his death in 1978.

"It's time to go home and see him," I said.

She passed a couple minutes later.

Becky and I continued to farm. I would arrive at the office early in the morning and work until about 11 a.m. Then I would race back out to the valley, get out of my suit and into some work clothes. I would change sprinkler heads, adjust venting in the greenhouse and handle all variety of jobs. I would then change back into my suit and hurry back to the office to finish out the afternoon. It was a hectic but rewarding life.

In 2006, Becky and I were at the Liberty Lake farmer's market selling our produce. A couple stalls down were a woman and her mom selling quilts. I recognized the woman and watched her for a moment.

"Why are you staring at that cute blonde?" Becky asked.

"I know her."

"Who is she?"

"That's Sue Davis from high school."

"Go say hi to her."

I walked down and reintroduced myself to her. She didn't recognize me until I told her my name. The next time we were at the farmer's market I dropped off a couple of Café Blue CDs for her. Becky and Sue's mom hit it off and they exchanged tomatoes for pot holders. It was nice to catch up with Sue.

In May 2008, after selling the farm and moving, I was diagnosed with Prostate cancer.

After receiving two additional opinions and reading a book about cancer all within one week, Beck and I decided the best course of action was surgery.

To this day, I'm still cancer free.

My sister, Carol, suffered from emphysema for several years like my father in 1978.

It became so bad that she was hooked to oxygen all the time.

On February 4, 2009, as she underwent tests for the transplant list, she suffered a heart attack and passed away.

In September 2009, upon return from a Hawaiian vacation, I thought I strained myself working out. I was extremely uncomfortable for three days with chest pains.

In a meeting at Sterling Bank, my Purchasing Manager mentioned he was going to the hospital to visit his brother. I asked him to drop me off at the ER so I could get checked out.

After they examined me, Becky arrived to take me home. The hospital planned to release me since my heart appeared fine. At the last minute, the hospital staff decided to do an MRI. It was then they discovered blood clots. It saved my life. They told me I wouldn't have lived another twenty-four hours.

As I recovered from the blood clots, Becky showed signs of liver failure again.

Through the holidays, she became fatigued and mentally confused. She described it as "feeling dull."

On a Saturday in March 2010, Becky slept late, something she never did. When she came downstairs, she had no robe on and was only in her pajamas, which again she never did. She acted distant and out of touch.

I found her in the kitchen putting a metal coffee pot into the microwave. I tried to explain that she couldn't do that. She became agitated and yelled, "Stay away from me."

I was concerned that she may have been suffering a stroke. I finally convinced her to let me take her to the hospital.

While there they ascertained that she was suffering from encephalopathy and was indeed on the path of needing a new liver.

To make matters even more burdensome, she needed a kidney.

It made music trivial.

Around this time, Pat Coast and Out of the Blue ended up rebranding as The Pat Coast Band. Members shifted and my old friend, Eric Lindstrom, joined the group. It was good to have him around.

As much as I loved playing with Pat Coast, the music wasn't bringing me the happiness it once did.

After one practice, I broke down my equipment and took it to my truck. A couple of my bandmates said something that wasn't complimentary about me while I wasn't around. Eric came to my defense and said they needed to show some empathy because of how sick Becky was. I appreciated him looking out for me just like he did in the Stone Johnny days.

Throughout 2010, Becky continued to worsen.

In the late spring, I stepped down from my Vice-President position at Sterling Savings Bank to take care of Becky. By the end of the summer, we relocated to Seattle and moved into the Residence Inn.

The first week of October, the hospital said her liver and kidney transplant were imminent and to stay in the area. She was admitted to the University of Washington ICU the first week of November and stayed there through January.

We all had very high hopes.

Becky did everything she was supposed to do while there. Unfortunately, the transplant never came. If you've never registered to be an organ donor, maybe now is the time.

She fought so hard, but we never got the call.

Becky passed away on January 30th, 2011.

She was always there for me and the kids, as we moved from state to state, enduring hard times when I'd leave good jobs to go back to music.

She was an incredible partner, wife, and mother.

I was lucky to be married to Becky Bancroft for 30 years, 5 months, 10 days, 4 hours, and 35 minutes.

EPILOGUE
THE REST OF MY LIFE

Sitting behind the kit for The Bobby Patterson Band
photo courtesy of Rhonda Patterson

After Becky's passing, I started a new job as a Contracts Manager with a company at Fairchild Air Force Base. My office was in the same building where Organized Crime rehearsed.

Sterling Savings Bank had let me go after I took the time off to care for Becky. I have a lot of anger over that turn of events and have fought the instinct to vent it here.

I had to start the new job the Monday following Becky's funeral. I was in such a bad place. I could not concentrate and didn't care about anything. As you can imagine, I didn't stay long at that job.

That was the darkest of times.

I drank too much. I didn't eat right. I contemplated horrible things.

My children and Becky's memory kept me from doing something completely selfish and stupid.

Becky fought so hard to live that I had to keep surviving.

In September 2011, Spokane Mayor Mary Verner asked me to fulfill a one-year contract as Conservation Resource Manager for The City of Spokane. While at Sterling Savings, I had sat on her Conservation Resource Sounding Board.

I accepted the contract and put together a plan to create a functional centralized Facilities Department for the city.

Following a tough election campaign, a new mayor was elected and my contract was terminated as part of a house-cleaning effort by the new administration.

I struggled with music throughout 2011 and played a New Year's Eve gig at The Knitting Factory. Afterwards, I let Pat Coast know I was done playing.

I didn't drum at all in 2012.

In May, I accepted a job with Avista Development as a property manager for Steam Plant Square and Courtyard Office Center.

I worked there for over a year and a half before leaving in 2014. I had put things in order for the properties and became essentially lost in my depression again.

I spent time riding my bicycle and being on my boat, the *Becky Anne*. I tried to date for a bit. It was strange. I felt so guilty. In time, it got a little easier.

It remained a bleak time.

I struggled with Becky's death and the loneliness.

If it wasn't for Erin, Cory, and Casey, I wouldn't have made it through this period.

Eric Lindstrom was no longer with The Pat Coast Band and wanted to start a new group. He invited me to join with Dennis Higgins (guitar) and Dave Olsen (harmonica) to form a blues band called Bakin' Phat.

Looking back, I probably shouldn't have done it. I wasn't ready to play music, but the drums have always been my happy place. Unfortunately, no matter how hard I tried I couldn't find the joy in playing.

I attended all our practices and liked the music we were working on. I figured if I kept banging away, I would rediscover some of the contentment I had before. I just needed to get back on the horse as Jeannie Carter had said so many years before.

Following a couple paying gigs, however, I was fired after a practice. Dennis said he was taking control of the situation and confronted me. He said, "We don't know what to say to you, Bill. It's so damn depressing with you around."

Eric didn't stand up for me then like he had with the guys in The Pat Coast Band. In fact, he didn't really look my way as Dennis fired me.

Eric is my friend today. We've shared too much history not to be, but I can't stress how deeply hurt I was by that moment. When I needed the music and my bandmates most, I was let down. I carried that hurt for some time. It still bothers me when I talk about it.

That moment pushed me further into my personal black hole.

During one of my darkest moments, I played at a local club called The Blues at the Bend, filling in with a rather weak country band.

I wish I could have worn a mask we were so bad.

An old band member came to see the show.

He walked out to the parking lot as I loaded my gear. He was drunk and tried to justify why we didn't get along.

"You're a rocker and you don't know shit about the blues," he said.

"Shut up, asshole," I said and continued to load my gear.

"Everyone thinks you're so great, but I know better."

I stopped and turned to him. "What I've been through the last year, I have no qualms knocking you out."

He continued to berate me.

"You need to leave right now because I want to hurt you," I said.

He laughed. "You don't have the balls.

With my go-to move, I punched him in the throat and he hit the ground. I got on top of him and hit him in the face several times more. I then stood as he lay there, his legs splayed open. I swung my leg back before shoving my cowboy boot up his ass.

I looked around for witnesses, realizing I'd crossed a line. Being in the darkest place I'd ever been, I was surprised at how I reacted. I got in my truck and pulled away. As I left, he lay there in the parking lot. I drove home, scared of police lights dropping in behind me.

I later heard that he was okay and I finally relaxed. He was a complete asshole and deserved to be punched, but that should have been enough. It was completely unfair what I did to him.

I later saw that former bandmate at The Inland Empire Blues Awards in late 2014.

We shook hands.

"Hi, Billy," he said. "How are you doing?"

"Hey," I said, flatly.

"You're sounding good," he said, nicely.

It's amazing what a punch in the throat will do to a man's demeanor.

Life moved on and I witnessed the birth of my grandson and my two granddaughters. I gathered my wits and learned how to relax again.

That allowed me to come back to work in April 2015 as facility manager for the company that owns all the properties in the "Metro Block" of downtown Spokane. Their main tenant is The Knitting Factory, Spokane's largest concert venue outside of the arena. All sorts of major acts have come through that venue since it opened.

Occasionally, I would stand on the sidewalk when tour buses pulled up outside. I would be dressed in a suit with a set of keys clipped to my belt, the classic facility manager look. The band would exit the bus, laughing and joking, involved in their own world.

They wouldn't notice me. I was background noise to them.

Yet it was okay they didn't see me.

I was lost in the smell of the exhaust from the bus. The burning diesel fuel lifted me back to my days on the road. I remembered the excitement these guys and girls felt as they headed inside to prepare for their show.

I must admit I missed that feeling.

Leon Russell once pulled into town for a show at The Knitting Factory and his tour bus parked outside. Leon Russell was the first concert I saw in 1973 at the old Coliseum.

As facility manager, I made my morning rounds to check for new graffiti on the walls or unsightly piles of puke from the previous night's concert.

Next to the bus, a scooter sat on the sidewalk. A small, portable step was placed on the sidewalk below the last step from the bus.

I knew they were for Leon. His health hadn't been good. He needed the scooter to get inside.

I stood there for a moment and thought, "Good for him." He was still out on the road, touring and doing his thing. Soon, another thought crept into my mind. I now wondered what he had to sacrifice over the years, how many relationships were ruined and how many friends were lost.

It made me glad that I made the decision to step away from full-time music when I did.

In late 2014, I joined up with guitarist Bobby Patterson. We'd been mutual fans of each other for many years. Bobby fronted The Fat Tones, a popular blues/rock trio in Spokane, and they needed a drummer. The bass player for The Fat Tones, Bob Ehrgott, was set to retire at the end of the year.

Bobby Patterson and I decided to let the band evolve into something featuring more rock and roll.

Rebranding as The Bobby Patterson Band, we moved forward with Tom Norton on keyboards and our new bass player, Randy Knowles.

I hadn't been that stoked about a band in a very long time.

Being a drummer has taken its toll on my body. I've had three foot surgeries, the result of playing barefoot and trying to grip the pedals all those years.

I've had my hip replaced.

There have been several back surgeries (some of that was caused by the injury lifting soda bottles).

I've lost most of the hearing in my left ear. I've only fifteen percent left. My right ear is at seventy-five percent.

But I still get on stage whenever I get the chance and pound the skins.

The passion is still there.

My youngest child, Casey, has marched to the beat of his own drum throughout the years. While his brother played the trumpet, and became quite good at it, Casey picked up the guitar and bass. He played in one local band and, like me, he had a *feel* for playing music. Casey fell in love, married, had three beautiful children and does not pursue music any longer. Becky used to confide in me her fears of Casey trying to have a family while chasing a musical career. We paid a toll to walk that journey and she didn't want Casey to pay that same price.

I am so very proud of the man, husband, and father Casey has become. In some ways, I have *almost* envied him in his ability to walk away from "professional" music to maintain his home life at such a relatively young age. I see my father in him.

I'm so very happy and proud to say that my middle child, Cory, has grown into a good, hard-working, decent man, husband, and father.

When Cory was very little, I taught him how to fish. His uncle later taught him how to fly fish. Now, when we go fishing (which doesn't happen enough), he is the teacher. He's patient with me like I was with him so many years ago. While my happy place is behind a drum set, Cory's is walking a stream looking for the perfect spot to lay in a self-tied fly.

I consider him a true friend and we never run out of things to talk about. I see so much of his mother and my father in him each time we're together.

I think I loved Erin even before I fell in love with Becky. From the start, I was so taken by her spirit and tenacity, just like her mother's. Erin still has that today. She reminds me so much of her mother in looks, attitude, sense of humor, and sense of family. She's also fiercely protective of whom she loves. Erin and I had our struggles, especially since I was absent during so much of her formative years.

Being gone for weeks while on the road and then returning home was perceived as invading her and her mom's space. This created many challenges over the years. Erin has always been very smart and was good in school. She played sports and was quite popular. When Erin puts her mind to something such as going to college, or pursuing a career, she is relentless. The loss of her mother was especially devastating to her.

Becky and Erin were quite a team the first three and half years of her life. That stayed with her. They were so very close up until the end. Erin and I are in a good place now. I know she loves me with all her heart as I love her with all of mine. I am so proud to have her as my loving daughter and friend.

My brother, Chuck, passed away in 2017. In my life, no one had been there longer for me than him. He looked out for me growing up and was a confidant as I struggled to spread my wings. He was the one who gave me the early encouragement to move to Utah when things had grown stale with my early music career. His unwavering confidence in me, even as I made repeated mistakes, was never lost on me. I loved him not only as my brother, but as my best friend.

The position as the facility manager for the Knitting Factory didn't last long. What they needed was a maintenance man, but they hired me instead. They were paying me a great salary to do part-time office work while the rest of the time I was in jeans, turning screwdrivers. After a while it didn't make financial sense for the company, so they let me go. I can't blame them, but at this point in my life it creates a new reality.

I'm older than the target employee most companies want. They see me and my gray hair and think I'm only going to work a few more years before I ride off into the sunset. It's an interesting problem since, according to the Bureau of Labor and Statistics, the median length of employment in our country is just slightly over four years. There's definitely ageism in our culture. I wonder now if my kids have ever listened to Neil Young's *Old Man* and thought about me like I did my dad.

There's not much I can do about my age. I've earned these years.

Something funny happened with those years piling on. I was encouraged by a friend to apply to a modeling agency. Supposedly, old guys are in. I grabbed a few photoshoots around town before landing a small part in the television show, *Z Nation*. I was referred to as Billionaire Number Two in the scripts.

I've now been on multiple auditions for various gigs. Al Pacino doesn't have to fear anything from me, but suddenly I'm an actor and model. Just saying that makes me laugh out loud. What a life.

As I slowly came alive again after Becky's passing, I reactivated my Facebook account and stumbled upon a familiar face.

It was Sue Davis, the girl who walked the halls of Central Valley High School on that last day of my senior year in the yellow jumper and the same woman we had run into at the farmer's market years before.

She looked just like I remembered. I sent her a friend request and she accepted. For the next year, we "liked" many of the same things and occasionally commented on each other's posts.

To this day I'm not sure what compelled me, but one afternoon I sent her an email asking if she'd like to meet for a cup of coffee. She declined my first invitation but later offered to meet on a Tuesday morning.

I arrived early and was quite nervous. I watched her drive up and walk towards the door. I immediately got in line and did my best to be nonchalant. She walked over to me and we hugged. I think it surprised us both.

We sat and talked for five and a half hours. I was so enamored with her that I lost track of time and failed to even offer her a second cup of coffee or some food.

I had plans to meet with some buddies for a beer in the afternoon so around 3:30 p.m., I told her I had to go. I'm sure she thought it was a "line," but I never expected to stay so long and to be completely entranced by the multitude of things we had in common – our sense of humor, music, family, politics, religion, and more. Not to mention she was still gorgeous.

We walked out to the parking lot and gave each other a polite, friendly hug. I thought about kissing her. I *wanted* to kiss her but didn't want to scare her away. As I drove toward downtown to meet my friends, I was in a daze. I kept saying to myself, "What the fuck? What just happened?"

Sue had spun my head around and, at that moment, all the other women seemed to pale in comparison. Yes, some old habits can return. I had been seeing at least three women prior to her.

Now, all I could think of was Sue Davis. Over the next few weeks our relationship grew and I quickly stopped seeing anyone else.

One evening, while having dinner at my apartment, Sue opened a kitchen drawer in search of a pot holder. "Are those my mom's pot holders?" Sue asked. They were the ones her mom had traded Becky for tomatoes years before at the farmer's market. Sue started to cry. It was a sign that we were meant to be together.

I never thought I could ever fall in love again. I did, though, and I couldn't deny it.

I've been blessed to call her my wife since April 30, 2016.

In looking back, it's clear now that the road was a cruel mistress. Every time I went home to be with my wife and family, to build something that I so desperately wanted, the road would beckon again. At her calling, I went running, most often with my Becky's blessing.

When the road damaged my marriage to the point of breaking, I would leave it and go home. I would beg my wife's forgiveness but when my day jobs became scarce or intolerable, I would walk out the door once more, drum kit in hand.

I found real happiness when I broke the spell that the road had on me and focused on my family. I would not trade that time with them for anything.

However, that itch remains. Like an alcoholic who still misses the taste of whiskey years later or the gambler who gets the shakes when he walks by a craps table, I get the rush when I stand next to a tour bus and smell the diesel fuel burning.

I'm fortunate that my life is finally good again.

I'm happy.

I've got a great woman who loves me.

My kids are fantastic with growing families of their own. My grandkids are so precious.

I'm in a band of guys I dig being around.

I know that after all I've experienced and put others through, I'm extremely lucky to be at this point in my life.

However, if a band that really spoke to my soul offered me a drummer's chair at the cost of going on an extended tour away from family and home, I just might join in for one more journey along those highways.

DO YOU WANT MORE TALES FROM THE ROAD?

For updates, pictures, stories, and links, join the community at

facebook.com/TalesFromTheRoad2018/

It's never too late to go on tour!

THANK YOU TO FRIENDS AND FAMILY

This book started as an examination of my years as a musician on the road. It grew into much more than that.

In preparing this manuscript, I reread it many times, more than I can remember. It is clear to me that I was an immature, narcissistic, and shallow person for many years.

I had serious doubts about this book ever seeing the light of day.

To say that I am profoundly ashamed of many of the antics described is an understatement. I cannot attribute it to being a kid because many of these stories occurred while I had the responsibilities of both husband and father.

It is a very scary feeling to have a portion of my life laid bare. I fear being judged, ridiculed, or ostracized by friends, family, and even total strangers.

I sincerely hope that I didn't hurt anyone in the retelling of some wild times. That was not my intention. Many in this book can rightfully be embarrassed by our actions.

In recalling some stories, I laughed at my immaturity as I hope you did.

I enjoyed sharing other moments of shear euphoria, (musically, not drugs – well, maybe some drugs) and many great accomplishments both professional and personal.

There are *too* many people in my life to thank them all, so if I fail to mention someone, please know that I'm sorry. Hopefully, they will know that they had a profound impact in my life.

Mom, Dad, Bonnie, Cathy, Carol, Chris, Chuck, and Laurie. My god, how lucky can one man be to have parents and siblings like them?

My late, extraordinary, beautiful and loving wife, Becky Anne Bancroft (1952-2011). Her unwavering support while I pursued my dream, enabled me to have success in music and more importantly, a successful, happy, loving family. Her foresight and encouragement to start "committing my memories" to tape in case I ever wanted to write a book cannot be overstated. Her strength, her "never give up" attitude, her tenaciousness, her incredible sense of humor and her unwavering love and support for me and the kids will continue to resonate within me until my last breath. My love forever, Beck.

My daughter, Erin Marie, and my sons, Cory John (and his girlfriend, Teresa, and their daughters, Willow and Juniper) and Casey William (and his wife, Natalie, and their kids – Balen, Joss, Simon and Jorah).
Thank you for still loving dad after all those years away on the road. When I worked day jobs and then raced home from work to play some club that weekend.
For understanding my absence at events, birthdays and time normally spent together because of my "career," I am forever humbled and grateful for you. I love you!

All my nieces, nephews and cousins – there are too many to list.

To all my bandmates; *in alphabetical order,*

Bob Allen, Jennifer Anderson, Doug Artist, Brett Ashley, Kurt Baumer, Linda Beach, Duane Becker, E.J. Bell, Al Bevan, Blue, Tom Brewster, Tom Brimm, Steve Brody, Larry Brown, Chip Bush, Charlie Butts, Pat Coast, Mike Coman, Rob Conway, Ron Criscione, Jan Danielson, Rob DiPietro, Mark Doleman, Mark Douty, Ted Dussor, Paul Elliot, Bob Erghot,

Sammy Eubanks, Blake Gardner, Chad Gardner, Mark Gilmore, Ty Green, David Griffith, Steve Hanna, Linda Heath, Frank Hewitt, Russ Hoffer, Mark Johnson, Kevin Jones, Richie Kap, Robbie Kap, Bones Kasune, Randy Knowles, Tim (Too Slim) Langford, Tom Lapsansky, Jay Lee, Mike Lenke, Keith Lewis, Eric Lindstrom, Little Buzzy Foo, Dave Love, Dave Low, Chet Martz, Ken Martello, Paul Mata, James McElwain, LuAnn Miller, Donny Mills, Chuck Montes, Terry Morris, Dan Murphy, Tom Norton, Bob Parsons, Bobby Patterson, Dale Peterson, Eric Rice, Rick Roadman, Joe Scribner, Gary Smith, Rick Smith, Professor Bob Spitahl, Chuck Swanson, Tommy Taylor, Ramiro Vijaro, Tim Wassen, Joe Webber, Dave Winslow, Gary Yeoman, and Ray Yount.

To my bandmates/agents/managers no longer with us;

Cordell Baird, Jeff Benson, Jessie Bishop, Jeannie Carter, Mike Cavender, Bruce Chaffon, Greg Clary, Dave Dieter, Bo Diddly, Freddy Fender, Mike Medeiros, Greg Pendleton, Randy Peterson, Darren Robinette, and Billy Tipton.

To the many others that I had the privilege to step on stage with…

THANK YOU SO VERY MUCH!

To Colin Conway, without his talent, enthusiasm, and perseverance, this book would have remained a bunch of cassette tapes with the narcissistic ramblings of some corporate guy, drunk in his hotel rooms.

Last, but most certainly not least, my love, my best friend, my wife, Sue (Davis) Bancroft.

I sometimes wonder if you're really an angel disguised as a statuesque model with a heart of gold. How else could I be so lucky to have known you since third grade and now be married to you?

When you reappeared in my life, the veil of sadness and darkness was lifted. What I felt and experienced with you, because of you, was a resurgence in my soul.

You were, and are, a healing presence to me and the kids. I have seen that special bond grow between you and them. That is truly precious to me.

I am amazed by your strength and grace and want you (and the rest of the world) to know how much I love, respect, and adore you.

I will forever love you.

THANK YOU FROM THE CO-AUTHOR

The Bill Bancroft I now know is a man I call a very close friend.

You can't go through this journey of writing a deeply personal history and not know his inner thoughts, secrets, and deepest regrets.

I've also shared my personal failings and secrets with him through this process. I hope it's brought us closer and he doesn't think any less of me, like I don't think less of him.

Thank you, Bill, for sharing your journey with me.

Carla Warren, who I mentioned earlier, captured my heart and my imagination.

I can't thank her enough for her patience while I worked on this project. There were many nights and weekends when I disappeared into my office to write only to reappear, bleary eyed and tired, with another tale that would start, "Oh my god, you won't believe what Bill did."

I love you.

-    Colin Conway

APPENDIX I
BANDMATES

Cold Smoke was:

    Jesse Bishop – lead guitar / lead vocals
    Mike Coman – rhythm guitar
    Dave Low – bass / vocals
    Bill Bancroft – drums

Organized Crime was:

    Bob Allen – lead vocals
    Linda Beach – lead vocals
    LuAnn Miller – lead vocals
    Randy Peterson – lead guitar / lead vocals
    Brett Ashley – rhythm guitar / vocals
    Steve Hanna – lead guitar / rhythm guitar
    Chet Martz – bass / vocals
    Dave Low – bass / vocals
    Bill Bancroft – drums / vocals

    Dan Murphy – sound

Raven was:

    Randy Peterson – lead guitar / lead vocals
    Steve Hanna – lead guitar / vocals
    Dave Low – bass / lead vocals
    Bill Bancroft – drums / vocals

    Dan Murphy – sound / lights
    Rick Wise – lights / sound

Clear Sky was:

Frank Hewitt – lead vocals
Jimmy McElwain – lead guitar
E.J. Bell – lead guitar / keyboard
Jeff Benson – rhythm guitar / vocals
Chuck Montes – bass / vocals
Billy Bancroft – drums / vocals

Utah: The Group was:

Frank Hewitt – lead vocals
Jimmy McElwain – lead guitar
Dave Love – lead guitar / vocals
E.J. Bell – lead guitar / keyboard
Chuck Montes – bass / vocals
Billy Bancroft – drums / vocals

Stone Johnny Mountain Band was:

Eric Lindstrom – bass / lead vocals
Rick Roadman – lead guitar / lead vocals
Dave Griffith – everything / vocals
Paul Elliott – fiddle
Billy Bancroft – drums

Mark Douty – sound
Cowboy John – lights

Secrets was:

Mike Medeiros – lead vocals
Darren Robinette – acoustic guitar / lead vocals
Rob DiPietro – lead guitar / vocals
Blue – lead guitar
Jimmy McElwain – lead guitar
Cordell Baird – lead guitar
Chuck Montes – bass / vocals
Billy Bancroft – drums

Ray – lights

Hotspurz was:

Al Bevan – rhythm guitar / lead vocals
Doug Artist – guitar / pedal steel / vocals
Dave Love – lead guitar
Bob Parsons – lead guitar / vocals
Greg Clary – bass / lead vocals
Terry Morris – piano / vocals
Tommy Taylor – piano / vocals
Joe Webber – piano / lead vocals
Billy Bancroft – drums

Mike Medeiros – sound
Chad Gardner – sound
Ray – lights

Raz was:

Ray Criscione – guitar / lead vocals
Linda Heath – keyboard / lead vocals
Mark Gilmore – lead guitar
Ray Yount – bass / lead vocals
Bill Bancroft – drums

Too Slim and the Taildraggers was:

Tim Langford – lead guitar / lead vocals
Tom Brimm – bass guitar / vocals
Greg Pendleton – saxophone / vocals
Billy Bancroft – drums

Wind Chill was:

Ted Dussor – guitar / lead vocals
Blake Gardner – guitar / keyboards / lead vocals
Greg Clary – bass / lead vocals
Joe Webber – keyboards / bass / guitar / lead vocals
Billy Bancroft – drums

Chateau was:

Joe Scribner – guitar
Donnie Mills – guitar / vocals
Jennifer Anderson – keyboard / lead vocals
Dale Peterson – bass / vocals
Billy Bancroft – drums / vocals

The Ty Green Band was:

Ty Green – lead vocals / rhythm guitar
Rick Roadman – guitar
Ted Dussor – guitar / vocals
Eric Lindstrom – bass
Joe Webber – keyboards / vocals
Kurt Baumer – fiddle
Duane Becker – pedal steel
Billy Bancroft – drums

Yo and De Cats was:

Gary Yeoman – rhythm guitar / lead vocals
Eric Rice – lead guitar
Slim Medina – bass
Eric Lindstrom – bass
Billy Bancroft – drums

J.R. Boogie was:

Eric Rice – lead guitar / lead vocals
Ramiro Vijaro – bass
D.K. Black – harmonica / vocals
Billy Bancroft – drums

Café Blue was:

Pat Coast – lead guitar / lead vocals
Tom Brewster – bass
Keith Lewis – keyboards / vocals
Chuck Swanson – saxophone / vocals
Russ Hoffer – saxophone / vocals
Bob Spitahl – saxophone
Mike Lenke – trumpet
Buzz – trumpet
Peter Rey – trumpet
Gary Smith – drums
Billy Bancroft – drums / percussion

Chip and the Bushwackers was:

Chip Bush – lead vocals / harmonica
Rick Roadman – lead guitar / vocals
Eric Lindstrom – bass / vocals
Billy Bancroft – drums

Pat Coast and Out of the Blue was:

Pat Coast – lead guitar / lead vocals
Jan Danielson – piano / vocals
Larry Brown – bass / vocals
Tom Brewster – bass
Billy Bancroft – drums

The Pat Coast Band was:

Pat Coast – lead guitar / lead vocals
Ramiro Vijaro – bass
Rick Smith – bass
Eric Lindstrom – bass
Kevin Jones – bass
Bruce Chaffon – bass
Dave Winslow – keyboards
Keith Lewis – keyboards / vocals
Chuck Swanson – saxophone / vocals
Mike Lenke – trumpet / vocals
Billy Bancroft – drums

The Fat Tones was:

Bobby Patterson – lead guitar / lead vocals
Bob Ehrgott – bass / lead vocals
Bill Bancroft – drums

The Bobby Patterson Band is:

Bobby Patterson – lead guitar / lead vocals
Tom Norton – keyboards / vocals
Randolph Knowles – bass
Billy Bancroft – drums / percussion / vocals

APPENDIX II

VENUES NOTED
(in alphabetical order)

121 Club – Boise, ID (OC)

Ahab's Whale – Spokane, WA (TS&TT)
Armadillo, The – Greenacres, WA (TS&TT)

Baceceks Lounge – Liberty Lake, WA (OC)
Baldy's Apartment – Milton- Fife, WA (Raven)
Bigfoots – Ogden, UT (Hotspurz)
Billy's Country Music Emporium – Evanston, WY (Hotspurz)
Boot Hill Saloon – Gillette, WY (Hotspurz)
Boot Hill Saloon – Rapid City, SD (Hotspurz)
Bouquet, The – Boise, ID (TS&TT)
Bronze Boot, The – Cody, WY (CS)

Capricorn Lounge, The – Moscow, ID (CS)
Charlie's – Casper, WY (CS)
Chelsea's – Coeur d'Alene, ID (CB)
Chrissy's Disco – Moose Jaw, Saskatchewan (SJMB)
Cowboy, The – Vancouver, British Columbia (SJMB)
Curley's Alibi – Lewiston, ID (TS / Chateau)

David Thompson Motor Inn – Kamloops, BC (OC)
Dispensary, The – Moscow, ID (Raven)
Doc Holiday's – Spokane, WA (Raven)
Dug-Out, The – Post Falls, ID (TS&TT)
Dumpiest Hotel Around, The – Missoula, MT (Raven)

El Patio – State Line, ID (Raven)

Fizzie O'Leary's – Priest Lake, ID (TS&TT)
Fort Spokane Brewery – Spokane, WA (Y&TC / CB)

Gentle Ben's – Boise, ID (Hotspurz)

Golden Drift, The – Nelson, B.C. (OC)
Goofy's / Gatsby's – Spokane, WA (Raven)
Grand Illusions – Eugene, OR (CS / SJMB)
Gramma's – Billings, MT (Raven)
Green Triangle, The – Pocatello, ID (Hotspurz)

Hermitage, The – Ogden, UT (CS / U:TG / Secrets)

Judge's Chambers – Spokane, WA (Raven)

King Cole's – Colville, WA (SJMB)
Knitting Factory, The – Spokane, WA (PCB)

Land's Inn Tavern – Spokane, WA (OC)
Little Bear's – Evergreen, CO (SJMB)
Little Opry Hall – Troy, MT (OC)
Loose Cabooze, The – Rossland, B.C. (Raven)

Million Dollar Cowboy Bar, The – Evanston, WY (SJMB /
    Hotspurz)
Mint Lounge, The – Wallace, ID (OC)
Muskogee Civic Auditorium – Muskogee, OK (Hotspurz)

Nickelodeon – St. Maries, ID (OC / Raven)
Night Hawk, The – Lewiston, ID (Raven)
North 40 Club – Saskatoon, Saskatchewan (SJMB)

Our Place Too – Cheyenne, WY (Raven)
Outlaw Inn, The – Kalispell, MT (OC)

Packers Roost – Coram, MT (SJMB)
Paddock – Regina, Saskatchewan (SJMB)
Palace, The – Winthrop, WA (TS&TT)
Panama Red's – Fort Collins, CO (SJMB)
Pine Shed, The – Spokane, WA (Raz)
Performing Arts Center – Walla Walla, WA (TTGB)

Rainer Beer Fest – Priest River, ID (SJMB)
Rathskellers – Coeur d'Alene, ID (Raven)
Rathskellers – Pendleton, OR (OC)
Red Barn – Great Falls, MT (Raven)
Red Lion Barbeque – Spokane, WA (TS&TT)
Reggie's Rockin' R – Salt Lake City, UT (U:TG)

Sandbox Lounge, The – Smelterville, ID (OC)
Shamus O'Toole's – Breckenridge, CO (SJMB)
Shy Clown Casino – Reno, NV (SJMB)
Silver Cloud – Salt Lake City, UT (Raven)
Silver Dollar Bar – Rock Springs, WY (SJMB)
Spokane Opera House – Spokane, WA (SJMB)
Supertramps – Ogden, UT (U:TG / Secrets)

T.J.'s Lounge – Creston, B.C. (OC)
Thunderbird Lounge – Ellensburg, WA (OC)
Top Hat, The – Missoula, MT (CS
Trading Post – Missoula, MT (Raven)

Victor's Barn – Victor, MT (Clear Sky)
Victorian – Casper, WY (Raven)
Village Green – Vernon, BC (SJMB)

War Bonnet Saloon, The – Nespelem, WA (OC)
Washboard Willies – Spokane, WA (SJMB)
Western Star – Salt Lake City, UT (Hotspurz)
Westerner – Salt Lake City, UT (Hotspurz / WC)
Whiskey River – Boise, ID (SJMB)

... and many, many more that are lost in time of a fading memory...

APPENDIX III

BAND TIMELINE

1974-1975	Cold Smoke (rock)
1975-1977	Organized Crime (rock/country-rock)
1977-1978	Raven (rock)
1979	Clear Sky (country-rock)
1979	Utah: The Group (southern-rock)
1980	Stone Johnny Mountain Band (bluegrass)
1981	The Kap Brothers (southern-rock)
1982	Secrets (hard rock)
1982-1984	Hotspurz (country-rock)
1985	Raz (top 40)
1985-1987	Too Slim & The Taildraggers (blues)
1987-1988	Wind Chill (country-rock)
1989	Smooth Moves (top 40)
1989	The Stetson (country)
1989-1990	Chateau (country)
1990	The Ty Green Band (country)
1991	Yo and De Cats (blues)
1992-1993	J.R. Boogie (blues)
1993-1997	Café Blue (blues)
1997-1998	Chip and the Bushwackers (blues)
1999-2010	Pat Coast and Out of the Blue (blues)
2010-2011	The Pat Coast Band (blues)
2014-2015	The Fat Tones (blues)
2016-	The Bobby Patterson Band (blues)

ABOUT THE AUTHOR

Bill Bancroft lives in Washington. He continues to play professional music and is now acting on stage, TV and film as well as modeling. You can follow along with his career at *www.facebook.com/Inmytrailer*.

ABOUT THE CO-AUTHOR

Colin Conway lives in Washington. Besides regretting the decision to quit playing the drums in the 9th grade, he now also regrets having never been on tour.

Find more at *www.colinconway.com*.